TARVES LANG SYNE

The Story of a Scottish Parish

ISBN No. 1871125 324

Printed in Great Britain by
MAXIPRINT
Kettlestring Lane, Clifton Moor,
York

TARVES LANG SYNE

The Story of a Scottish Parish

by

WILLIAM A. PORTER

Published
by
MAXIPRINT, YORK
1996

BY THE SAME AUTHOR :

A BACKWARD LOOK
(at the forefolk of Lord Thomson of Fleet and North Bridge)

ONE HUNDRED YEARS IN YORK
(Centenary of the St Andrew Society of York, 1994)

CAVALCADE REFLECTIONS & CAVALCADE RETROSPECT
(150th anniversary of the Stockton-Darlington Railway, 1975)

WHAT DO YOU KNOW ABOUT RAILWAYS ?

QUEST FOR SPEED
(Official story of East Coast railway enterprise)

A BRUTAL INHERITANCE
(The story of a Scottish crofting family)

OUT OF THE PAST...
A PRESENT FOR THE FUTURE

by Arthur Watson

TARVES has existed since before 1000 AD. It grew around a vital trade artery linking the Earldom of Buchan with Aberdeen and was also situated on the drove road along which cattle from the heart of Buchan passed on their way to the Trystin' Fair at Falkirk.

With improvements in animal and crop husbandry, as well as more enlightened land management,Tarves emerged as an important agricultural district. The 19th century saw development of the village Square - the Old Inn, built in 1800, the Aberdeen Arms Hotel (1810), and the School and Schoolhouse (1837). A church has stood on the site of the present building (completed 1798) since about 600 AD.

Tarvesians, whether born here or recently moved in as a consequence of expansion to meet the needs of new industries, value the past but confidently anticipate a future where old and new continue to harmonise. The historic core of the village is already a Conservation Area and there is much evidence of a collective desire to work for the benefit of both the village and parish through preserving the best of the past, enriching the present and participating in planning the future.

Bert Porter's book comes at an opportune time. It will provide a platform from which people, once stimulated to learn more about our community, will hopefully wish to become more involved in influencing its destiny. The author has a long association with Tarves and his interest and fondness for the area shine through the pages of this book. I believe that Tarves folk would wish me to record publicly our thanks to Bert for donating all proceeds from the sale of the book to worthy causes in the parish.

Tarves Lang Syne is probably more comprehensive than any similar parish story in Scotland. For members of the older generation, like me, it is a unique chronicle of the past; for younger folk, it is both that and an opportunity to learn from the past while charting the way ahead.

Tarves
July 1996

*"How can the story of a small village in an odd corner
of Aberdeenshire be of interest to anyone ?*

- from an essay by J. Duthie Webster (1866 - 1944)
Tarves banker, farmer and historian

Bringing in the sheaves...

COWS graze where a cornfield once waved in the late summer breeze. Time in that quiet place has all the essence of standing still. The track which I trod as a small boy, gripping a grandfather's hand while hunting for burrows among rubble dykes, has long since melted into the pasture.

Here, on a croft called *The Doulies*, my great-grandparents brought in the sheaves more than a century ago and supped from a stone bottle of honey ale hidden in a stook from the glare of the sun. Their smallholding, near the village of Tarves in Central Aberdeenshire, has been tastefully renovated and rebuilt to create a comfortable retirement home for a hospitable English couple. Yet, it looks oddly out of kilter with its surroundings - too well-dressed, as it were, for the landscape which I recall from half a century ago.

Nearby, the farm of *Raitshill* glowers down from its height where John Porter was once a ploughman and another of his ilk sold mulled ale to womenfolk who gathered there to barter with stocking merchants from Aberdeen. The farm on the brow was home, too, to kitchen 'quine' Helen Kelly who pursued the runaway father of the ploughman through the courts and had him declared an outlaw at the Mercat Cross in Aberdeen.

Over at *Northseat* and *Braeside*, now comfortably clad in stone and cement instead of the mud and turf of old, are the sites of long-vanished 17th century hovels which were the homes of my ancestors. More than three centuries have elapsed since Jim Porter, my earliest traceable forebear, faced oblivion during the famine years of King William III.

When I embarked on a family project some years ago to write the story of Jim Porter and those who followed him, it was as one totally unversed in the intricacies of genealogical research, though well-armed with enthusiasm and the naturally enquiring mind of a journalist. It was perhaps inevitable that I should become bewitched by the wider history of the parish and district in which my ancestors struggled to make a living.

The leap from what became an obsession to publication of this book was made possible by the generosity of an international businessman whose long-ago folk also had their hearths in this remote landscape. Though he does not wish to be named publicly - a condition which I am obliged, albeit reluctantly, to respect - he has chosen this means to celebrate his Scottish roots. Moreover, with all proceeds from the sale of the book going to deserving causes in Tarves, both of us may be entitled to feel that we have put something back into the parish which nurtured our kinfolk.

It may sound trite to claim that the sources of research for this book were legion - but that is how it seemed. Grass-roots co-operation by members of the Tarves Heritage Project - notably Arthur Watson, Lindsay Cook, Bill Rattray and Ian Davidson - and by the parish minister, the Rev Leslie Barrett, and head teacher, Marek Gorski, has been inestimable. It must be said, too, that on my visits to the parish, Arthur Watson was a delightful host, companion and tireless pursuer of loose ends, enabling me to bring this history to a satisfactory conclusion. His strong civic conscience and energetic guardianship of all that is desirable in the parish environment were truly infectious.

I owe a special debt of gratitude to Professor T.C. Smout of St Andrews University (*A History of the Scottish People,1560-1830*, and *A Century of the Scottish People,1830-1950*), and to Robert E. Tyson of the University of Aberdeen (*From Lairds to Loons*) for permission to use extracts from their valued works. Another inspirational source was the late W. Douglas Simpson's *A Short History of Tarves*, as were extracts from the *Statistical Accounts of Scotland* in the 18th, 19th and 20th centuries.

I am profoundly grateful to the Special Collections Department at the Library of the University of Aberdeen for permission to use photographic extracts from the original 1696 *Poll Book of Aberdeenshire*, which is in their care, and for photographic contributions from Historic Scotland, the National Trust for Scotland and the parish heritage project.

The expertise of the ladies of the North of Scotland Family History Society in Aberdeen enriched my tale, as did meticulous groundwork by staff of the former Grampian Regional Council in kirk session, parochial board, census and educational records. A similar debt of thanks is due to staff of the North East Library Service at Oldmeldrum for painstaking identification and retrieval of invaluable sources of information. For vital leads from the labyrinth of the Scottish Records Office, and permission to use some of her own genealogical research, I am thankful to Edinburgh history researcher Diane Baptie.

That doyen of 19th century commentators on the North-East agricultural scene, William Alexander (perhaps best known for his *Johnny Gibb of Gushetneuk*), was a source which I visited again and again. My cousin, Tarves-born author David Kerr Cameron (*The Ballad and the Plough, Willie Gavin Crofter Man*, etc) was manifestly generous, both with encouragement during the lengthy period of research and with permission to quote from his own evocative works. Treasure troves of local historical detail were encountered in the Rev Thomas Mair's *Extracts from the Records of the Presbytery of Ellon*, Gavin Turreff's *Antiquarian Gleanings from Aberdeenshire Records 1871*, the anonymous *Aberdeenshire Black Kalendar*, and that sheet anchor for history-seekers in the North-East, *The Thanage of Fermartyn*.

The *Tarves Letter*, a publication issued by J. Duthie Webster of the Tarves Literary Society at the turn of the 19th/20th centuries was a mine of interesting detail. An interview by him with William Duncan of Boghouse, which has long outlived both of them, was a delightful source of reverie about times long gone.

Newspaper reminiscences (*Aberdeen Bon-Accord & Northern Pictorial*, 1938) by another son of Tarves, Charles Davidson, who was a Lecturer in Spanish at the University of Aberdeen, were a rich and charming seam of commentary about childhood in Tarves at the turn of the century.

The final proof-reading of my manuscript was undertaken voluntarily by fellow Aberdonian Frank Paterson. It says much for true North-East grit that at the conclusion of this daunting task our long and valued friendship remained unscathed.

For thousands of miles driven on motorways and on rough farm tracks in pursuit of the facts which make up much of this book, and for tolerance when the word processor appeared to take precedence over urgent dometic issues, I am much obliged to Helen, my wife.

I dedicate this book to Tarvesians everywhere.

William A. Porter,
Dunnington, York

Summer 1996

CONTENTS

Chapter 1   In The Beginning   1

Chapter 2   Off The Beaten Track   9

Chapter 3   Feudal Fetters   17

Chapter 4   On The Seamy Side   24

Chapter 5   A Melancholy Land   35

Chapter 6   Famine and Bitter Harvest   42

Chapter 7   Removing History's Veil   51

Chapter 8   Witches, Warlocks and Hangmen   70

Chapter 9   The Tarves Kidnapper   78

Chapter 10   Penury and Parsimony   83

Chapter 11   Fire and Brimstone   89

Chapter 12   Anatomy of a Kirk   97

Chapter 13   Castle in the Air   109

Chapter 14   In Great Hooses   117

Chapter 15   A Class Of Their Own   128

Chapter 16   A Time For Renewal   141

Chapter 17   Animal Farms   159

Chapter 18   Country Claik   171

Chapter 19   A Terrible Price   180

Chapter 20   A Public Place   184

Chapter 21   A Brave New World   186

Chapter 22   Birds of the Wilderness   199

Chapter 23   Church and Community   208

Index   217

ILLUSTRATIONS

Standing stones, South Ythsie	4
Memorials, Tarves Kirkyard	4
Map of Scotland, 1610	5
Tarves Kirkyard; Tolquhon Castle	23
Tarves countryside; Prop of Ythsie	41
Pages from 1696 Poll Book	57,59
Map of Aberdeenshire, 1807	69
Panoply of death, Tarves	96
Effigy of William Forbes	98
Site of the Bede-House today	99
Tarves Kirk; Tolquhon Memorial	102
Plan of Tarves, 1900	103
Tolquhon - Ancient Pile	110-116
Haddo House	118
Pitmedden Garden	123
Schivas House	127
School Days	131
George Melvin, eccentric genius	134
Plaque at Cottage Hospital	136
The new school logo	140
The welcome 'piece'; harvest-time	150
Power-houses of farming	151-152
The family wares	153
A loon and his horse	153
Jog-trot days	154

Crofting, old style	155
Croft and cottage	157
Faces from another time	158
Shorthorn champion	163
Shorthorn trophy winners	165
A boy and his horse	169
After the war	181
Village streets	182-183
Conservation sites	196
Tarves from the air	209
Ministers in time	213
Church folk, 1862	214
Church folk, 1996	215

Thankyou

The illustration on the front of this book's dust-jacket is of a painting of Tarves Square in 1860 by an unknown artist. It was kindly loaned by Mr & Mrs John Presly of Tarves.

" There be of them, that have left a name behind them,
that their praises might be reported.
And some there be, which have no memorial;
who are perished, as though they had never been."

Ecclesiasticus XLIV

Sentinel over the Central Aberdeenshire landscape, Bennachie is believed to
have been the site of the ancient battle of Mons Graupius. Picture - the author

Chapter 1

In The Beginning

WHEN the last Ice Age retreated, the wilderness turned to grassland and forest. Hunters who had survived in more temperate climes followed the deer, the boar and the wild ox into the northern fastnesses of Europe. Dug-out canoes fashioned from tree trunks brought the first post-Ice Age hunters to North-East Scotland, eight thousand years before the birth of Christ.

Burial sites and midden heaps of shells, bones and flint unearthed by the plough in modern times are frail though compelling clues to those Stone Age nomads who, in animal skins, fished Grampian's rivers and stalked the wild beasts of its forests. In time they were succeeded by others - the first farmers - who brought new forms of stone tools and implements, along with a basic form of animal husbandry. The plough was unknown to those pioneering tillers of the soil who used pointed digging sticks and crude hoes made from the antlers of deer in their attempts to create primitive settlements. Trees and undergrowth were hacked down or burned to the ground to make forest clearings for their dwellings, rough pasture for their beasts and small plots for growing corn. The long stone cairns in which they buried groups of their dead have been uncovered at various sites throughout the North-East. Indeed, when stones were being carted away for building purposes from several large cairns on the farms of North and South Ythsie, Tarves, last century a large quantity of human bones was found.

Four thousand years ago, these settlers were supplanted by a new race of people who dragged their flimsy wooden craft into the dunes overlooking the long empty strand between the mouths of the Don and the Ythan and moved inland along the river valleys. They were the outriders of a horde of warlike broad-headed 'beaker' folk who crossed the sea at its narrowest point between the Low Countries and the fragmented island kingdoms that would one day be called Great Britain.

Many of these skilful navigators made landfall in the marshes of East Anglia, which had been joined to the Low Countries by a land bridge before the glaciers departed. Others reached the rocky shores of Yorkshire, and the most intrepid of them hugged the island coastline until curiosity, rough seas or the need to replenish their stores of food and drinking water drove them ashore in North-East Scotland.

As the 'beaker' folk followed the river courses into that backward countryside all those years ago, the world elsewhere was shaking itself loose from the torpor of pre-history. Farming communities all over Mesopotamia, for instance, had long since harnessed the annual floodwaters of the Tigris and the Euphrates to irrigate the desert and grow cereals upon it. In that same land, the world's first libraries had been set up and the first known legal code established. Everyday life in Egypt was being recorded on papyri. The Sphinx and the Pyramids of the Pharaohs at Giza were complete, and work was well advanced on the massive Temple of Karnak at Thebes. The Chinese had mastered the art of silk weaving and the production of bronze artefacts. The plough was already in widespread use in India and the Assyrians had built trading settlements with their own shops and banks. Closer to home, the construction of an impressive circle of standing stones had just been completed at Stonehenge.

Yet, what we call Aberdeenshire was at that time a dismal and profoundly inhospitable place. Forty centuries on, we do not know if any resistance was offered to the contingents of 'beaker' folk heading for the land now known as Tarves. Indeed, we are not even aware if there was anyone still there to offer it. There is no doubt, however, that the 'beaker' folk settled in that dour landscape. Vestiges of their individual burial cists and of the ornate urns which gave them their name came to the surface at a later age in locations throughout today's parish - at South Ythsie, Mains of Tolquhon, Shivas and Craigies. The 'beaker' folk's distinctive pottery, particularly their elegant drinking cups fashioned in the shape of an upturned bell and decorated with incised patterns, was clearly prized by its owners. It followed them to their stone-lined graves, along with their bows, daggers, arrow and spear heads, flint scrapers and knives, bone needles and ornaments of copper, amber and jet - all, presumably, intended for use in the expected after-life. From about 1700 BC they were making tools and weapons of bronze and were learning how to weave cloth from wool and flax. Their urns, usually stuffed with food to nurture their owners on the long journey to that after-life, served another useful purpose during life here on earth, for the 'beaker' folk had discovered how to make an alcoholic drink from fermented barley! A drop of the hard stuff would not have gone amiss in that grim land.

In his delightful little book, *A Short History of Tarves*, sponsored by Tarves Literary Society 40 years ago, the distinguished Aberdeen historian, W. Douglas Simpson, wrote: " Geology is the womb of history. Upon the rocks of a land and upon the soils derived from the rocks, depends the life that men can live. It cannot be said that in this respect Tarves has offered any outstanding advantages to the generations of human beings who for some four thousand years have won a living from its haughs and braes."

With the Bronze Age came the sword and the axe, and other cutting tools which accelerated the clearing of the countryside. A bronze sword found at Shivas in 1834 was presented by Mr Alexander Forbes Irvine, the laird, to the Society of Antiquaries of Scotland. A remarkable hoard of bronze relics was revealed by the plough at South Ythsie in 1858, the find including four leaf-shaped swords, the end of a scabbard and two 'sunflower' pins. Another significant discovery at Braes o' Gight, Methlick, included three rings linked by the remains of a bronze ribbon, six huge armlets and three jet necklets.

The gradual merger between the Bronze and Iron Ages (400 BC -100 BC) is associated with the arrival from France and Belgium of Celtic-speaking tribesmen, ancestors of the Picts, in the area north of Scotland's central plain. Their burial cairns, and those of their predecessors, once peppered the Tarves countryside, and names familiar to us today, like Cairnbrogie, Cairnfechil, Coucher Cairn and Tillycairn, are echoes of that far-off time. Fragments of early habitations littered the humps and hollows of the parish until land reform reached the North-east in the 18th and 19th centuries - here in a hollow a weather-scarred Celtic cross, teetering there on the moss a sculptured Pictish stone, or up on the slope the remains of a Roman marching camp dating from the invasion of Caledonia by Julius Agricola.

Much of Aberdeenshire's woodland was denuded by the Celts as they established permanent farming communities, raising cattle, pigs and sheep as well as cultivating grain crops, hunting deer and wild birds and gathering shellfish, nuts and berries to supplement their diet.

The folk of that raw landscape were obliged to form a fighting confederation shortly after the time of Christ when Agricola and his legions, having subjugated much of England and Southern Scotland, swept northwards to threaten their remote communities. The Roman invasion reached a climax in 84 AD when the tribes were routed at the Battle of Mons Graupius. The journal of the Roman historian, Tacitus, alluded to 30,000 tribesmen pouring on to this bloody battlefield, though his account rings of fantasy, probably in the interests of glorifying his general's triumph. His mention, too, of a tribal hero named Calgacus is also considered by historians to have been a literary licence serving to garnish the tale he wrote for a gullible Roman audience.

Where Mons Graupius was actually fought has for long been a matter for conjecture among historians, though the site now generally accepted is one on the northern slopes of Bennachie, whose peaks straddle the horizon in much of central Aberdeenshire. This has been derived from aerial and ground surveys carried out in the 1970s by Professor J.K. St Joseph. A huge Roman marching camp identified by him at Durno, between Pitcaple and Old Rayne, is the largest known site of its kind north of the Antonine Wall.

The invaders failed to extinguish the threat from the stout-hearted tribesmen, however. During a gap in the Roman intrusion the painted warriors staged a series of punitive raids in the south, crashing through Hadrian's Wall to bring mayhem to legionary and peasant alike. The Romans responded with a vengeful

Stones of Destiny

The Tarves countryside abounds in relics of bygone ages, like these standing stones (above) at South Ythsie farm.   Picture - the author.

These ancient slabs (below) rest against the parish church wall at Tarves. They are dated 1584 and 1617 and commemorate early members of the College of Heralds - Thomas Craig, Pursuivant, and William Craig, Rothesay Herald.   Picture - THP

An Ancient Kingdom

This section of a map of 'The Kingdome of Scotland,' drawn by John Speed in 1610, depicts North-East Scotland. The district of Formartine, described as 'Froumartena,' is situated just above 'Buquhan' (Buchan). The North Sea was then known as the 'Germane Sea' and the town of Aberdeen as 'Aberdone.'

expedition in 209 AD and the tribes were saved from annihilation only by the death of Severus at York. After that time, the Romans abandoned their intermittent and wasteful occupation of the northern fastnesses.

Most of Scotland north of the Firth of Forth became Pictland, with the country between the Dee and Spey forming a confederacy of the Taixali and other Celtic groups. Arable land was distributed among members of the tribe, and pasture was allocated according to the number of cattle possessed by each family. Tribal districts were divided into homesteads, to each of which belonged as much land as was required for the subsistence of a family. These divisions, or 'raths' (fortified farms) as they were known, are suggestive of Tarves place-names which have come down to us today, like Raitshill, near Tolquhon. According to the *Thanage of Fermartyn*, a 19th century treasure trove for the historian, the homestead usually comprised a dwelling-house, an ox stall, a sheep pen, a hog house and a calf house, and was surrounded by a ditch or rampart, with wooden pallisades for protection against rival tribes. The Pictish enclaves lived on in this fashion for almost a thousand years until they were engulfed by Norse invaders in the 9th century AD.

Christianity arrived in the North-East with a mission to the Picts, led by St Ninian in about 400 AD from a monastic base at Whithorn in Galloway. The remains of a chapel he established at Andet, in the adjoining parish of Methlick, were visible until they yielded to the plough at the end of the 18th century. St Ninian was a disciple of the French St Martin of Tours, and Formartine - the name given to the wider district in which Tarves is situated - has been said to signify 'Martin's Land'.

The Irish missionary, St Murdebur (or Muirdebar) arrived from Leinster in about 600 AD to found a chapel close to where the village of Tarves now stands. In his *Short History of Tarves*, W. Douglas Simpson debunked the once-popular association of 'St Englatius' with Tarves. He wrote:

> " St Murdebur is the founder of our church. The so-called
> dedication to St Englatius is a piece of nonsense, and the
> name of this fictitious patron has been compounded from
> the old Gaelic word oenglais - 'choice brook.' The good
> folk of Tarves should forget about St Englatius and do all
> they can to preserve the memory of their real apostle."

Being monastic in its origin, the Celtic church was a succession of preaching outposts rather than the parochial entity with which we are familiar today. The parochial system arrived much later with the Roman Catholic church, its priests supported by tithes which became a crippling imposition on the peasantry. Christianity reached the heathen tribes slowly but surely through the itinerant teachings of St Murdebur and other saints, perhaps better known than him - St Ternan, St Drostan, St Devenick, St Machar, St Colm and St Mungo - who were associated in Aberdeenshire with the evangelical missions issuing from Galloway, Ireland, Iona and the West of Scotland.

Theirs was a peripatetic calling, travelling in groups, preaching and teaching as they went. When remaining in one location for a period it was their practice to put up a chapel - a mud-and-wattle erection, windowless and without seats or steeple, to serve as a humble headquarters of the mission. There they preached, studied, taught and prepared manuscripts, and from there they went out to work the land, shoulder to shoulder with those they sought to convert.

Little is known about the impact of freebooting Viking raids on the communities of North-East Scotland between the 8th and 12th centuries. Though skirmishes with Norsemen are richly featured in the folklore of the North-East, there is a frustrating dearth of written history with which to corroborate events or erase myths. The Scandinavian sagas of the time are blatantly unreliable sources of information for those in search of historical fact. There can be little doubt, however, that the Norsemen harried and destroyed much of Pictland. Most of Scotland was at the mercy of these fierce warriors who sailed in their longboats from the Viking earldoms of Orkney, Caithness, Sutherland, and the Western Isles.

The Pictish people's grip on the land became more and more feeble and was virtually extinguished by a massive defeat in 839 AD (the precise location of this rout is lost in the mists of time). The old nationality and culture of the Picts was wiped out at a time when Viking conquest was at its peak and the first steps towards a unified Scotland were being taken.

Of the four constantly warring kingdoms of Scotland, Dalriada and Pictland merged in 843 AD to become the kingdom of Alba, with the Gaelic Kenneth MacAlpin as king. In 1034 the others - Bernicia and Strathclyde - came into the national fold, with King Malcolm II's grandson, Duncan, as the first King of Scotland.

Thanages* emerged in the period between the tribal organisation and the Norman feudal system established by William the Conqueror, with 'Fermartyn' (Formartine) extending to the eastern seaboard between the Ythan and Don rivers and having Fyvie Castle as its principal seat. The District of Formartine, which it eventually became, included within its boundaries all or parts of the present parishes of Udny, Tarves, Methlick, Foveran, Oldmachar, Newmachar, Fintray, Kinkell, Monkeggie, Bourtie, Bethelnie, Fyvie, Auchterless, Forgue, Ellon, Drumblade, Belhelvie, and Logie Buchan.

Enmity between the rival houses of Canmore and Macbeth in the 11th century and, later, the Balliols, the Comyns and Robert the Bruce, spilled over the Formartine landscape, heaping repression and despair on a countryside where struggle with the elements was a recurring certainty. They were an ill-starred breed, the medieval Tarves farmers and crofters, whose war was not with the aggressor but with the stony ground from which they sought an existence. Their concerns were the price that the crop would bring at market or the storm clouds which, careering in from the 'Germane Sea' (later, the North Sea), so often threatened to make a mockery of their year-round toil.

* **Thanage** - tenure of lands held by a Thane (chieftain) in return for military service to a king or other superior.

Tarves was included among gifts which the pious and scholarly William the Lion made to the Abbot when founding the great Abbey of Arbroath in 1176. History records that these embraced the lands of 'Carrinbrogyn, Milton, Newton, Smiddiehill, Brechullath, Tulicarthyn and Tulielt.' They were incorporated into the Barony* of Tarves, which was raised to a regality by Robert the Bruce a century later. The monks of Arbroath exercised an almost royal - and often corrupt - control over their feudal tenants.

The medieval *Calendar of Supplications Relating to Scotland* records the extent of the bounty which the monks came to expect of Tarves: "From the vicarage of the church of Tarwas (sic), taxed at 32 merks, the whole altarage with one acre of land, reserving 8 marks to be taken up annually from the teinds** of wool or of lambs or of both, with the teind sheaves of the whole parish with the whole church lands to remain with the Abbot and convent foresaid."

In 1178, Matthew, Bishop of Aberdeen, issued a confirmation charter relating to the church of Tarves and chapel of Fuchill with their tithes - "given to God," he said, "and the Church of St Thomas the Martyr, of Arbroath, and the monks there." The charter was confirmed again in 1192 by John, Bishop of Aberdeen, in 1207 by his successor, Adam, and by later bishops down to 1247. In 1357, Pope Alexander VI ratified the provision made for the vicarage of the church, for which there was to be a "yearly stipend of 15 merks, the whole altarage and six merks in teind scheaves and a yearly rent of 50 Pounds Scots."

(When the Scottish and English currencies were stabilised at the Union of the Crowns in 1603, £ 1 Scots was worth only about one-twelfth of £ 1 English, ie 1s 8d. In the 14th century, however, the ratio was only 2:1. The merk, or mark, was not a Scots coin but a unit of value equalling two-thirds of £ 1 Scots ie 13 shillings and 4 pennies Scots.)

Records of the 13th century reveal that the 'parson of Tarves' was one by the name of Maurice who had been among witnesses to the foundation of St Peter's Hospital in Aberdeen's Spittal by Bishop Matthew de Kyninmund during the reign of King Malcolm IV. Another, Galfridus (Geoffrey) de Wellys - from about as far south in England as it is possible to get from Tarves - was mentioned in a 1322 deed concerning "a pension of eight merks due to the monastery from the vicar teinds of Tarves." His successor, John Munro, was mentioned ten years later in connection with the same 'pension.' Other early Tarves priests included Sir Alexander Abercrummy, who died in 1493, and was succeeded by John Lumsden of St Andrews. In 1496 the incumbent was Edward Cunynham, Rector of Cluny. He did not have the charge for long, for just four years later Sir Thomas Myreton demitted the vicarage in favour of Sir Archibald Balconny. William Sympill was succeeded as vicar in 1534 by Henry Lumsdsen, and the last of the Roman Catholic priests at Tarves was Alexander Ogilvy, appointed in 1540. It is difficult to resist the conclusion that these priests, with their smattering of knighthoods, living off the fat of the land and being rewarded handsomely for the efforts of luckless others, were close to being the medieval equivalent of the 'fat cats' of British industry today.

* **Barony** - freehold estate whose principal had sweeping jurisdiction over the peasantry
** **Teinds** - tithes, or tenths, a tax paid towards the upkeep of the clergy.

Chapter 2

Off The Beaten Track

THE remoteness of Tarves in medieval times, and even later, meant that the great movements in Scottish history largely passed it by. Evidence available to us today suggests that epochal events like Bannockburn and Flodden, and anarchy and rebellion during the Stewart reigns touched the parish but lightly. Apart from records revealing the extent to which the monks of Arbroath swelled their coffers at the expense of parishioners, Tarves scarcely rated a mention in the hand-written chronicles of the age. Rather, it was life's little squabbles at parochial level that coloured and shaped the destinies of those in the clustered crofting communities of Formartine.

Like fleeting breaks in a leaden sky, however, there were exceptions when the grey bucolic existence was thrown into confusion by events played out on a wider canvas. A May day in 1308 provided one of these. The enmity between Robert the Bruce and the Comyns of Buchan over succession to the Scottish throne was coming to a head. Bruce had declared himself King at Scone two years before, though dubious diplomacy in earlier years had ensured he did not have the general approval of the Scottish nation at that time. In fact, he had been on the run in the West of Scotland during the winter of 1306-07 and, now a sick man after another winter spent largely out of doors, was recuperating at Inverurie.

The tide was now turning in his favour, however, and the number of supporters rallying to his cause was growing. His convalescence was interrupted at dawn on 23 May when a detachment from Sir John Comyn's army, encamped near the farm toun of Meldrum (Oldmeldrum today) just four miles from Tarves, staged a foray into Bruce's defences around the small market town but could not sustain the attack.

Bruce retaliated by ordering his brother, Sir Edward Bruce, to attack Comyn. The enemy was unprepared for such a rapid riposte and quickly wilted when the armies clashed on swampy ground between Barra Hill and the Lochter burn. One account has it that Robert the Bruce was present among his men, propped in the saddle by a man on either side. Whatever the facts, Comyn's force disintegrated, hundreds of deserters fleeing east and northwards to their Buchan homeland.

There followed what has become known as the "harrying of Buchan". Tarves folk would have been terrified observers or would have hidden behind their doors as Sir Edward and his men pursued the hapless deserters, rooting them out from woodlands and ditches, cutting them down as they ran. Castles were burned and dismantled, farms and crofts razed, crops levelled, livestock butchered or stolen, their owners killed or put to flight. As an old poem tells us, the King's brother.....

> " gert his men burn all Bouchane
> Fra end to end and sparit nane."

Comyn fled to England where he died soon afterwards and the family's century-long lordship of the North came to an inglorious end when the remnant of the Comyn army was wiped out at Aikey Brae near Old Deer. Vengeance satisfied, Bruce now faced the future with much restored confidence. Indeed, within a year he was holding the first Parliament of his reign at St Andrews.

The Battle of Barra had been fought on what is now pastureland on the North Mains of Barra farm by the side of the Oldmeldrum-Inverurie road. In the fields of another well-known Inverurie farm, at Balhalgardy, two miles north of the town, lies the site of Harlaw, one of the bloodiest battles ever fought on Scottish soil. It is extremely unlikely that the remote peasant communities of central Aberdeenshire were untouched by this savage encounter on 24 July, 1411. For most of the great families of North-East Scotland, with their feudal levies, responded to a call by Alexander Stewart, Earl of Mar - son of the notorious Wolf of Badenoch - to defend the lowlands from invasion by Donald, Lord of the Isles.

Fearing the mounting influence of the Stewarts under Scotland's Regent, the Duke of Albany, Donald led 10,000 unruly clansmen towards Aberdeen, burning and looting as they progressed through Moray. Keeping to the high ground, they marched by Culsalmond and Rayne and, finding their route blocked by Mar's forces at Inverurie, took up position at Harlaw, a stony plateau commanding a great sweep of the surrounding countryside.

Sir Henry Preston of Fyvie led a strong contingent of men from the Formartine district - at the centre of which lay Tarves - and Mar's army was also joined by the Lairds of Balhalgardy, Auquhorthies, Pitmedden and Lethenty, as well as Provost Robert Davidson and 36 burghers from Aberdeen. On hand, too, were landed gentry, lairds, and their followers from Kincardine, Angus and both Donside and Deeside. Though outnumbered by the Highlanders, the Lowland army was better armed, better disciplined and better led.

The carnage at the end of the confused day-long struggle, fought entirely on foot, was so colossal that it found a place in history as 'Reid Harlaw'. Although the outcome was still undecided when darkness fell, the Highlanders withdrew during the night, leaving the victory to Mar.

The result had clearly been a stalemate but Donald, suffering even heavier casualties than Mar, may have reached the conclusion after the heat of battle was over that plunder of the Lowlands was not worth the sacrifice.

The ballad recalls:

> "An' sic a weary buryin'
> The like ye never saw,
> As wis the Sunday after that
> On the muirs aneath Harlaw.
>
> An' if Hielan' lasses speer at ye
> For them that gaed awa'
> Ye may tell them plain, and plain enough,
> They're sleepin' at Harlaw."

And, as Scott recounts in *The Antiquary*:

> " The cronach's* cried on Bennachie,
> And down the Don and a',
> And hieland and lawland may mournfu' be
> For the sair field of Harlaw."

In the following year, the Duke of Albany pursued Donald into the Highlands and compelled him to submit to the Scottish crown. The Government's gratitude for the role played by Mar's army in bringing about Donald's downfall was enshrined in a special act by which the sons of men who had perished at Harlaw were excused from paying their feudal taxes.

A 44-foot-high grey and pink granite obelisk was erected by the City of Aberdeen in 1911 - 500 years after the battle. Today, the site of 'Reid Harlaw' is covered by fields of barley enclosed by drystane dykes.

Though the Civil War of the 17th century did not bring slaughter to the North-East, the rage and disgust of country folk folk were provoked by the savagery of marauding Covenanters. Locally, Sir John Gordon had become a persistent thorn in the side of the zealots. They had occupied Aberdeen after the Battle of Brig o' Dee in June 1639, at which another popular Formartine figure, John Seaton of Pitmedden, was shot dead while riding upriver with a Royalist detachment in an attempt to outflank the invaders. The Gordons and their followers returned home while the Covenanting force lived on the townspeople and pillaged the countryside. Contemporary accounts allude to "daylie deboshing, drinking, hureing, nicht-walking, combating, sweiring and bringing sundry honest women-servandis to gryte miserie."

*** Cronach** - lament*

The regiment of Covenanters, the record adds, left the countryside "manless, moneyless, horseless and armsless."

The garrison took its leave of Aberdeen in early 1644 and the town returned to comparative quiet. This was soon shattered, however, by incidents which had their beginnings at Kintore. There, Sir John Gordon had encountered and wounded Aberdeen's Bailie Alexander Jaffray of Kingswells, a former provost, and his brother John. Alexander, a magistrate, had earlier been obliged to sentence one of Sir John's retainers and the attack upon him was an expression of the laird's resentment that anyone other than himself should discipline one of his servants.

The town council resolved to impose a mighty 20,000 merks fine on Sir John. Ignoring the censure, however, and cocking a snook at the night patrol and artillery pieces assembled to greet him, he rode into town at dawn on 19 March, 1644, with the Laird of Drum and other associates to seize Provost Sir Patrick Leslie of Iden, Provost-elect Sir Robert Farquhar of Mounie and the Jaffray brothers.

A commentary by Spalding states:

> "The like seldome hes bein sein, that so few men so pertlie and publictlie sould have disgraced sic a brave burghe, by taking away thair prouest and the rest without any kynd of contradictioun or obstacull."

Clearly, the eminent recorder was not amused! Nor, as might be imagined, were the town council, the townspeople or the religious marauders who saw in Sir John and his papal adherence a dire threat to their own mission in Scotland.

On his way out of town, the laird halted in Old Aberdeen to collect some of his children who were attending school there, then stopped for drinks at a hostelry in Kintore before staying overnight at Leggatesden. By next morning his captives were imprisoned in Strathbogie and did not regain their freedom for another five weeks until the arrival of Argyll and his Covenanters in North-East Scotland forced their release. Soon afterwards, Argyll caught up with Gordon.

The goal of the intruders, in 1644, was the Place of Kelly, Sir John's great mansion-house which straddled the boundary between the two parishes. Sir John, who was of the Roman Catholic faith, stoutly defended the house until forced to capitulate to Argyll who put a garrison of 36 men into the building to destroy and plunder it, carrying away the victuals and killing or driving away the horses and sheep belonging to Sir John and his tenants. The peasantry were obliged to stare impotently from the sidelines as the well-armed troops rampaged over the property. The venom of the Covenanters knew no bounds. Although Sir John had surrendered on honourable terms, he was whisked off to Edinburgh where he was imprisoned in St Giles Church before execution for his loyalty to King Charles.

By many accounts, Sir John was a man of profound ability and loyalty. He had been second in command to the Marquis of Huntly in leading the King's forces - with, no doubt, Tarvesians among them - against the Covenanters in 1639. At a skirmish commonly known as the 'Trot of Turriff,' he had behaved with great courage, for which he was created a Baronet by King Charles. On 10 July, 1645, he was executed along with Captain John Logie, son of a learned and loyal clergyman, the Rev Andrew Logie, minister of Rayne and Archdeacon of Aberdeen.

Sir John's friends had petitioned to wait upon him on the scaffold and six of them were allowed to do so. A contemporary report informs us:

> "When they mounted the scaffold, they were attended by some of the town's ministers. One of them, addressing himself to Sir John, desired him to make open and full confession of his sins to God, upon which he acknowledged that he had been a great and grievous sinner, and hoped that God would graciously pardon him.

> "The minister went to the side of the scaffold and told the people that this unfortunate gentleman had confessed himself guilty of rising in arms against the country, in opposition to the covenant.

> "Haddo, overhearing, went to the same place and with the like voice answered 'Not so. I confess myself to be a great sinner to God, but never transgressed against the country or any in it, and what I did in that case, I thought good service, and bound to do as my duty by the laws of God and man.'

> "After which he returned to his private devotions, using among others this short prayer - ' I commend myself to God, and my six children to his Majestie's care, for whose sake I die this day.'

> "And so he passed boldly and calmly unto death. His body was buried in the Greyfriars Churchyard, Edinburgh."

William Seaton of Shethin also fell foul of the Covenanters. Though evading the axe, he was imprisoned in St Giles and his Shethin home "pitifullie plunderit and spolzeit" by the forces of Argyll. The Scottish Parliament ordained that the house should be "cassin doun* to the ground" but the order was not carried out.

Soon there followed the iron-fisted rule of Cromwell, whose helmeted troops, far from their general's surveillance, caroused around the district, using parish kirk clocks for target practice with their muskets after revelling in local alehouses.

On a happier note, peasant folk from miles around, in carts and on foot, had travelled the moorland paths into Tarves on a July day in 1589 on the occasion of an extremely rare Royal visit. It was made by King James VI, who came as the guest of William Forbes, the cultured and scholarly seventh Laird of Tolquhon

Cassin doun - demolished

Castle. The occasion was the completion of a five-year programme of extensions at the stately hilltop pile near the village. William, who was to enjoy the comforts of his new home, one of the finest of its day, for only another seven years, would have proudly shown his monarch the Royal coat of arms displayed along with his own on the gatehouse facade. William died at Tolquhon in 1596. He and his wife Elizabeth were buried in the south aisle of the parish church. Although that church building has long since gone, their exquisitely detailed monumental tomb has survived. The story of the castle, which is now in Historic Scotland's care, is told in a later chapter.

The pomp and circumstance of the King's visit can only be guessed at - the brightly coloured pavilions, the courtiers, the carriages and the strutting horses, the swaggering of the nobles and the graceful deportment of their ladies in exotic costume never before seen in that poor man's land. The visit would have been talked about for many years to come, would have been handed down the generations, have become grander, even, through the embellishments of time.

Much talked about at this time, too, were the depredations of a Tarves parishioner, John Gordon of Tillyhilt. A man with no redeeming traits and a son of the laird of Tillyhilt, Gordon had become a notorious bully and profligate in the district. This branch of the Gordon family was apparently a troubled and graceless one, with a catalogue of misdemeanours bridging 50 years of the 16th and 17th centuries. In 1621, despairing and helpless, John Gordon's father sought the Presbytery of Ellon's compassion and guidance at a crowded meeting in Tarves Kirk. Tarvesians thronged the kirkyard, awaiting news of the 'meenisters' censure.'

Old Man Gordon told a woeful tale - of desperate letters to judges and justices of the peace, even to the Marquis of Huntly, Sheriff Principal at Aberdeen. He was quite unable to restrain his offspring whose threatening behaviour worsened by the day. For 14 years, the old man told the thronged ministers and elders, his son had been:

> "ane nicht walker and extraordinar drunkard, committing daylie very mony ryotts be tulzeing* and oppressing of all quhom he may overcum, and that he wald cam within his awn hous of Tillielt and thair in the presence of his parents wald miserablie abuse the haill familie, and so vilipend** and disdane his auld father in his face that mony nichts throw greif of hart he wald be forced to ryis fra his tabill and go to his chalmer***and bed unsoupit."****

Old John complained bitterly, too, that the Tarves minister had lately shown "over-mild countenance, and sufferit ye said John now and then in his societie and wald eit and drink with him." It seems, however, that the incumbent, the Rev Thomas Gardyne had little choice in the matter, since the bully would lurk in some dark corner of the village until he judged that supper was due to be served at the Manse. As Mr Gardyne averred in his own defence, the uninvited and unwanted guest:

tulzeing - brawling; **vilipend** - abuse; ***chalmer*** - bedroom; ****unsoupit**** - unfed "wald peirtlie cum in at the durs* and sit doun at the heid of his buird** and wald not be restraynit except he wald have swaggerit with him or useit violence, qhilk*** wes very far to the said Thomas's discontentenment."

No doubt - for, from his vantage point at the head of the table, the scoundrel would have seen to it that he did not want for the best of the minister's food and strong ale, whatever his unwilling host thought of it.

The catalogue of charges levelled at Gordon was comprehensive. With accomplices - John Mill, described as a 'commissioner's officer', and John Lowrie, a less than admirable Tarves schoolmaster - Gordon had ranged over the district, inflicting an astonishing imposture on the peasantry.

John Beg, of Bracklay, told the assembly that Gordon had produced a parchment purporting to be a commission from the king to raise soldiers for a campaign in Bohemia. Beg was ordered to go with Gordon immediately or pay a £ 3 ransom. When the shame-faced Lowrie was dragged into the crowded kirk, he confessed all but insisted that he had been forced to co-operate at pistol-point - "be ane bend (cocked) pistoll haldin to his breist." Although the presbytery was unable to bring Gordon to heel, the sycophantic schoolmaster's sentence was salutary - he was discharged from office and his house demolished.

The unsavoury trio had been plying their trade industriously for some time and, to judge from the contemporary narrative, much of their activity was conducted under cover of darkness to ensure that they laid a personal hand on their victims. By ambushing small farmers like Beg, they had everything in their favour. Faced with the choice of buying himself off or of hastily decamping from friends and fireside to cross the sea and shoulder a pike in a strange land, the victim would inevitably seek out his savings, however reluctantly, and pay down as many of his hard-earned merks as would keep the trio roistering merrily for a time in the alehouses of the district. Buchan was their principal hunting ground. It is easy to imagine how Gordon, with his unscrupulous attendants and his rapier and sinister-looking pistols, had become the scourge of the coastal regions. With word that he was on his rounds, the peasants would hurry from their homes to hide in the mosses until the danger had passed. A record of the time states:

"This sort of deilling put the haill countrey pepill, speciale of the commoun sort, baith maisters and servands, in sic feare that for the space of 14 or 20 dayes they ran fra thair awn houssis in the nicht tyme to the montains, dens, mossis and craigis of the sey(sea), and in fisch boitts remaneit on the sey in gryt multituds, as is notoriouslie knawn."

The demeanour of the people with whom Gordon dealt - dour but essentially peace-loving - would have been slow to comprehend the nature of the imposition being thrust upon them, but if he had returned among them once too often, he might well have been given a rather different reception. The worst charge against him was that, along with others, he had gone to Robert Johnston's home in Tarves and there "perpetrated an outrage that cannot be mentioned."

* **durs** - doors; ** **buird** - table; *** **quilk** - which

The Presbytery of Ellon considered it "sic a obshenous* actioun" that they suspended the proceedings until the truth could be determined. Thomas Gardyne, the maligned minister, along with Gordon's father and villager William Craig, were sent to investigate and returned to confirm the accuracy of the report. The presbytery decided at once to advise the Bishop of Aberdeen of Gordon's enormities and to exhort the justices to arrest Gordon and Mill "for thair allegit commissioun of Bohemia."

History is coy about the nature of Gordon's unmentionable violation, but with the united front ranged against him he made himself scarce - a common practice with delinquents at that period. The record does not attest to him again until five years later, but there is nothing to demonstrate that he had been to Bohemia. By 1626, he returned to his old haunts, for there was then a memorandum to the synod urging the bishop yet again to intercede with the officers of the law. Gordon avoided arrest and disappeared once more, only to return in the following year to ruffle, debauch, bully and bluster among the quiet dwellers of the Tarves district - a bloated 50-year-old reprobate with the ban of the kirk and the censure of the law hanging over him. Unfortunately, the records do not disclose how he met his end.

Violence and death in that raw land were often self-inflicted. Tarves tongues were kept wagging for many a day, for instance, about an incident in 1621 when two men drank themselves to death at Tilliecorthie in a neighbouring parish. It was a sorry tale, recorded for posterity in the annals of the Presbytery of Ellon:

" anent ye drinking in Tilliecorthie when tua men drank them selfis deid."

The drinking spree, featuring a tailor and a gardener from Tilliecorthie and a crofter from Belhelvie, occurred at a public house on the boundary between the nearby parishes of Udny and Foveran. The 17th century scribe reported, with a degree of levity which was scarcely in keeping with the appalling outcome of the incident:

> "They haid drunken so extraordinarlie that not onlie haid they drunkin sic drink as wes on ye gantreis** there for the time, but haid also drunkin a geill fatt *** full of new beir wharthrow**** tua of them wes deid, for they never drank mair."

The scribe went on to recount how the survivor staggered home to Belhelvie to fight with his brother " wha brak his heid and sched his bluid." He appears to have survived, however, for the reporter added:

> " So he lyvis. This being a grievous accident and sin, it is refarit to ye bischope and assemblie what sall be the censure of the man that lyvis and of them wha sald the drink."

History does not reveal the fate of the toper who weathered that fatal tryst with Bacchus. It is certain, however, that interest in the trio's exploits would have transcended for a time any news that might have reached the crofts and farms from the outside world.

---

* **0bshenous** - obscene; ** **gantreis** - shelves; *** **fatt** - vat; **** **wharthrow** - whereby

Chapter 3

Feudal Fetters

MUCH though it would have been merited for endless toil on their stubborn acres, the early Tarvesians were not honoured with a place in the Hall of Fame. The paucity of contemporary records has cast a frustrating veil over their lives, though there are tantalising glimpses which serve to put some pieces of the historical jigsaw together.

The boulder-strewn land of the parish was of little interest to the land-hungry or the opportunist seeking to pile up the 'merks.' The people who laboured on it led a hard, numbing existence. Nor were they beneficiaries of the scholarly research and high-tech communications which make all of us so well informed today. Their knowledge of what had gone before them would have been elementary, much of it harvested from folk lore. Their knowledge of current affairs - if, indeed, they actively sought news of the outside world - would also have been rather limited, though some reliable information would have been imparted by the learned clergymen of the day whose presbytery responsibilities entailed regular travel in both town and country.

There would also have been tales from itinerant tinkers and scraps of information garnered on trips with pannier-slung ponies along the pot-holed moorland tracks to Aberdeen, a score of miles away, the bustling little port of Newburgh, 10 miles distant, or the markets at Inverurie, Ellon and Oldmeldrum. At Aberdeen, they bartered their knitted stockings, skins, hides and corn for fish, cloth and whatever else the townspeople were able to offer. Fisherfolk from the Don and the harbourside village of Footdee at Aberdeen would offer their catches of salmon, whiting, codling, herring and mackerel - salted, smoked or semi-cured. During the season, fishwives with creels on their backs visited the inland parishes like Tarves with bounty from the sea at Collieston, 12 miles away.

Most farmers and crofters in the Formartine landscape paid a portion of their rent in corn, the remainder in money. They were tied to the local landowners and obliged to support them with money, corn, peats, thatching and other services in kind. They were bound, too, by the canons of their heritor's Baron Court, established to settle disputes and dispense justice - for trespass, assault, unpaid rents and the like. It also laid down the rules of husbandry and generally ensured observance of the heritor's rights and whims.

Heritors' rights had been extensive from distant times. At a sitting of the baron court of Tolquhon, for instance, held at 'Lytill Eithsie' (Little Ythsie) on 6 October 1608, with William Forbes of Tolquhon presiding, the peasantry were up in arms about a local meal miller, Alexander Arthur. The proceedings were recorded thus:

> "The haille tennentes of the insuken of the milne of Tolquhon complenit upon Alexander Arthour, milner, for not holden in of the watter to the samen on the watter-gait thereof, and not putting of ane lock on the mill door, qlk was tried to be of trouth for the quilk, he was convict and decernit to amend ye samen in tyme cuming, and pay fourtie shillings for his bye-gane wrang and unlawe."

The not insubstantial charge for that time was that he had allowed the water supply to the meal mill to dry up and had left the precious meal at risk behind an unlocked door at the mill. The penalty was a heavy one. Bringing a miller to book for neglecting his responsibilities would have delighted those who toiled in the fields, for after the harvest they were compelled to take their grain to the mill to have it ground into meal, sacrificing a substantial portion of it - the multure - to the often grasping miller. The peasantry had long regarded this way of doing business as a form of daylight robbery which they must accept through necessity and the force of the heritor's law.

Though an important figure in the community, the miller was usually an unpopular one and Baron Court proceedings reverberate with cases of poor farmers striving to evade this brand of servitude. Moreover, the dice were heavily loaded in the miller's favour for the peasantry were also required to carry out running repairs at the mill and to transport new millstones to it when the old had broken or outlived their use. Small wonder that the miller, clearly on to a good thing, was tempted to take advantage of his fellow man, earning their enmity in the process. A number of Tarves peasants who were clearly seeking to avoid obligations, both to the laird and their miller, were also reprimanded by the Tolquhon court. This is what the record said:

> "William Beg is ordenit be his own consent to set w'in the corneyard at Ythsie, be the advyse of George Mar at ye milne of Ythsie, Duncan Marr in Newseitt, John Mowat in Caldhame, and John Smythe in Boghouse, as much cornes, beir (barley), and aittis(oats) as they think will satisfy the laird for his ferme meil and malt of this instant crap, and as will satisfie George Mar, at ye milne of Ythsie for his insuken multures of his beir and aittes the said yeir, and crop, qlk suld be peyit to ye said miller."

James Walker was in trouble for his amateurish shoeing of a horse:

> "James Walkar, be sufficient trial, was convict of shoeing an horse in a wrang manner, quareby the said horse was made crippell, and decernit to amend in time coming , and to pay fourtie shillings for his bygane wrang to the pairty."

Also in bad odour were members of the Brechin family on a charge which is somewhat unclear to today's reader (though believed to refer to a matter of drainage):

> "James and Duncan Brechin are decernit of thair ain confession to red and haud red ye marche watter gange betwixt ye lands of Ysie and Drumbeck fornent their occupationnis of the saidis landis of Ysie."

The business at another sitting of the same court was largely taken up by late or non-payment of rents, rules to be observed by the tenants and a number of cases of assault. On this occasion, the heritor was respresented by Bailie George Meldrum of Achnive, and the Procurator Fiscal was named as John Duncan. James Man was Notary Public and Clerk of the Land, Alexander Murray was Officer, and Gilbert Chrystie was Demster (Constable). Scores of tenants were ordered to pay their rents "under pain of poynding " (sale of their goods).

They were also ordered to pay their respective debts of meal to John Duncan. Failure to do so would produce a fine of seven merks for every undelivered boll of ferme' meal and eight merks for every boll of 'whyt' meal. Tenants were accused, too, of unwillingness to pay "the sixth part of their silver duty at Whitsunday, Lammas, Martinmass and Candlemass." They were instructed to pay up immediately and to attend all future Martinmas and Whitsunday courts "upon 24 hours advertysement by the ground officer."

Among the defaulters listed as owing rent were:

Ythsie - John Myll & William Geerie	Laverockland - James Allan
Raitshill - Robert Gavin	Balgave - John Lendrum & Gavin Hunter
Newseat of Tolquhon -Thomas Watt	Coldhom - George Gaven
Cairdseat - Robert Myln	Cutchercairn - James Cocker
Mylne of Fuchell - John Gaven	Braesyd -John Smith & Robert Smith
Newseat - William Byres	Mossyd - William Moir
Mill of Tolquhon - Robert Gaven	Myln of Ythsie - Robert Forbes
Overboghouse -Robert Steiven	Boghouse -James Smith/George Douged
Meikle Ythsie - William Gow	Fuchell - Alexr Gray & Alexr Thomson
Old Balgove -Gaven Hunter	Little Ythsie - Isobell Smith

Oldtown of Fuchell - David Beans, George Walker & Alexander Gray

The law was also laid down about the manner in which tenants should transport their meal dues to the laird's victual house:

> "The haill tenents due and lyable in pay of whyt and ferm meall shall cary and transport the samen imediatly after grinding to the maner place of Tolquhon without going to their houses and yt the sd meall shall

be in all tyme coming siffted at the sd victuall house of Tolquhon with certificat that who ever shall contraveen this present act shall and are heirby americat (fined) in the soume of ten pounds Scots toties quoties."*

So much for the laird's trust in the peasantry - he was clearly plugging all the loopholes through which any recalcitrant peasant might seek to avoid delivering his newly-ground meal to the manor house. Sundry instructions which the Baron Court issued to Tarves tenants included the following examples of extra work expected of those who already had on their hands the dawn-to-dusk task of taming the soil:

- ◆ " erect dycks of the road of Blairsoull "
- ◆ " send in six thack sheaves of straw with three winlings of each pleugh" **
- ◆ " attend at Tolquhon to adjust their accompt "
- ◆ " use John Smith for all smith work "
- ◆ " carry ferm meal to the house of Tolquhon and also cut peats "
- ◆ " carry two bolls of lime and eight stone leat of slates to the laird of Tolquhon and also slates and timber payable to the minister's manse within 48 hours "

Domestic rows and fist fights were also on the baron court menu. Among those in the dock at the Tolquhon court were Robert Steven of Overboghouse -already in trouble for not paying his rent - with his sons John and George, and James League and James Bramber of Mill of Tolquhon: " they beat and stirk ane another to the great effusion of their blood "

Their sentence is not given in the dog-eared record. Similarly, there is no published outcome to a domestic row in which Alexander Clerk of Boghouse and his wife, Janet Edward, were accused of beating their neighbour, Patrick Smith. Apparently Clerk had called Smith a "whore's bird" and attempted to strike him with the branch of a tree but was stopped by his wife. There was also a complaint against James Anderson for unwarranted and barbarous riding and the killing of a black horse belonging to John Steven.

In yet another edict to the peasant classes, the court declared:

" Tenants are to convert their terms preferred both for bondage and leitt piets. For each litt of peats consisting of 24 foot of length and 12 part of broad and so properintall for leser quantaties eight pund per litt for each pleugh's bondage qch (which) consists of four hors in harvesting a day and four hors a day lending in harvest, and it is declaired that the uper lands shall pay but ane yocking of mucking at Martinmas, sex hookes and ane bande for a day in harvest."

These extracts serve to demonstrate the zeal with which a heritor of the early 17th century could pursue his calling and the salutary manner in which the complaints of parties were tried and justice dispensed. The Baron Court clearly served as a venue where tenants could come together and interpret custom. It was also the laird's private court, through which he could exert a sweeping

---

* ***toties quoties*** - as often as something happens or occasion demands; repeatedly; ** **pleugh** - plough.

control over society, compel payment of rents and services due to himself and punish crimes committed by the peasants against himself or against the community. Inventories of the time, few though they are for the folk of that landscape, produce evidence of the high values placed on animals and farm equipment in those far-off days. As much as £ 18 Scots was being paid for a young broad-headed black ox. A bull was selling at £ 6 but a black horse fetched £ 16. About £ 11 would buy a mare and foal, while five ewes and lambs were sold at £ 9. 13s 4d. Five hogs fetched £ 6. 13s 4d, and a 'red cow' could be got for £ 6. A 'pleugh and pleugh geir' were worth about £ 8.

Seventeenth century Tarves reeked of sweat, unremitting toil and niggardly returns from stony acres. The names of many of the farms and crofts of that era live on today, albeit spelt to suit modern times, while others have vanished in time. The location of some will forever remain unknown, though the boulders that were their walls and gables may be with us still in the fabric of older farm steadings.

Last century, David Milne, a schoolmaster at King Edward, employed an intimate knowledge of Gaelic to bring to us his interpretation of the old place-names in and around Tarves. It was a bizarre sense of humour, for instance, that bestowed the name 'Doulies' on the eight-acre croft farmed by the author's great-grandparents last century. In the distant past, that drab little place had been known as 'Smiddyhill', but in the mid-1800s the name was changed to the 'Doulies' -' a place where a dwarf or fairies live.' It is doubtful that the little people would have found much to prance about in that gloomy corner of the parish.

According to Milne, 'Tarves' itself was 'an inn or place of hospitality on a height' (tor: a height; uis: hospitality, comfort).'Ythsie' was 'a farm town or a residence near a burn or water' (oth: a water; suidhe: a settlement or residence). 'Tillyeve' (tulach: a little green hill; ibh: a drink) was 'an ale-house on a hill', while 'Auchneive' (achadh: a field; na: of the; ibli: drink) was similarly a 'place of an ale-house.' Perhaps it is a commentary on the social habits of our forebears, but 'Auchinhoof' was also 'the place of an ale-house,' drawn from 'Auchinhiv,' an older form of its name.

'Tillyhilt,' seat of notoriety in the 17th century, was 'a hill frequented by hinds or deer' (tulach: a hill; eilid: a hind),'Tillycairn' was ' a hill with a cairn on the summit', 'Tillygonie' was 'a hill where young cattle were pastured', and 'Tillygreig ' was 'a sunny hill.' 'Boolroad ' was 'a cattle road to a fold where cattle were enclosed and watched at night by common herds.'

'Shethin' had some allegiance with the 'Doulies', being 'a hill frequented by fairies' (siothan: a fairy knoll). It was also, apparently, the place where a baron bailie held court.

'Gateside' was 'a windy town', 'Bronie' a 'glittering or pretty burn' and 'Tolquhon' a 'howe abounding in water rats', while 'Braikley' was 'a spotted hillside' and 'Raxton', or the older form of its name, 'Rawstone,' implied 'rows of houses.'

Not surprisingly, 'Keithfield' had the standing of 'an estate belonging to a Keith, one of the Earl Marischal family' and 'Pitmedden' (pit: a place; meadhon: middle) was 'the middle town.' Further afield, 'Oldmeldrum' was, rather aptly, 'high ground, round on the summit', 'Logiereive' was 'a cattle fold near a hollow', and 'Haddo' was 'a mains or farm occupied by the proprietor of an estate' (hall: proprietor's residence; davoch: a sowing or a farm). 'Cloister Seat' had claims to be 'a place where there was an abode of monks', and 'Auchedly' was 'half of a farm which had been divided' (achadh: field, ground fit for growing corn; leith: half). 'Dumbreck' was 'a spotted ridge' and 'Courtstone' was 'a stone at a circle.'

Being 'a level place on a height', the farm of 'Collynie' seems to have had inbuilt advantages which may have played a significant role in its fame as a cattle breeding mecca. 'Cairdseat' earned its name from 'the place where a smith or tradesman lived' (ceaird: trade or occupation), and 'Cairnbrogie' was a 'grey cairn' (brocach: greyish).

Another cairn - 'Cairnfechil' - was one 'at which a watch was kept and on which a signal was made by a fire' (faichill: guard, watch). 'Raitshill' had a formidable derivation - 'a hill of judgement' (raidh: decision, arbitration; reith: a ram), while it seems that 'Picktillum' was 'a pointed hill' and 'Ironhill' a 'hill where sloes grew.' The 'Gowlie Burn' was 'abundant in trout and eels' and 'Balgove' was 'a smith's town or residence.' Naturally, 'Thornroan' was 'abundant in sloes or thorns'.

Writing in the 17th century, Sir Samuel Forbes of Foveran penned this description of the Formartine district:

> "Whatever land lies between the Rivers Ythan and Don one hears called by the name of Formartine among the inhabitants, who disdain to consider themselves as belonging to Buchan.

> "There is no town in Formartine, for Aberdeen being in the neighbourhood intercepts all traffic. But if the nature of the soil, or the genius of the inhabitants be taken into account, it is worthy of consideration, and inferior to none of its neighbours. To most of them, it is superior in the number of its inhabitants, the richness of its soil, the number of its castles and villas, its amenity, and the refinement and culture of its manners."

It has to be said that Sir Samuel's almost Utopian view of the countryside is somewhat at odds with the commentaries of witnesses writing long after his time. Parish ministers writing as late as the 19th century described a persistent, hand-to-mouth contest with soil and season.

The Herculean efforts by which the land was cleared, drained, enclosed, manured and converted to the rich farming countryside of today was an endeavour covering centuries and all the evidence points to Sir Samuel having viewed his beloved countryside through somewhat rose-tinted spectacles.

" There was no place for these humble folk in the Hall of Fame, for history all but passed them by " - Tarves kirkyard today (above)   Illustration - Gordon D.C.

" One of the finest houses of its day" - ruined Tolquhon Castle, in today's sylvan setting.   Picture - the author.

Chapter 4

On The Seamy Side

THE middle years of the 16th century witnessed the sweeping ecclesiastical revolution called the Reformation. The church of Rome was on the run. Centuries of corruption and of flagging attention to the spiritual needs of the people were replaced by a church and a new brand of clerical tyranny.

When Alexander Ogilvy, last of the Roman Catholic priests, was forced out of his Tarves vicarage in 1574, Thomas Germok became the first of the Presbyterian ministers, responsible for three parishes - Tarves, Methlick and Fyvie. This reflected the dearth of men trained in the new discipline at that time, though he did have the assistance of a reader, Donald Reoch, at Tarves. Germok was succeeded by Thomas Gardyne from Fintray whose long and tempestuous ministry at Tarves ended in him becoming unable by age to discharge the duties of his office. He died in 1633.

Charles I appointed James Moir in his place. Soon, the Scottish nation was alienated by an attempt by Charles to foist an English-style prayer book on the kirk. The King's ploy was interpreted as yet another example of domination from London - a sentiment that still has its adherents in nationalist circles today.

 Apprehensive about the outcome, some bishops fled to England , though one - the Bishop of Brechin - read from the new book in his kirk, with loaded pistols pointed at the congregation! By introducing the prayer book, the king sought to bring Scottish forms of worship into line with those of England but most Scots held adamantly to their Calvinist traditions. The prayer book ignited a blaze of resentment, though in the strongly Episcopalian North-east, history's verdict is that there was no local covenanting zeal worthy of the name.

The virtues of the early Presbyterian Church - custodian of morality, protector of the poor and promoter of the earliest forms of education - were sometimes overshadowed by a pulpit tyranny which seeped into the privacy of ordinary mortals. Country folk walked in awe of the 'meenister' and strong men cringed at the scale of retribution which the Church could visit upon the wrong-doer. It must be emphasised, however, that the Church's interference in domestic affairs was fired by the lawless nature of the times and fulfilment of its own objective of raising the nation's moral standards. The Reformation had asserted a return to scriptural truth and was seen as an opportunity to purge the country of superstitution and to strengthen moral, religious and educational influence. Domination by the Church during the 17th and 18th centuries over the lives of its parishioners - especially their sex lives - screams out from the tattered records of the Presbytery of Ellon. That governing ecclesiastical body for the parishes encompassed by this history was established in 1597 when Roman Catholicism was on the retreat and superstition and persecution were rampant. Indeed, the presbytery's first ordinance was to a minister to provide himself with: "ane comelye and weill bound buik yairin to pen his discipline."

The die was cast - a formidable coterie of grey, often humourless men, who preached fire and brimstone in decaying kirks, among them Thomas Gardyne at Tarves, John Mercer at Methlick and Thomas Tullidaff at Foveran, was resolved to dispense domestic justice in the name of the Almighty.

As W. Douglas Simpson reveals in his *Short History of Tarves*, all of the Church courts in the 17th century were grossly abused by fanatics for their own ends:

> "The cruellest forms of government ever devised by man have been theocracies. There are no crueller or more revolting pages in Scottish history than those which were traced in blood and persecution when the Covenanters were in full control in Scotland, through the General Assembly of the Kirk, in the years before Cromwell's conquest. And even in the records of the lower church courts, we find revealed a tyrannical control over the lives and thoughts of men and women, an inquisitorial supervision of their private lives, and an organised system of detection and spying which no modern society, in this country at least, could tolerate. Inevitably, however, these records are over-much concerned with the seamy side of parochial life."

Indeed, scarcely was the Ellon Presbytery under way in 1596 than the first of a virtually endless procession of sexual offenders came under its opprobrium. William Mitchell, a Tarves parishioner, recorded as being "delinquent with Barbra Leslie", was sentenced to report to Tarves Church on six successive Sundays "in sack-cloathe, barefooted and barelegged and to sit lykwayes before he enter to his repentance in gowis* or brankis "- attached to the church wall by a square iron neck frame and chain as a warning to others who might contemplate similar adventures of the flesh. Since Mitchell's girlfriend was reported to be living in Old Aberdeen, the Tarves minister was instructed to make contact with the minister there to ensure that she suffered a similar penalty.

---

* **gowis or brankis** - *a scold's bridle; an instrument of punishment consisting of an iron framework for the head and having a sharp metal gag which restrained the tongue.*

On the same day a pair of Newburgh lovers were told that they would escape the "gowis or brankis" by paying "ten merkis of silver", and Patrick Hay of Haddo, who interceded for the absolution of Crystall Pratt, recently excommunicated, was advised of the Presbytery's refusal until "he has put away the harlot MacLannan and shows signs of repentance."

A four-year wrangle between the presbytery and George Gordon of Gicht, whose bitterness echoes in the dog-eared pages of the presbytery record today, began with an accusation that he and his wife Isobell Wood were professed enemies of religion and "had laitlye caused ane popish priest baptize ane bairne to them." Young Gicht, as a leading Roman Catholic, would have been a prime target for the clergy's wrath. He alleged that the Tarves minister had refused to baptise his child - a charge which Thomas Gardyne denied. In page after page in the record, Gicht is summoned to appear before the brethren but nothing will induce him to attend. Excuse after excuse is trotted out. Gicht spun out nearly four years putting off the evil day by one device or another, but finally, in September 1601, sentence of excommunication was pronounced.

About the same time, Barbara Gray, Lady Bonitoun, and her sisters-in-law Margaret and Lilias Wood suffered a similar fate for "avowed contempt of the Word and Sacraments " by arranging a Jesuit baptism at night in a local stream.

A scandal which brought many months of anguish to the clerical martinets turned the spotlight on other branches of the Gordon family - James Gordon of Haddo and his cousin, John Gordon, the "Guidman " (laird) of Tillyhilt. Tillyhilt's daughter Agnes had "cast her glamourie " over Haddo, though he was betrothed to the Laird of Udny's daughter, Helen. Haddo and Helen Udny had plighted their troth to one another solemnly with uplifted hands, as was the custom of the time, and banns of marriage between them had been proclaimed three times. Perhaps familiarity had bred a degree of disenchantment, but it is certain that Haddo had become a frequent visitor to the mansion at Tillyhilt where Agnes Gordon made him welcome as she best knew how. Now - in 1599 - when it surely seemed too late, Haddo craved the Presbytery to relieve him of his obligation to Helen. So often harsh in its treatment of simple sons and daughters of the soil, the presbytery was oddly circumspect, preferring to remit Haddo's predicament to the Presbytery of Aberdeen.

The delay did not suit Agnes. One of her brothers made out a fraudulent certificate purporting to be from the Methlick minister and claiming that the banns of marriage had been proclaimed between Agnes and Haddo. Armed with this document, the lovers took horse and rode off over the moors to Ruthven, near Forfar - an adventurous crusade of some days - where they persuaded the local minister, the Rev David Henderson, to solemnise a marriage between them. Among the witnesses were Alex Johnson of Tarves and Lawrence Cheyne of Bracklaw.

The intermittent and wasted records of the time do not reveal when the lovers returned to their native heath but it is clear that the Presbytery of Ellon did not let up in its determination to extract its pound of flesh.

For we find that the 'Guidman' of Tillyhilt was summoned by it "for tryall off ye counterfaite testimoniall," though he declined to appear on the grounds of "ane deadlie feud betwix Gicht and him." Ultimately, however, he was arraigned before the clerics at Foveran where he confessed that his eldest son James had forged the certificate at his mother's suggestion. The Presbytery ruled that he should be fined £ 20 and repent his delinquencies. The records are silent on the fate of the forger.

The 'Guidman' Gordon had sired a truly troublesome family. His son John, brother of he who forged the certificate of banns for his sister Agnes, became the notorious vagabond whose story was told in the previous chapter. And Agnes was not long in the wings. The glamorous Dame who had snatched the Laird of Haddo from under his fiancee's nose was back in the limelight a few years later, accused by the Methlick minister, the Rev John Mercer, of being guilty of infidelity to her husband with a retainer, Patrick Barclay. In the decayed pages of the presbytery record there lurks a drama which smacks of D.H. Lawrence, with Agnes cast as the 'Lady Chatterley' of Formartine.

After denying the charge upon oath, Agnes was ordered to "avoid suspicious societie" with Barclay and to remove him from the laird's service before next Whitsunday, a few weeks hence. She was told by the ministers that if she failed to dismiss him, she would be held as having confessed to adultery! She was also reminded of an affair a year or two earlier which had led to a tumult in the kirk of Cruden.

The Methlick minister, a quarrelsome and vindictive man, was a sworn enemy of Lady Agnes and was again in the thick of the fray when Whitsunday passed with Barclay still ensconced at Haddo. The lovers - for that they surely were - again appeared before the grim assembly and were ordered to "obey the voice of the kirk." Agnes offered the ingenious explanation that her husband - not she - had retained Barclay beyond the prescribed date. "It was his deed," she told the clerics. Mercer would have none of it, declaring that she had "gevin counsell and persuadit ye laird, hir husband, to reteine him."

Moreover, Mercer, sensing victory over the titled 'besom'* he had grown to loathe, told the gathering that she had been seen "riddin on horsbak behind the said Patrik betwix touns, and namelie betwix Kellie and Haddo." While admitting this to be the case, Anges emphasised that she had always been accompanied by others on these occasions. Mercer then played what he considered was his ace card. The record states:

> "Being inquyrit gif scho lay ane nicht in ane barne of Kellie, the Laird, hir husband, being in the Place of Kellie, the said Patrik lay in that barne also, confessit scho lay that nicht in that barne, but ye said Patrik lay in ane uther Bed there besyd the uther men with him."

Barclay denied having "his cloak cassin ower** hir." It is clear from the repetitious entries in the record that the presbytery members, led by Mercer, were determined

---

* **besom** - a low woman; ** **cassin ower** -thrown over

to spike the lady's guns. It was inevitable that the simmering feud between her and the Methlick preacher would boil over. Mercer alleged that Agnes had called him a liar and that she was a witch who had such a hold over her husband that "he culd not fle hir companie." She did not deny these accusations but counter-charged Mercer with having rebuked her as a "deboshit harlat." *

Cornered, Mercer conceded that he had used this description, but only after - he said - she had called him a "deboshit screinger" while he was in the company of other parishioners and friends. Clearly, Mercer was furious about being dubbed in public as a "screinger " - one who drifts about the countryside, eating and drinking at large and gathering in malicious gossip. It was characteristic of the daring and apparently shameless daughter of the Guidman of Tillyhilt that she should confront her enemy in the midst of his friends.

A year later, Barclay was still enjoying the comforts of Haddo and the presbytery was exhorting the Synod of Aberdeen - in vain it appears - to bring the wrath of the kirk upon the heads of the sinning couple. The record fades with the presbytery demanding that the lovers "mak their publict repentance on their kneis befoir the pulpit ". The end can only be surmised, though it seems unlikely that compromise or capitulation would even have suggested themselves to such a spirited and wayward lady.

The peasantry did not weep when they learned of the demise of the fiery Mercer who had taken pride in his self-appointed authority to "dang** the puir man" and "cudgel the contumacious." He was a man who almost continuously had strife or trouble on his hands. Even his daughter brought him angst. Margaret Mercer went astray first with Patrick Smyth at Slains, then with George Black at Birness, a married man, and a third time with John Beidie at the Mill of Brogan. Some might have felt entitled to view Margaret's sexual adventures as just deserts visited upon a pugnacious cleric who had kept his parishioners in perpetual fear.

The presbytery's predilection for sexual matters produced a seemingly endless trek of miscreants to its doors, there to receive the inevitable punishment of having to stand barefoot and in sackcloth on the stool of repentance over several Sundays at their own kirk. Sometimes, according to the severity of the offence or the mood of the ministers, there was the additional indignity of having half the head forcibly shaven - in the case of men, the beard too - or being chained to the outside wall of the kirk as a lesson to others who might be planning like brushes with damnation.

Again and again there are cases of excommunication - banishment from the church and sacraments - and women transgressing against the divine law were reproved as "prophane godless contumacious harlotts." The unending recital of sexual aberrations would be tedious to the reader today were it not for the sheer variety listed in the ancient record. Four hundred years ago, for instance, John Littlejohn incurred the presbytery's wrath for a "prophane mockerie of ye ministrie and prophanation of mariage "- he had taken it upon himself at nearby Foveran to marry John Nicoll to two women - Catherine Innes and Isobel Christie.

---

* **deboshit harlat** - *debauched harlot* ; ** **dang**-*struck, hit*

Nicoll confessed "yat he sat doun upon ye stuile appoynted for mairage and speired (asked) quha (who) wald sit doun with him." The record adds:" Isobell Crystie and Catharine Innes sat doun besyde him upon ye stuile and yat yairefter (then) he speired quha wald marye them, and ye said John announced yat never ane misthrave yat he maryed, efter ye quhilk (which) answeare he confessed to tougled (chose) ye said Isobell Crystie."

Nicoll was ordered to sit three Sundays dressed in sackcloth, bare-foot and bare-legged, upon the stool of repentance. There is no record of the punishment imposed on Littlejohn. Isobel Christie was ordained to "satisfie the kirk as ane fornicatrix " while Catherine Innes appears to have been let off the hook. One wonders what the presbytery's ruling would have been had Nicoll married both women, as was originally intended, instead of expressing a preference for Christie!

About the same period, Christine Ross who confessed delinquency with James Anderson, was "injoynit to make repentance sax Sondays in sackcloth and goneis (iron neck halter) with hir half heid schavin "(with her head half shaven). For a similar offence, James Fyfe was instructed to "make repentance sax Sondays in sackcloth and pay ten merks money, or else to stand the sax Sondays in the goneis ane half hour befoir sermone ilk Sonday and ane half hour efter sermone, bairfuttit and bairleggit." *

In 1622, the ministers of Tarves, Ellon and Foveran visited the home of James Ogilvie at Blerack to publicly warn his wife, Marjorie Gordon -the Gordons again! - to terminate her "suspicious behaviour " with George Hay, son of the laird of Brunthill. They reported that "efter lang and tedious expostulatiounis and recriminatiounis with her " she was given "publict admonitioun'. Nearly two years later, despite admonitions from presbytery and synod, the scandal between the two was reported to be worse than ever. Hay had been given a room in the house and Ogilvie, the husband, had apparently made him his heir! Three years on, the minister was under orders to "try cairfullie the scandelous conversatioune of George Hay and Marjorie Gordon, guidwyff **of Blerack," and sharply rebuked for being negligent about doing so in the past. It seems there was no letting up by the holy men, though the record does not bring this case to a conclusion.

A case of using a sledge-hammer to crack a nut is suggested by the arraignment of Captain William Barclay, held to be guilty of "a flagrant scandell and open prophanation of the Lord's day in the parioch*** of Tarves." He was charged with "lying in wait for and trubling the Ladie of Towie and her relations in their passage towards the Church of Methlick." The matter was referred to the Bishop of Aberdeen who ruled that nothing should be done "till the lords of his Majestie's privy council have examined that matter." Much ado about nothing?

While the Civil War was raging, James Reith of the Mains of Drumbreck was before the presbytery for harbouring a vagabond called Margaret Reidheid. He pleaded that she " hade possest hir selff within his barne " but that was held to be an inadequate excuse. Robert Seaton, his master, agreed, under a penalty of £ 5,

---

* **bairfuttit and bairleggit** - barefoot and barelegged ; **guidwyff** - laird's wife; *** **parioch** - parish

that they would " be more warie in tymes to cum." About this time, too, Robert Wood and Isobel Paul had to repent their affair, with the ministers declaring that Isobell should be "punishit in hir bodie efter ye strickest maner because of hir former affrontit lies." In 1686, George Wood was in trouble for "ane actione which had given great scandel and offence to many" - selling his wife, Margaret Donaldson, to James Pirie for £ 5. In defence, Pirie told the church court that he was "ane merchant and had libertie to buy any wares." As might have been expected, both men joined the long column of evil-doers craving absolution in sackcloth. This would surely have been a ripe item of gossip throughout the parish, as would have been the restoration to kirk membership of William Forbes of Craigie. Forbes, it seems, was at last absolved, having paid his penance for a "quintulapse" (having transgressed five times) with Janet Anderson which had earned him debarment from the communion at Tarves for a number of years.

John Marr of Moss-side of Fuchell, Tarves, appealed to the presbytery in 1735 to rescind their refusal to allow him to marry. His freedom to wed had been blocked by one, Elspet England, who alleged breach of a promise made to her while they were casting peats in a moss at Tarves. She alleged that after seeking marriage with her, he had gone to her home and offered her a guinea to stop troubling him - a charge which he denied. Marr produced witnesses who claimed they had heard Elspet England deny the existence of the marriage proposal. While revoking the prohibition against him, the churchmen recommended that Tarves Kirk Session should "be tender in proceeding upon mere fama clamosas of promises of marriage....and hereby testify their abhorrence of the practice in general of pretending to give promises of marriage before people in providence are in proper circumstances."

It may come as no surprise to readers today that the men of the cloth were themselves not entirely above reproach. On 19 June, 1605, for instance, the Rev Thomas Gardyne of Tarves was rebuked on account of his fondness for the public house -'oistlar hous '- and of playing at cards, rattling the dice-box and 'civill trysting '- conviviality. These are the terms under which he was admonished:

> "Heirupon Mr Thomas Gardyne wes chargit to forbeir ye oistlar hous, carting, dyceing, civill trysting - to await on his buik - to teich on ye Saboth at efternone, to censure and punisch absents fra ye kirk, drunkards, banneris and sweireris, and to labour for settling ane scuil maister."

Not to be outdone, the church officer, Thomas Moir, was also reprimanded for his 'drunkines'. The Rev Thomas Mair, to whom a great debt is owed for transcribing the Ellon Presbytery record, commented:

> "The charges against Mr Gardyne all point with no uncertain finger in one direction - that his failings lay much in line with those of the easy-going vicars or 'Mess Johns' from the Abbey of Arbroath, whose place he had taken in the manse and kirk of Tarves. In the lordly hall and great courtyard of Tolquhon, then in all its early and newly-erected grandeur, his jovial voice had been heard, and from the doors of his well-to-do parishioners on the fat lands of Tarves, when the hour for

parting came, he had turned not empty away, with a last hail as to the night of their next 'civill tryst. Lest there be any misunderstanding, however, it should be stated that there is no word or hint of any charge against Mr Gardyne beyond what is given here. Had there been any grounds for such, it would likely have been set down, for our ancestors seem to have been men, whether ministers or laity, who went straight to the mark in their language, either spoken or put on record.'

Two years after his arrival in neighbouring Udny in 1766, the Rev George Adams was accused of having fought with Alex Smith, a parishioner, late at night in a local public house. Adams admitted having ejected Smith from the inn, after being kicked and called a rascal and a liar. The presbytery found that Mr Adams had been greatly provoked and that there was nothing censurable in his conduct. The record does not inform the researcher if anyone asked what Mr Adams was doing in a pub late at night!

The Rev Thomas Tullidaff and fellow Presbytery of Ellon ministers survived accusations by parishioners early in the 17th century that they were "soukeris out of ye bluid of ye puir." The presbytery was told: " They preichit in pulpit against extortioun and sowking of ye bluid of ye puir, and sum of them selffis war the grytest extorsioneris and bluidsowkeris." The antics of the Formartine ministers were eclipsed in 1632 when the Rev David Rattray was removed from his kirk at Cruden. It had been alleged that :

"The Sabbath is profaned in Cruden universally by shearing and leading in harvest, and other handiwork. Stranger vagabond beggars are taken in, the burial silver is not duly taken up, the kirk is ruinous and the kirk yard dikes down, and Mr Rattray himself putts his cattell and hors in the kirk yard."

Fellow clerics also averred that they:

"Never knew him to cleith himself as becom him in his Ministrie and he had done na guid bot much evill in his calling in that place."

Rattray was in debt, too, in danger of being put to the horn (outlawed and his goods sold) by an Aberdeen burgess whom, he told the presbytery, he "haid narrowlie eschapeit within few dayis."

The charges mounted, one upon the other. The brethren "are informit to thair gryt grief that everie Saboth day there is a market at the kirk of Cruden." No accounts had been kept of church collections and the fees of the church reader and officer had been in arrears for five years.

The chronicler of the presbytery records commented:

"For the third part of a century he had hung upon their shoulders like a dead weight. Whatever other of his talents he had allowed to rust, he had cultivated a certain engineering gift by which he could make a kirk impregnable. The day before an expected visit from the presbytery had been a busy one with him and his officer in making fast the kirk door and in expeditions to the smiddy for new nails and 'stepills' for the purpose."

He added:

> "When the day of trial and visitation dawned, his strategy seemed to consist in making a masterly retreat with his family across the hills to some outlying quarter of his wide parish, leaving his kirk officer on the scene in the character of a simple innocent, but whose eyes and ears would have been alert enough to all that passed when the presbytery deputation arrived and a congregation of the people - amid them some wives with infants in their arms and eager to have them baptised. While these clamoured in the kirkyard and gazed blankly at the unyielding doors, or sieged away at them, using every endeavour to effect an entrance short of actually battering them in, David himself - 'far from the madding crowd's ignoble strife' on some upland heath - would have been free to linger and listen to the carolling of the lark.

> "When the day had run its course, David had again drawn in towards them with his wife and family - the congenial spouse and daughter who gathered in the 'lawing' on that market day in Cruden when he turned the manse into a public house. His first business on arrival had been to foregather with his satellite beside their fortified kirk, and the garrulous narrative may be imagined as he told how his heart misgave when some of the parishioners 'clam in at the windows' to take their fortifications in reverse, and the grim smile on the countenance of his chief as he learned how they had to climb down again, baffled of their purpose."

The Presbytery's patience was also driven to the limit many years later by the Rev Alexander Howe who in 1759 - the birth year of Scotland's bard, Robert Burns - chose to rebuke the Tarves schoolmaster, a mere stripling of just 18 years, by giving him a 'lunder'* on the shoulders with his staff. When called to account by his peers, he insisted that the schoolmaster, Archibald Davidson, had become a new man since receiving the violent chastisement!

The presbytery chronicler wrote:

> "The picture has an interest of its own as faithful to the time and its manners - the sturdy and somewhat domineering old minister, in cornered hat and heavy coat, with hosen only below the knee, and buckled shoes, in his administrative capacity sparing not the rod."

Howe stoutly refused to admit he had been wrong. Within a few years, he was taking his own will more and more and, as if deaf to the calls and appeals of the brethren, sat at bay in the Manse of Tarves, absenting himself from presbytery gatherings for some years without satisfactory defence or excuse. Finally, in the Spring of 1764, he advised the presbytery that he had "great pleasure in meeting

lunder - whack, blow

his brethren but since his advanced years was grown so tender in his health and particularly so distressed with the gout that he could not so regularly attend as he inclined." His death the following year avoided an embarrassing showdown with his colleagues.

Evidence abounds of the kill-joy nature of the clerics of that time. Down the years, peasant folk who on a Sunday went to market or danced or played football were assured of eternal damnation. "Drinking in houssis and fuitball and playing and dansing opinlie in the fields" were strictly taboo. So, too, was ingathering of the harvest, regardless of the weather, or the driving of cattle.

By such men - or at least some of them - was the laity judged. Retribution was visited upon the moral waywardness of courting couples in that stark countryside. Illegitimacy was almost a way of life then. Scotland had a higher illegitimacy rate than England and most of Europe. This, says Edinburgh history researcher Diane Baptie, writing in the *Manchester Genealogist*, is extremely surprising, with kirk sessions censoring those down the centuries who had committed the sin of fornication.

"Some session books," she writes, "consist almost entirely of such transgressions. Many of those in the 17th and 18th centuries contain pages of investigation, including witnesses' depositions. Punishment could be severe - heavy fines were levied and the parties would have to appear in sackcloth, often 'bare-leggit and bare-footed'. The couple is often recorded as having to appear before the congregation for endless Lord's days, and in those days almost the whole Sunday was spent in church. No wonder one or other of the parties absconded, being reported in the minutes as 'furth of the country.'* If he or she returned, an appearance before the presbytery would result, and this court could excommunicate church members."

Cases of abandoned children were legion,and according to Diane Baptie, the kirk session would employ midwives to go round the parish to identify anyone who had recently given birth. In this way, the mother was located and then the father's name would be found out and sentence pronounced. Pregnancy in its later stages is difficult to hide and the members of the kirk session would be on the lookout for this. Many couples did not wait to be summoned but appeared voluntarily and this often mitigated in their favour. Visiting troops and sailors caused problems when they moved on, their whereabouts being difficult to ascertain, and sometimes the army and navy would be recalcitrant in following up a letter from a minister.

It was only in the 20th century that the church abandoned its pressure on those accused of 'uncleanness,' as fornication was often called. Some records reveal that while the woman appeared before the kirk session, the man did not. Rather than persist in trying to persuade the man to appear, the church would grant the woman a Certificate of Poverty. This enabled her to pursue the man in the civil courts for 'inlying expenses' (confinement) and maintenance of the child. If he did not pay up, then she could have him 'put to the horn' - declared an outlaw and his belongings sold.

*** furth of the country** - abroad*

In just such a case in 1834, the author's great-great grandfather, John Porter, a Tarves labourer, was pursued through the courts by Helen Kelly, a 'kitchen quine'* at Raitshill. He denied the child she was expecting was his and fled the parish when she threatened to expose him to the kirk session. In her predicament, the 26-year-old Helen was granted a Certificate of Poverty which allowed her to pursue her erstwhile paramour through the courts as 'Poor Helen Kelly.' Quite how she contrived, as the asthmathic mother of an infant and with a tying job in rural surroundings, to track down the runaway in Aberdeen and persist with the chase for four years, is not alluded to in the records.

When the court's decision in favour of Helen was conveyed to the runaway's home in the city's Causewayend, he had flown the nest, leaving the court's messenger-at-arms, Alexander Milne, no alternative but to declare Porter an outlaw, signifying his new status with three blasts on the horn at the city's Mercat Cross. It is evident, however, that under the force of law Porter ultimately paid his debt to Helen Kelly, though he never consented to recognise her son. Little did the illegitimate son realise the problems he was setting future family researchers when he erected a memorial in Tarves kirkyard to his mother Helen Kelly, without any reference to a father. The memorial is still there today.

Clues to the high illegitimacy rate in rural Scotland are to be found in Professor T.C. Smout's book, *A Century of the Scottish People 1830-1950*:

> "It was always in the interests of farm workers to ensure that their future wives were capable of having children who would add to the family income and look after the couple when they got old. The significant point is not only that love was very physical, but that parental control was minimal. It was difficult to assert control since the children left home as teenagers and went to work on farms where the employer was generally very unwilling to stand in loco parentis. And was it ultimately in anyone's interest to prevent a girl having sex with her lover if that was the way to get a husband, start a family and set up a household when they were both young and at their peak earning levels as wage labourers?"

In a series of unusually frank articles in *The Scotsman* in 1870, Dr J.M. Strachan, a general practitioner at Dollar, said: "It was unusual for working class lovers to meet in public. The ordinary thing was to meet after dark, at the back of a haystack, in a barn or an outhouse, or, especially in the case of servant maids, in the girl's bedroom. Each meeting lasted for two or three hours and was repeated weekly, a girl perhaps having several such lovers and a boy not regarding it as wrong to visit different girls after this fashion."

It doesn't take an expert, however, to recognise the attractions of a maid servant's bed or the temptations of the hay-loft at harvest time to a labourer coping with spartan facilities in a cold, stinking bothy! During the closing years of the 18th century, many instances were reported of erring couples offering to pay sums of money to the kirk session to avoid the usual form of repentance and this practice ultimately took hold all over the North-East countryside.

quine - girl or young woman

Chapter 5

A Melancholy Land

VIEWED from the convenience of the 20th century, the well-ordered vista of lush farmland that is Tarves today bears little resemblance to that in which our forebears sought to make a living. Three hundred years ago, it was a melancholy land, a truly insignificant blip on the map of Scotland, wedged between the lowlands of Buchan and outlying knuckles of the Grampian Mountains.

The obdurate acres which ensnared our ancestors rank today, in a paradox bordering on mockery, with the richest and most productive farmland in the world. Our forebears did not savour its Midas touch. The fruits of their valiant toil were to be enjoyed by others in a later age.

Like all the neighbouring parishes, 17th century Tarves was a gloomy place, existing almost in a time warp. For beyond Formartine's boundaries, the century was a period of spectacular progress in scientific belief, a watershed between the old and new worlds. It was the age of Sir Isaac Newton, Galileo, and Kepler, challenging and debunking the medieval approach to knowledge. The British philosopher, Bertrand Russell, was to write of it:

> "Almost everything that distinguished the modern world from earlier centuries is attributable to science which achieved its most spectacular triumphs in the 17th century."

In backwaters like Tarves, however, the feudal shackles of the medieval age were still firmly in place. No historian has researched this period more keenly than Professor T.C. Smout of the University of St Andrews.

In his *History of the Scottish People 1560-1830*, he describes the countryside of the time:

"In place of a chequer-board of separate fields, one must imagine the ground everywhere lying as open as moorland, studded with thickets of broom and gorse but unprotected from the sweeping winds by woods or planted rows of trees and seldom divided in any way by hedge, wall or dyke, apart from the broad earthen head-dyke which marked the perimeter of the cultivated area around a settlement. The pastoral land beyond the head-dyke was all more or less rough brown waste: there was no question of grass being cultivated as a crop. The ploughed land within was a series of undulating strips or rigs, divided into blocks by weedy baulks, studded with large boulders, which have been mostly cleared today. Except where knolls presented a chance of island cultivation, the narrower valleys had to be neglected except as a source for a little rough and rushy hay."

The drainage which made the Tarves farmland what it is today was far beyond the capacity of the peasant folk of that time. Professor Smout comments:

"The contemporary English travellers who wrote about this countryside, squelching through it on a wet horse from one dirty inn to another, found it all intensely depressing and greatly inferior to the neat, prosperous enclosed farms of much of their own country. Outsiders also noticed the absence of villages as they were known in England. In Scotland the unit of settlement was a hamlet centring on a notional farm, the size of which was determined by the area that one or sometimes two or three plough teams of horses or oxen could keep under cultivation."

Another very reliable source is the *New Statistical Account of Scotland,* to which the Rev Francis Knox of Tarves brought an intimate knowledge of the local scene. Though writing in 1842, he drew from the experience of generations of his own farming family. This is what he reported:

"The stagnation of water on the low ground utterly precluded tillage, while the arable lands were over-run with noxious weeds, and chilled from November to May by innumerable land springs. The cultivated ground was divided into what was called infield and outfield. The former received all the manure of the land and was perpetually in crop. The latter consisted of rig and baulk - arable ridges, between every two of which there was an interjacent space termed a baulk which the plough never disturbed.

"The arable part was cropped with oats five years in succession and then permitted to lie in pasture for the same number of years to recruit its exhausted powers of production. Green crops, with the exception of a few potatoes and colewarts* in the gardens of the farmers and peasantry, were unknown.

"The implements of husbandry and the mode of using them were equally crude. Two men with ten or twelve oxen yoked in a team barely

* *colewort* - any plant of the cabbage kind, eg kail.

accomplished the work which one man with two horses in a plough can at present perform without difficulty. The horses employed in agriculture were diminutive in size and used merely for burden, never draught. They carried out manure, and home peats, in paniers or creels, and the meal to be sold was conveyed to market in sacks laid across the horses' backs.

"Carts and wheel carriages were only to be found in the possession of landed proprietors. Depressed by bad seasons and deficient in capital, the peasantry had neither the courage nor the means to attempt expensive innovations."

Writing half a century earlier, one of Mr Knox's predecessors - the Rev Thomas Mitchell - listed the crops of the parish as oats, peas, turnips and potatoes. Any surplus grain was sold at Aberdeen, Inverurie or Oldmeldrum, or was exported through Newburgh to England, the Low Countries or Scandinavia. Butter, cheese, eggs and poultry were also sold in the city. Oats sown in March or April were generally reaped in September or October, and barley, sown a month later, was harvested towards the end of August.

Mr Mitchell shared Mr Knox's view of why the peasantry were unwilling to experiment with new methods of husbandry:

"As the leases are seldom longer than 19 years and many of the tenants pay fines or grassums, they have no encouragement for improvement."

In the adjoining parish of Udny, the Rev John Rose had this to say:

"The farmers are far from being in comfortable circumstances. Few of them have money for purchasing a sufficient flock of cattle and are never able to improve them. By following the old mode of farming, though they work hard along with their servants, and live with great sobriety, they can scarcely pay their rents. The women and children are employed in working stockings for the manufacturers in Aberdeen. They or their servants come once a fortnight, give wool to be spun, and worked on the wires into stockings. A woman gains from 1s 6d to 2s a week. Some few spin lint, by which a little more may be gained."

According to Professor Smout, the clustered settlements in the North-East were known as 'ferm-touns' - or 'kirk-touns' if they contained the parish church, 'mill-touns' if they had a mill, or 'cot-touns' if the settlement was largely occupied by poor cottars. Thanks to highly skilled research by professional historians like him, it is possible to visualise how Tarvesians looked and lived in their crude 17th century dwellings. These were built mostly of turf or stone, of which there was a profusion in the vicinity, and of skin and brushwood, thatched with heather or straw and partly subterranean as protection against the bleak climate. It was probably very like the 17th century lowland peasant dwellings described by English army chaplain, the Rev Thomas Morer, about 1690:

> "The vulgar houses and what are seen in the villages are low and
> feeble. Their walls are made of a few stones jumbled together without
> mortar to cement 'em, on which they set up pieces of wood meeting at
> the top, ridge-fashion, but so order'd that there is neither sightliness
> nor strength ... they cover these houses with turff of an inch thick and
> in the shape of larger tiles which they fasten with wooden pins and
> renew as often as there is occasion; and that is very frequently done.
> 'Tis rare to find chimneys in these places, a small vent in the roof
> sufficing to convey the smoake away."

Floors were earthen, with straw in the main living space. Glazed windows were
then a luxury not enjoyed by the peasantry, and the source of light was no more
than small square openings in the walls, the ever-present wind ineffectually
excluded by boarding or crude curtains of sacking or other primitive material.
There is overwhelming evidence that people and animals shared the same living
space but it is probable that the cattle byre was separated from the hearth by
boards. This may have contributed to the much-needed warmth but would have
done nothing to improve the stench in these shared quarters.

Professor Smout:

> "It would be fair to picture the head of the family and his wife sleeping
> at night in a box bed, with the children and servants curled up in their
> plaids on straw pallets around the fire, though sometimes there would
> be more division of the house, more box-beds and more privacy. Apart
> from the bed, the meal kists and a stool or two, the husbandman had
> little furniture."

Indeed, the household possessions were unlikely to have included more than a
few pots, a kettle, a chest or two, a table, one or two chairs or stools, some rough
bed-clothes, and some cups, spoons and wooden plates.

Thomas Kirke described Scottish crofter homes thus in 1679:

> "The houses of the commonality are very mean, mud-wall and thatch
> the best; but the poorer sort lives in such miserable hutts as never eye
> beheld; men, women and children pig together in a poor mouse-hole
> of mud, heath and some such like matter; in some parts where turf
> is plentiful they build up little cabbins thereof with arched roofs of turf
> without a stick or timber in it; when their houses are dry enough to
> burn it serves them for fuel and they remove to another."

The historian might suspect Kirke of exaggerating if there were not also accounts
from the early eighteenth century of lairds depositing their cottars' houses on the
dunghill after they had evicted their occupants, and illustrations from the same
period of Highland homes that were simple tents of wattle with no opening other
than a hole at ground level through which a man would have had to crawl on
hands and knees to gain entry.

In a reference to the earliest architectural drawings of rural housing in Scotland, dating from 1701 and thought to be a pair of stone cottages flanking the entrance to a laird's home farm, Professor Smout comments:

> " One is described as the henwife's house, the other as the foreman's hall: each consisting of a single room thirteen foot by nine, lit by an unglazed window two foot by three, with a chimney-hearth in one corner and what appears to be a box-bed in the other. Adjacent to each house is a separate raised privy with three seats, from which the excrement fell into an open midden yard to accumulate until cleared away for use on the farm. Apart from the curious and insanitary toilet arrangements, there can be no doubt that this represented something a little superior to the standards of cottar housing described by Kirke. At least the external appearance did the architect credit."

In the rugged fashion of the time, the men wore trousers under a belted plaid - a woollen blanket that served as somewhat basic protection from the elements during the day and as a bed-wrap at night. Women invariably wore a linen skirt with plaid draped over head or shoulders, pinned at the bosom and falling to the knees. Like the children, the women went barefoot.

Thomas Morer had this to say about the practice:

> "The husbands have shoes, and therein seem unkind in letting their wives bear these hardships."

Even then, however, there was some pride in appearance, for the Rev Alexander Knolls at Methlick wrote of his parishioners:

> "They are generally frugal, more expensive in dress than in diet."

And John Ray wrote in 1682:

> "They lay out most they are worth in cloathes, and a fellow that hath scarce ten goats besides to help himself with, you can see come out of his smoaky cottage clad like a gentleman."

Oatmeal was life's staple, whether in the form of porridge, brose*, gruel, oatcakes or bannocks. Cows and goats produced a steady source of milk, butter and cheese. Kail, grown in yards close to the dwellings, was used to make broth.

The rutted paths which served as Tarves's communications with the outside world rumbled frequently to the passing of great herds of cattle. For Tarves was situated on the old drove road from Aikey Fair in Buchan to the great cattle sales at Falkirk Tryst in the Central Lowlands of Scotland. The ancient way crossed the Ythan at Tangland Ford to reach Tarves by the Lindsay Hills. It went on over the Hill of Craigdam to fords on the Don at Thainstone and the Dee at Kincardine O' Neil, before scaling the Cairn O' Mounth and heading south to Stirling and Falkirk.

* **brose** - a meal made by pouring boiling water, or milk, on oatmeal seasoned with salt and butter

Great herds had been driven over this route from the earliest of times and there were occasions when a drove coming through Tarves would have its leading animals at Craigdam and the tail-end coming up the Lindsay Hills, three miles away. The records of the ancient Abbey of Arbroath allude to one drove of 6000 head. In these great animal treks many dealers joined forces for driving and safety along the pot-holed way. At intervals on the road were great "commonties" for resting the cattle overnight, one of which was at Raxton Howe in Tarves. The dust and excrement left in the animals' wake, and the damage caused by strays wandering from the main body made them thoroughly unwelcome in the village. As early as 1625 the kirk resolved that "if any beast be got in the kirkyard in time coming, the owner will have to pay two merks."

Water supplies were hand-drawn from a number of wells in the district - pumps would come later. Stone and clay thatched houses squatted around a nondescript village square which one heavy shower of rain would transform into a quagmire. Without drainage or any other form of utility, the backyards of the houses were indescribably filthy.

No-one had yet troubled to officially measure the parish. Indeed, writing for the *Statistical Account of Scotland* as late as 1790, the Rev Thomas Mitchell of Tarves described it as being "sixty ploughs of land" - the computation by which tenants paid for services and public burdens. The parish was still largely treeless. Rent for the entire parish was put at £ 2000 but Mr Mitchell had some difficulty defining it precisely since much was paid in oatmeal, barley, and several customs and services.

The curious manner in which Mr Mitchell's own services to the community were financially rewarded would baffle the best of accountants today:

> "104 bolls 3 pecks oat-meal; 12 bolls 2 firlots 3 pecks bear and £ 40 Scotch paid from the lands of Tolquhon as the converfion of 9 bolls meal."

(For the mathematically-inclined, the Britannica World Language Edition of the Oxford Dictionary describes a 'boll' as 'a measure of capacity for grain, containing in Scotland six imperial bushels; also a measure of weight = 140 pounds.' There are 4 pecks to a bushel. An imperial bushel contains 2218 cubic inches. A firlot is a quarter of a boll.)

The 17th century Tarvesians were honest but raw farming folk who had not freed themselves from the chains of medieval tradition. Theirs was a brutal living, in the shadow of hopelessness and penury. They were an independent race who, in their quest for survival, would neither have courted nor welcomed our compassion today. For in their contest with soil and season there was no place for condolence, however well intended. It would be easy for us, in our favoured circumstances, to censure those early folk, to dismiss them as short-sighted, pig-headed even,but that would be to overlook the nobility of their truly monumental endeavours to redeem the land from a defiant wilderness. Their true grit was surely a powerful ingredient in the prosperity which Tarves enjoys today.

The Tarves Landscape

Tarves, once at the centre of a melancholy land, is now in the heart of lush farm country, renowned throughout the agricultural world. The parish church (above), on its tree-lined knoll, has dominated the valley for centuries. The granite Prop of Ythsie (below) is a landmark for miles around. It was erected in the 19th century by a grateful tenantry as a memorial to the 'Premier' Earl of Aberdeen.

Pictures - the author

Chapter 6

Famine and Bitter Harvest

UP on the hill, the monotonous toll of the Tarves Kirk bell summoned the bereaved to yet another muddy hole in the ground. It had been a bitter harvest. The corn rotted in sodden fields. Summer had not come that year. April, bright and full of promise, had surrendered to leaden May skies and, in June, to rain driven by a soul-numbing wind that was the coldest in memory.

The Tarvesians watched, dumbstruck, as their life-sustaining crop was destroyed by incessant storms. Famine, too, and fear, stalked the flooded byways. Nature, it seemed had plumbed new depths of perfidy.

The Ythan river, until lately an irresistible lure to youngsters hunting for the fabled pearl or guddling for the wily trout, now spewed into the hollows, an ochre torrent ripping at the land. Where the Yowlie Burn had gurgled on its pebbled course, now there was hideous disfigurement, a creeping invasion of rough fields won from the wilderness by centuries of toil. The putrefying carcases of farm beasts trapped by the flood bobbed in the current.

Snow had lain all year round in the high places. Out on the Western rim, when fleeting light punctuated the storm, Bennachie's Mither Tap pointed an Arctic finger at the heavens. The land was in the grip of what would become known as the 'Seven Ill Years' of King William's reign.

The peasant folk were close to imprisonment in their stone and turf hovels, staring calamity in the eye. This had been the cruellest Autumn of all. Much of the seed corn, stored in more benign times for the next season's crop, was already gone - consumed in the three lean years since blight first struck the parks in the Autumn of 1695.

Blight had sent the price of meal - the staple of life and the means by which the rent was paid - into an agonising upwards spiral. Fresh in the memory was the surge in that first bad year, with the price doubling to £ 8 Scots a boll. Now, rumour ran in that unhappy landscape, it was likely to soar above £10.

(At the Union of the Crowns in 1603, the 'pound Scots' was equal to one-twelfth of a 'pound Sterling', being divided into 20 shillings, each of the value of an English penny. A 'boll' - variation of 'bowl' - was a measure of grain weighing 140 pounds).

Though Tarvesians would survive the famine rather better than folk in some of the neighbouring parishes, starvation, pneumonia, and typhus played havoc in the cheerless countryside. Danger lurked, too, in the guise of marauding rogues who had deserted their crofts and taken to the tracks in search of food.

Some had resorted to eating wild radishes and nettles and a tale ran through the parish of a Monquhitter farmer found dead near the coast, with raw flesh in his mouth. Thieves and beggars abounded but there was little to take, even less to give in that hapless landscape.

Throughout the North-East, one in five would perish during the "Ill Years." At this distance in time, there is little on record to provide a comprehensive understanding of the famine years, though a learned anatomy of it has been assembled by Robert E.Tyson, Senior Economic History Lecturer at the University of Aberdeen, in *From Lairds To Louns* (Aberdeen University Press 1986).

Tyson describes it as the last major famine in Scotland, though there were many lean years yet to come. Starvation on a massive scale afflicted many countries across Europe for a decade. In Scotland, the period was dubbed 'The Seven Ill Years', 'King William's Dear Years', or 'The Black Years of King William.'

The crisis lingered from 1694 to 1700 and varied in its severity between one region and another. Because of its nearness to Ireland which was able to provide food and refuge to the hungry, the West of Scotland did not suffer the full ravages of the shortage.

But in Aberdeenshire, says Tyson, the mortality crisis was exceptional even by the standards of the pre-industrial period, and may have been more severe than anywhere in Scotland, except the Highlands.

Years of serious scarcity, followed by a widespread murrain among the cattle, caused the heaviest famine mortality for a century. The emergency was provoked by the impact of foul weather on successive harvests and a subsequent escalation in food prices.

During the first five years of the 1690s, the price of farm meal hovered around £ 4 Scots a boll. Because of the months-long downpour in 1695, the crop was so contaminated that the price doubled. Hard on the heels of this disaster came a second atrocious harvest and, in 1698, the most bitter harvest of all.

Winds, rain and snow combined to decimate the crop. Some salvageable corn was cut as late as January 1699 but most was beyond harvesting. The price of £ 13. 6s 8d in August 1699 was the highest recorded before the end of the 18th century. It was not until the autumn of 1700 that prices returned to their pre-crisis level.

Tyson's narrative states:

> "From the middle of the 16th century onwards there was a worsening of the weather throughout Europe which is usually referred to as 'the little ice age'. The movement south of Arctic sea-ice produced colder winters and cooler, wetter summers. This probably explains travellers' references in this period to permanent snows on the tops of the Cairngorms and lochans covered with ice during the summer months."

Other factors combined to make the crisis even worse than would have been expected from the lean harvests :

> "Aberdeenshire in this period was a major producer of coarse woollen cloth (plaids) and stockings which were largely made in rural areas, particularly in a broad belt of parishes which stretched westwards from the Buchan coast to Strathbogie. In some parishes a fifth or more of the adult males listed in the *1696 Poll Book* had trades, 60 per cent of them as weavers and shoemakers. The Poll Book does not give the occupations of women but the proportion engaged in spinning and knitting was probably much greater. Some tradesmen were also tenants but the great majority were sub-tenants, cottars and grassmen*, or had no land at all. Such people were clearly dependent upon their trades for part or even all of their livelihood; to quote a contemporary account of Buchan, it was the manufacture of the plaids and stockings 'which bringeth money to the commons, other ways of getting it they have not.'

> "A bad harvest meant that they had to spend proportionately more of this money on food at a time when high prices caused their customers both at home and abroad to purchase less cloth and fewer stockings. The problem of these and other Aberdeenshire exports, however, was made much more acute by the consequences of the war with France between 1688 and 1697. Exports of cloth from Aberdeen had been in difficulties since at least 1680 but the decline seems to have become really serious from 1694-95 and continued throughout the famine years, so that by 1700 they were at little more than half their previous level.

> "This fall in exports, as well as lowering the income of producers and exporters, reduced the ability of Aberdeen to purchase what grain was available abroad, while French privateers roaming off the coast impeded imports."

* **grassmen** - farm labourers, with no land of their own

The effects of the disastrous harvests were aggravated by the depression in trade and the financial demands of the government during a period of soaring prices. In these circumstances, the availability of poor relief could literally mean the difference between life and death. Yet, at the same time as kirk sessions needed more and more money to deal with growing numbers of the poverty-stricken, collections and other sources tended to diminish while money lent out on bond to heritors proved difficult or even impossible to recall.

The distribution of poor relief in the North-East, however, was made more difficult by the consequences of the religious settlement of 1690, which had re-established Presbyterianism. Many ministers were deposed for their Episcopalianism and some pulpits remained vacant for years. Sometimes there were no services, collections or distributions. The funds available to parishes were not sufficient to shield the poor entirely from the impact of famine.

Sweeping measures to deal with the plight of the poor were taken in Aberdeen where the problem was worsened by hordes of beggars who had moved there from the countryside.

Tyson:

> "Frequent attempts were made to expel them, beginning as early as September 1696, when 'extraneous beggars' were given a fortnight to leave 'and this tolerance is allowed because of the great scarcity.' Shortly afterwards all merchants and tradesmen who refused to make a reasonable weekly contribution to the poor were taxed and the elders and deacons of St Nicholas Church were ordered to list all persons and their condition 'but especially the poor and by whom they are served.'

> "As the crisis worsened, further measures were taken which culminated in the 'Overtures for the Poor' in April 1699. Those receiving monthly pensions were ordered to appear every three months before a committee to explain their circumstances; they were also obliged to attend church regularly and sit on seats reserved for them. Preference was to be given to 'such as have been most serviceable and honest traders' and wherever possible the poor were to be set to work. There was concern that 'there be not multiplied benefices bestowed upon one and the same person' and no-one was allowed to receive money from more than one fund.

> "All those resident in the town for fewer than seven years were to be expelled and every effort was made to keep out strangers; two people were to be appointed for this purpose in each of the town's quarters and a guard set at each gate, while anyone harbouring poor from the countryside was to be punished or fined. It was also agreed 'that some effectual method be taken to keep out the poor begging children and to transport them to where their nativity hath bene."

The town council also tried to influence the supply, distribution and price of food. But even these devices were not entirely successful and the Aberdeen meal mercat, in fact, appears to have collapsed at the height of the famine in 1699. Many left their parishes to find food either by begging or theft.

In Drumoak, near Aberdeen, church elders complained:

> "that a generalite of the people were become so unchristian and inhuman as would not so much help to the churchyard with the dead bodies of the poor persons who were daily dying before them."

Large numbers of strangers were buried in communal graves in both town and countryside and at the height of the crisis the Commissioners of Supply for Aberdeenshire ordered that the poor should be buried where they fell.

At Methlick during 1698 the number of deaths was four times higher than in pre-famine days, and the worst was still to come. The number of free burials (averaging three in normal years) leapt to 40 out of a total of 92 burials at Methlick in 1698. Unfortunately, the Methlick register petered out before the climax of the famine, and there was no register at all for Tarves. The clerk may well have succumbed or been too pre-occupied with his own survival.

Famine was not the only or even the principal cause of high mortality. Contemporary accounts, as Tyson remarks, refer frequently to 'fevers' which were most likely typhus, a disease always closely linked to famine. Conditions in Aberdeenshire were probably very similar to those in Ireland during the Great Famine where, to quote one medical historian:

> "The lack of cleanliness, the unchanged clothing and crowding together, provided conditions ideal for lice to multiply and spread rapidly. In such circumstances an initial case or two of fever could serve to infect a whole district. In general, the worse the famine in any part, the more intense the fever, and crowds of starving people forsook their homes and took to the road, thus carrying disease with them wherever they went."

According to Tyson, another frequently famine-related disease was the 'flux' or dysentery which was probably caused by eating rotten food and, like typhus, was spread by beggars. Other diseases like measles and influenza were undoubtedly made much deadlier as a result of malnutrition, while pneumonia was probably caused by a combination of hunger, bad weather and a shortage of peat fuel.The number of births plummeted during the 'ill years.' The most obvious explanation, says Tyson, was a combination of lessened sexual activity, loss of marriage partners, an increase in spontaneous abortions and famine amenorrhea (a temporary loss of fertility in women).

Writing in *Northern Scotland*, the journal of the Centre for Scottish Studies at the University of Aberdeen, Tyson concludes:

"The population of Aberdeenshire in 1695 was actually 7.7 per cent higher than in 1755. Although Aberdeen grew by over 50 per cent between these years, even this was not sufficient to counterbalance the decline in the remainder of the county. If the major explanation for the decline is the famine of 1696-99, it must have been exceptionally severe for the population not to have regained the 1695 level half a century after it ended. The tendency in recent years has been to treat contemporary and later descriptions of the famine with some scepticism. For the North-East, at least, these accounts should not be dismissed lightly. The region clearly underwent a massive reduction of population that must have had great economic and social repercussions. These still await their historian."

If all of this was not enough to crush the resolve of the bravest in that oppressed landscape, King William supplied additional gall in the form of an in iniquitous Poll Tax, to be levied on all.

The money which he needed to continue a pointless war against France made an obscenity of the mighty weight already dragging the peasantry down. Their predicament would be described today as 'Catch 22' - to pay up or face a salutary fine, to be evicted, even, from the thatched slums which were their only shelter from the elements. And the same armed conflict was also muzzling the stocking trade and the production of coarse woollen plaids upon which landless weavers and knitters were especially reliant as a means of swelling their paltry incomes. Peasant folk were already in bondage and though deprivation and disease were on the march, the single-minded king, it seemed, must exact his ransom.

The commissioners who came in the king's name were estimable local land-owners, James Keith the Elder, of Tilliegonie, and his son James, who were appointed for 'ingathring' the Poll. Their elevated position in the society of the time would have commanded considerable deference from the peasantry but unless they were entirely heedless of the plight of their fellow men, the Keiths would have suffered pangs of conscience about the task they had undertaken. The record does little more than invite surmise. The 'Act for Pole-Money', dated 27 June 1695, warned of dangers from 'forraign enemies,' of the 'Designs of Evill Men' and of 'Coasts not sufficiently Secure against Privateers.' It was "therefore necessar," Parliament declared, that "a compleat Number of Standing Forces be maintained and Ships of War provided for its necessary defence." Parliament therefore "freely and chearfully" offered to the king "a subsidy to be uplifted by way of Pole-money."

The Act stated:

"All Persons of whatsoever Age, Sex or Quality, shall be subject and lyable to a Pole of Six Shilling, except Poor Persons who live upon Charity, and the Children under the Age of Sixteen years, and in familia of all these Persons whose Pole doth not exceed One Pound Ten Shilling Scots. That beside the said Six Shilling imposed upon all the Persons that are not excepted: A Cottar having a Trade shall pay Six Shilling more, making in the hail Twelve Shilling for every such Cottar. That for Each Servant shall be payed by the Master, for which the Master is impowered to retain the fourtieth Part of his yearly Fee, whereof Bountieth to be reckoned a part (excepting Livery Cloaths) in the Number of which Servants are understood, all who receive Wages or Bountieth for any Work, or Imployment whatsoever, for the Term or the Year as they have, or shall serve."

The Legislation added:

"In Case they be not Alimented in familia with their Masters, then if they be not above the Degree of a Cottar or Hynd, they are to have two third Parts of Wages and Bountieth, or if above the said Degree one Third part of Wages and Bountieth, first deduced for their Aliment."

Few, it seems, were to be exempted, though it is logical to assume that in those devastating times many devised means of evading payment of the tax. The king's commissioners would also have encountered serious difficulty imposing the tax in such a remote area of the realm at a period when minds were concentrated on survival itself.Their task, in modern parlance, was tantamount to "getting blood out of a stone."

Yet, the Act insisted:

"All Seamen pay Twelve Shilling Scots in name of Pole. All Tennents pay in name of Pole to the King, the hundredth part of the valued Rent, payable by them to the Master of the Land, and appoints the Master of the Ground to adjust the Proportions of this Pole amongst his Tennents, according to the respective Duties payable by them in Money or Victual, effecting to his valued Rent."

In 13 years William III was to raise more than £ 58 million through new taxes on commodities like salt, alcohol and the land itself. The Poll Tax levied throughout Tarves amounted to "fyve hundredth and fourtein punds, eightein shillings and nyne pennies." The anguish it caused the law-abiding but destitute peasants was incalculably greater.

In these troubled times, Tarvesians would have cared little about events in the wider world. Even had they heard about the profligacy of the 'Sun King ' Louis XIV in his magnificent new palace at Versailles, they would merely have been bewildered, though the news would have served to highlight the hideous social imbalance of that era. What would they have known or cared about the golden age of culture then sweeping China under the enlightened rule of Emperor Kangxi of the Manchu dynasty? What would Isaac Newton's new theories about something called gravitation have meant to them? Even had they been able to read, acquisition of a new book like John Bunyan's *Pilgrim's Progress* was merely a pipe dream. They might have heard garbled tales about the 'Bloody Assizes' where Judge Jeffreys sentenced 320 supporters of Monmouth to be hanged and more than 800 to be sent as slaves to the plantations.

Or they might have heard about the flight of the Lincolnshire Quaker, William Penn, to Philadelphia to escape religious persecution at home. Or the revolt in Russia where one thousand members of the Praetorian Guard founded by Ivan the Terrible were publicly put to death by order of Peter the Great.

Did it matter much to starving Tarvesians that Henry Purcell had just been buried in Westminster Abbey where he was organist at the age of 20? Or that the Dutch scientist Christian Huygens was predicting the existence of intelligent life on other planets?

Closer to home, though there was no great love affair between Lowlander and Highlander, the peasantry would be unlikely to forgive or forget King William's involvement in the treachery that had led, just six years before, to the infamous Massacre of Glencoe. With 128 soldiers, Campbell of Glen Lyon, in league with the king, enjoyed the hospitality of the remote Glencoe Macdonalds for 12 days before turning on them in a surprise dawn attack. Their excuse was the apparent failure of MacIan of Glencoe to take an oath of allegiance to the king before 1 January 1692. Of the 200 occupants of the glen, 40 were slain and others fled to the mountains to die of want and exposure. Their homes were destroyed by the soldiers. Tarvesians then, as now, had a strong sense of fair play.

That same king was responsible for the fiscal problem now compounding the physical miseries of folk in the cluster of parishes that made up the North-East corner of Scotland. Ploughs and their gear lay useless in the quagmire of that terrible autumn in 1698.

Sir Robert Sibbald (1641-1722), naturalist and geographer, wrote in the following year about the devastation he had seen throughout the country:

> "For want some die in the wayside, some drop down in the streets, the poor sucking babs are starving for want of milk, which the empty breasts of their mothers cannot furnish them. Everyone may see Death in the face of the poor that abound everywhere; the thin-ness of their visage, their ghostly looks, their feebleness, their agues and their fluxes threaten them with sudden death if care be not taken of them.

> "It is not only common wandering beggars that are in this case, but many householders who lived well by their labour and their industry are now by want forced to abandon their dwellings. And they and their little ones must beg, and in their necessity they take what they can get, spoiled victual, yea, some eat these beasts which have died of some disease which may occasion a plague among them."

The floodwaters swirled in the haughs, lapping even at the door of the Beid-House on its little hump near Tarves village. Founded and endowed for four poor men by the Forbes family of Tolquhon, the tiny hostel shared the decrepitude of the nearby kirk and manse. The Beid-men, whose shelter it was, depended on the promise - now often broken - of "ane peck of meal and 40 pennies each in the week, ane grey gown the one Martinmas and a Coat and Breeches the other."

Their kailyard lay saturated and useless. The missing slates above their quarters were an invitation to the storm. The tenants of Meikle Ythsie, suppliers of peat for their fires and lime for their yard, had more pressing issues on their minds. The Beid-men possessed a large chest with four locks and lids for their meal, pots and pans, four beds and bedclothes and an annual hide for making shoes. Of late, however, with the tempest showing no signs of blowing itself out and calamity looming over the land, those tenants who were obliged to supply the Beid-men with fuel and other necessities, had shirked or been unable to perform these duties. Misery ruled at the Beid-House where sacking plugged into holes in the roof and walls was a hopeless gesture to the elements.

The most bitter harvest of all was upon the land - more awful even than the worst in memory. That had been in 1684 when the Bishop of Aberdeen decreed a fast and humiliation:

> "seeing that by the severitie of the last winter, the estream drought of this summer whereby the fruits of the ground wer in hazerd to be burned up, and by great and continued inundationes in and since the harvest, whereby the cornes in the yards and fields have been greatly indamnaged by rotting."

The rotting time had returned, with a vengeance that reeked of the Devil's work. In that far country the crop was dead, many of the animals gone or wasting, hope at a low ebb. The simple tenant farmer's or crofter's trust in the Almighty God was subjected to its severest test. A fiery God, the cottar man might have reflected, but apparently a feckless one . We shall never know the extent of the toll exacted by the famine and fevers at Tarves for the records of burials at that time, if they ever existed, have been lost in the mists of time.

The little-lamented William III, whose crippling taxes, wasteful wars and flamboyant lifestyle were blamed for many of the peasants' ills, died in March 1702 as the result of injuries suffered when his horse stumbled on a mole-hill in Richmond Park and threw him to the ground. He was succeeded by Anne, sister of the late Queen Mary.

Chapter 7

Removing History's Veil

T HROUGH good fortune, the Poll Book - *Ane List of Pollable Persons in the Shire of Aberdeen, 1696* - is preserved in the Special Collections Department at the University of Aberdeen Library in King's College. Besides being a goldmine for the family or social researcher, it contains *Ane List of Pollable Persons within the Pariochen of Tarves* - an indispensable 300-year-old roll of names and addresses which enticingly lift a corner of history's veil on the early Tarvesians.

The smallholdings scattered about the countryside were known by names which are easily identified in the prosperous parish of today. The imprecise nature of spelling in that far-off time, even by the few who had enjoyed the privilege of an education, is clearly demonstrated in the list of properties visited by the king's commissioners when the parish was facing the ravages of famine and disastrous harvests.

The valuation of the parish of 1800 souls - laboriously but meticulously penned by an un-named clerk to the Keiths - was put at £ 4880. Major land-owners included the Earl of Aberdeen whose broad acres were calculated at £ 1680, Sir Alexander Forbes of Tolquhon at £ 1500, George Johnston, Cairnbrogie, and George Gray, Shivas, at £ 600 each, James Keith himself at £ 300 and John Forbes of Auquhorthies at £ 200.

The lowly country folk were compelled to find a one hundredth part of their heritor's valuation - a pittance today but an intolerable imposition at a time when the once changeless community was being propelled towards oblivion. Besides the Tarves farming tenants in that long-ago time, 105 households were listed as cottars and 20 as weavers, though most womenfolk in the parish and men with trades rather than work on the land were also engaged in spinning, weaving and knitting. There were 14 shoemakers, 11 tailors, five gardeners, three smiths and two apprentices, five merchants, four tradesmen, two who described themselves as 'gentlemen' and six millers - Gavin Hardie at Shivas, Jim Dickson at Fuchell, Arthur Milne at Tolquhon, Bob Forbes at Ythsie, James Keith at Shethin and Alec Johnston at Tillyhilt.

The parish also boasted two 'grasswomen' (widows working as farm labourers), - Isobel Rae at Old Toune of Fochell and Helen Ferguson at Fullford - while Isobel Jack in the village followed the unusual calling of ' chyldkeeper', caring for the abandoned waifs and strays allocated to her by the kirk session. One can only surmise that in these 'killing times' her hands were full. James Fraser of Wedderbyres was listed as a 'pyper' - much sought-after in better times for weddings and the fairs which had long been a regular feature of parish life. Apart from the mournful lament by a sodden graveside, however, there was a dearth of opportunity to call on his services during these distressing days.

As the 'nottar publict' - writer - in Tarves, James Middleton lived in some style and paid a tax of £5. 4s for himself, his wife, daughter and servant Isobel England. Much lower on the social scale were a 'tinker, packman, pickman, walker* and wright.'

The Tarves merchants were men of means. Those with stock valued above 500 merks (a merk being worth about 13 pennies at that time) and paying tax in the region of £ 4. 00 included James Duguid, Robert Fiddes and Gilbert Middleton. John Gray and William Mitchell were in business on a rather more modest scale.

John Brown, described as a doctor, and schoolmaster William Greig, were low in the pecking order of the time, paying only 6s and 12s respectively, though humble shoemakers were charged 18s. John Brown's status was almost certainly not that of a medical doctor; rather, his was a qualification that permitted him to serve as an assistant to the schoolmaster.

Up at the Manse, on the brow where tumbledown village houses huddled like chickens around the mother hen, the Rev George Anderson was liable for £ 5 .14s to cover himself, his wife and their seven children - James, William, Robert, Gilbert, Margaret, Anna and Elspeth. Also living with them in the ruinous property was Isobel Middleton, widow of the Rev Alexander Garden, former minister of Forgue, who was expected to pay a further £ 1. 6s. According to the scribe:

> "She is lyable for the third pairt of her husbands poll, which (if allyve) would have been £ 3, and the generall poll of 6s."

Anderson, soon to become Professor of Divinity at King's College, Aberdeen, was one of the first Scottish ministers to conform to the new Presbyterian establishment, though Episcopacy persisted in the North-East. Indeed, Tarves was for a time the regular meeting place of the Presbytery of Ellon since the minister at Ellon, adhering to his Episcopalian beliefs, was in the habit of locking the presbytery brethren out of his church.

walker - fuller, worker in cloth

It was from Anderson, in his bare kirk perched on a knoll dominating the surrounding country, that Tarves folk had for the past 15 years received regular and generous helpings of fire, brimstone, and damnation, delivered with a venom approaching the apocalyptic.

Like much of the parish, the kirk was then in an advanced state of decay. Its walls were supported by props without which, the presbytery record states:

> "The same would inevitablie fall to the ground, whereby many of the people were frightened from comeing to the publick worship at the said church by manifest hazard of their lives, to the great scandall of religion."

Once a building of some architectural dignity, the kirk had become a place of impassioned preaching but cold and sodden comfort in these impoverished times as the rains found their way through its tattered defences. It had been rudely shaken and metamorphosed over the years by the erection of lofts and the knocking out of new windows and doors.

Sixty years on, when the dire threats that the 'ill years' posed to hearth and home had passed into parish lore, the state of the kirk was again described as 'ruinous.' Anderson's thatched manse, to which the peasant class were required, despite the rigours of the time, to deliver peats, thatch and portions of their farm meal, was also dilapidated. It, too, would have to be propped up soon for the safety of the inmates.

It was a dwelling of substantial proportions, comprising a hall, two chambers, a kitchen, pantry and cellar, as well as two stables, a barn, a byre, a victual house, a hen-house and two 'chalmers' (bedrooms) all valued at £ 578 Scots.

A thoroughly depressing picture of the 17th century Tarves Manse was painted in *Extracts from the Records of the Presbytery of Ellon,** meticulously assembled and published last century by the Rev Thomas Mair. This is what he recorded:

> "The hen-house is in ruins and the forewall of the byre outside the gate - dry stone work - is in a bad way. All the roofs are of thatch, in different stages of decay. An embodiment of the manse of Tarves and its offices as they stood may yet be found in some backland forlorn region of the county neglected by a needy proprietor - the steading of some single-ploughed farm, modelled in the fashion of a bygone time yet lingering on. But on closer acquaintance there is an assertion of dignity, as of one who, though attired in tarnished corduroys, takes his stand in a dress hat which has seen better days. It is to be feared that the whole establishment was a happy hunting ground for the old black 'rottan' (rat) of the country, which vanished before the still more repulsive gray one about the middle of the present century. If the west wall of the pantry was a faill or sod one, as stated, he must have been a hungry man who could have relished whatever cold provisions were stored in it overnight, unless they had been under special protection -the rats would have engineered through such a wall at will."

* **Presbytery** - the ecclesiastical court next above the Kirk Session and below the Synod.

In that God-forsaken parish, the village school had also fallen on bad times, though its neglect was said by the presbytery to be down to William Greig, the schoolmaster, for keeping a 'change' (alehouse) to which he devoted overmuch time. He had also been rebuked by the presbytery clerics for employing "a doctor too young and inexperienced" (presumably the Dr John Brown who paid a poll tax of 6s) and was instructed to find for his school a "doctor of learning, prudence and some considerable experience."

Greig was to survive the 'ill years' but in 1713 a much more serious charge would be brought against him - that of embezzling kirk session funds. The session's affairs had been plunged into confusion by the defalcations and negligence of Greig over a period of 20 years. The presbytery found him guilty of "falsehood, unfaithfulness and Sacraledge in embazeling the poor's money."

The sentence that followed was merciful in the circumstances. Although ordered to demit all his offices, it was ruled that his successor should pay him 100 merks yearly for life. Should he die before his three youngest children reached the age of 18, each should be paid 20 merks until then, and their mother should have 20 merks yearly for life. Greig's successor could not have had much left for himself, according to the rates of pay then in vogue.

At this time of pestilence, Tarves folk saw little of Sir George Gordon, 1st Earl of Aberdeen, and former Chancellor of the Exchequer,who lived out a semi-reclusive existence between Castle of Gight and the partially repaired Place of Kelly which had fallen foul of the Covenanters 50 years before. Indeed, he would not properly emerge from his retirement until after the accession of Queen Anne when he became a leading figure once more in the negotiations leading to the Treaty of Union between England and Scotland in 1707.

In their debt-ridden castle atop the Hill of Tolquhon, partially obscured by the few trees in that bare parish, Sir Alexander Forbes eked out a gloomy dotage with his spouse Dame Bathia, encumbered by the financial backlash of rash participation in the Darien Scheme - a disastrous Scottish attempt at colonisation - and other foolish speculations.

Once a colonel in the Scottish army of Charles II, Sir Alexander had played a heroic role at the Battle of Worcester, giving up his own horse to aid the king's escape from the field. Soon, his castle would be sold by order of the Court of Session but Sir Alexander did not survive to witness that sad transaction. His surviving relative, William Forbes, the 11th laird, would refuse to quit the castle until it was attacked by a body of Redcoats and he wounded and taken prisoner (the story of Tolquhon is told in a later chapter).

On the pages that follow is the list of pollable persons in Tarves in 1696, reproduced in its entirety by kind permission of the University of Aberdeen, custodians of the original Poll Book. The forms of spelling belong to the clerk who acted for the king's commissioners, James Keith of Tilliegonie, and his son James. Under the heading of "Paroch of Tarves", the introduction reads:

"ANE LIST of the POLLABLE PERSONS within the PARIOCHEN of TARVES, given up be JAMES KEITH of Tillegonie, Elder, and JAMES KEITH, Younger, of Tillegonie, two Commissioners nominate and appoynted for that effect, and be (blank) Clerk and Collector appoynted and chosen be them for the ingathring of the Poll of the said Parioch."

The People of Tarves, 1696

Those required to find the "hundredth pairt" of Lord Aberdeen's valuation were:

	£	s	d
Imprimis, John Walker, tennent in Raakstoun	1	0.	0
James Hay in Mayns of Shithin		16.	8
William Thomson, tennent ther		16.	8
William Breichen in Achedlie	2.	0.	0
James Porter in Northseat		13.	0
Alexander Peirie, at the Mill of Achydlie		6.	8
Andrew Barclay in Burnend		6.	8
John Breichen in Craigie of Schithin		6.	8
Adam Leith in Overhill		13.	4
James Couper in Thomven		12.	0
James Midletoun in New Toun of Tileilt		6.	8
James Watson in Overheids of Tilielt		6.	8
John Smith in the Maynes of Tileilt		13.	4
John Charles at Overmill of Tileilt		6.	8
John Leask in Neather Tilecarne		13.	4
Helen Findlay in Mayns of Auchinive		13.	4
Alexander Johnstoun in Wester Craigie		13.	4
Magdaline Findlator in Maynes of Craigie		13.	4
George Leask in Craigdarra		13.	4
Alexander Peirie in Overtilecarne		6.	8
John Birnie in South Craigie of Tarves		6.	8
Helen Walker in Sneall of Tillelt		4.	0

John Keith at the Mill of Shithine is £ 1, Alexander Johnstoun at the Mill of Tilleilt, is 6s 8d, William Mitchell in Tarves is 13s 4d, James Duguid ther is 13s 4d, Robert Furres ther is 13s 4d but being hyer clased in another place, is not lyable.

These were the general poll charges for individual property holdings or farm touns:

AUCHEDLIE

William Breichen, tennent ther, his generall poll for himselfe, his wyfe and sone, 18s 0d; James Skeen, his servant, 13s 0d; William Kynach, 13s 0d; John Charles 12s 8d; Isobell Charles 10s 8d; Elspeth Neill, 10s 8d; Robert Wilson, 13s 4d; Margaret Hog, ther servant, 10s 8d; Subtennents - William Christall, his wyfe and daughter in familia, 18s 0d; William Smith, and his wyfe, 12s 0d; John Auld, cottar, and his wyfe, 12s 0d; William Charles and his wyfe, 12s 0d; William Peirie and his wyfe, 12s 0d; John Forsyth and his wyfe, 12s 0d; and James Forsyth and his wyfe 12s 0d.

NORTHSEAT

James Porter, tennent ther, his wyfe, his sones , Johne, George and William, their generall poll £ 1. 10s; John McKie, 8s 8d; Margaret Todd, 10s 8d; Agnes Gray, 10s 4d; Gilbert Lawrance, cottar, and his wyfe, 12s 0d.

MILL OF ACHEDLIE

Alexander Peirie, tennent ther, and his wyfe, 12s 0d; William Kirktoun, 12s 8d; Christian Findlay, 10s 0d; Patrick Peirie, 6s 0d.

RAAKSTOUNE

John Walker, tennent, his wyfe and daughter, 18s 0d; Patrick Umphray, 14s 8d; George Ironsyde, 10s 4d; John Chrystie, 10s 8d; John Knox, 10s 4d; William Gray, cottar, and his wife, 12s 0d; Thomas Gray, wyver ther, his wife, and two children, to wit, Alexander and Jean Grays, £ 1. 10s; John Smith, elder, and his wyfe, 12s 0d; James Smith, his sone, ane taylor, 12s 0d; William Sandie, cottar and his wyfe, 12s 0d; John Divertie ther, and his wyfe, 12s 0d; William Smith, cottar, and his wyfe, 12s 0d; Jannet Smith, his sister, 6s 0d; Alexander French, and his mother, 12s 0d; and John Smith, younger, and his wyfe, 12s 0d.

THE MAYNES OF SHITHIN

James Hay, tennent ther, and his wyfe, 12s 0d; Patrick Hay, his servant, 14s 8d; Jean Chrystie, servant, 10s 8d; Agnes Knox, 10s 8d; William Cruickshank, cottar, and his wife, 12s 0d; David and Jean Mars, 12s 0d; Jannet Johnstoun and her daughter, 12s 0d; William Cassie, his wife and daughter in familia, 18s 0d; John Cranna, and his wife, 12s 0d; William Thomson, tennent ther, and his wife, 12s 0d; Andrew Archibald, 14s 8d; and Jean Hay, 10s 0d.

CRAIGIE OF SHEITHIN

John Breichen ther, and his wife, 12s 0d; Anna Leisk, his servant, 8s 0d; James Breichen ther, and his wife, 12s 0d; and Christian Boddy, cottar, 6s 0d.

MILL OF SHITHIN

John Keith, gentleman ther, and his wife, their poll is £ 3. 12s 0d; Margaret and Mary Keiths, his daughters, 12s 0d; George Gordon, 6s 0d; Robert Lamb, 12s 8d; Walter Cumming 10s 4d; Margaret George, 10s 8d; Mary Gray, 8s 4d; Janet Mathewson, 10s; Alexander Symson ther, and his wife, their generall poll (tradesman), 18s 0d; Alexander Myrdon, shoemaker in Litle Meldrum, and his wife, 18s 0d; - Wilsone and James Charles, two aprentises, 12s 0d; Ane servant woman, 9s 6d; James Philp, cottar, and his wife, 12s 0d; James Whyte, cottar, his wife and daughter, 18s 0d; John Hay in Badinhar, his wife and daughter in familia, 10s; James Todd, cottar, and his wife, 12s 0d; and Alexander Harvie, and his wife, 12s 0d.

OVERHILL

Adam Leask, tennent ther, and his wife, 12s 0d; Patrick Bruce, 14s 8d; Arthur McKenzie, 8s 8d; Margaret Neill, 10s 8d; William Daunie, shoemaker, and his wife, 18s 0d; and William Killo, cottar, and his wife, 12s 0d.

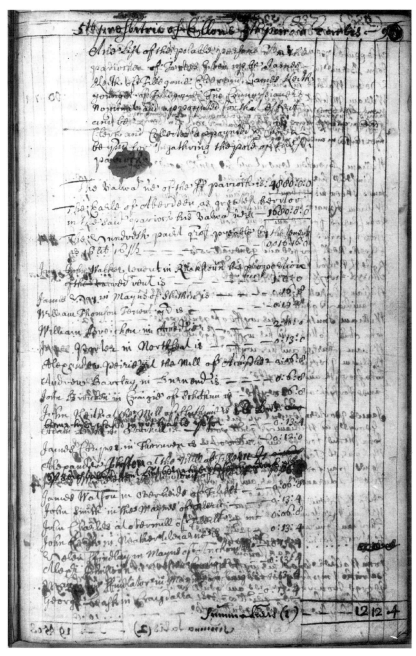

Though blotted and disfigured by time and writing on the reverse, the names of 17th century Tarvesians can still be read on this page from the 1696 Poll Book, reproduced here by kind permission of the University of Aberdeen. In the middle of the page is James Porter at Northseat, a direct ancestor of the author.

THOMVAN

James Couper, tennent ther, and his wife, 12s 0d; John Ferguson, 14s 8d; James Raynie, 11s 4d; George Watson, cottar, and his wyfe, 12s 0d; John Symson, wyver ther, and his wyfe, 18s 0d; and John Cobler, cottar, and his wyfe, and Christian Mutch, 18s 0d.

NETHERMILL OF TILLEILT.

Alexander Johnstoun lyeable for his stock £ 2. 10s, with own and his wyfes generall poll, is £ 3. 2s 0d; Alexander Johnstoun, his sone, wright, 12s 0d; Adam Johnstoun, sone, in familia, 6s 0d; James Sutor, 13s 4d; John Duguid, 8s 4d; Jannet Cumming, 10s 8d.

MAYNS OF TILLELT

John Smith, tennent, and his wyfe, 12s 0d; John Watson, his servant, 15s 0d; James Smith, 11s 4d; Helen Chalmers, 10s 6d; Jean Smith, 10s 6d; Patrick Gordon, 9s 0d; John Coming, shoemaker ther, and his wyfe, 18s 0d; Adam Low, cottar, and his wyfe, 12s 0d; John Gray, cottar, and his wyfe, 12s 0d; William Chyne, and his wyfe, 12s 0d; William Scott, wyver ther, and his wyfe, 18s 0d; James Mill, taillior, and his wyfe, 18s 0d; and William Lind ther, and his wyfe, 12s 0d.

NEUTOUNE OF TILLELT

James Midletoun, tennent, and wyfe, 12s 0d; William Midletoun ther, his wyfe and sister-in-law, 18s 0d; and Robert Cuie, gardner, his wyfe and two children in familia, £ 1. 10s.

OVERHEIDS OF TILLELT

James Watson, tennent ther, and his wyfe, 12s 0d; Patrick Irving ther, and his wyfe, 12s 0d; John Neill in Bondagefoord of Tillelt, and his wife, 12s 0d; and Margaret Brown, widow ther, 6s 0d.

MILL OF TILLIECAIRNE

John Charles, tennent ther, and his wife, 12s 0d; Alexander Lucktoun, his servant, 13s 0d; Elspeth Gray, 10s 0d; and Andrew Hass, cottar, and his wife, 12s 0d.

NETHER TILLECAIRNE

John Leask, tennent ther, and his wife, 12s 0d; Margaret and Jean Leasks, their daughters in familia, 12s 0d; John Horne, 14s 8d; George Cruickshank, 11s 8d; William Scott, cottar, and his wife, 12s 8d; Alexander Black, cottar, and his wife, 12s 0d; and William Taylor ther, and his wife, 12s 0d.

OVER TILECAIRNE

Alexander Peirie, tennent ther, and his wife, with their sone in familia, 18s 0d; James Doverty ther, and his wife, 12s 0d; Alexander Doverty ther, and his wife, 12s 0d; John Davidson ther, and his wife, 12s 0d; John Kirktoune ther, and his wife, 12s 0d; and Elspet Peirie, widow ther, 6s 0d.

MAINS OF ACHINIVE

Helen Findlay, tennent ther, 6s 0d; John Gordon, her servant, 13s 4d; Margaret Maitland, 9s 8d; Jean Paterson, 9s 8d; James Croudie, and his wife, 12s 0d; Donald Young, cottar (no trade) 6s 0d; and William Robertson and his wife, 12s 0d.

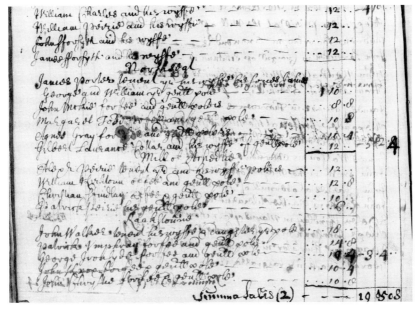

More names from the pages of the Poll Book. The left-hand column shows the tax to be paid, and the right is the running total owed for the properties.

Pictures kindly provided by Special Collections Dept, University of Aberdeen

WESTER CRAIGIE OF TARVES

Alexander Johnstoun, tennent ther, and his wife, 12s 0d; Alexander, James, and Jean Johnstouns, his children, 18s 0d; Kathirine Lesslie, his servant, 0s 0d; and Isobell Gordon, cottar woman, 6s 0d.

MAYNS OF CRAIGIE OF TARVES

Magdaline Findlater, tennent ther, and her mother in familia, 12s 0d; Magdaline Clerk in familia, 6s 0d; Elspeth Smith, 10s 8d; Margaret Abernethie, 8s 8d; William Abernethie, 9s 4d; William Auchinleck, younger, 9s 10d; William Kirktoune, 8s 0d; William Auchinleck, elder, cottar, and his wyfe, 12s 0d; and George Catto, cottar, 6s 0d.

SOUTH CRAIGIE OF TARVES

John Birnie, tennent ther, and his wyfe, 12s 0d; Alexander Allan, and his wyfe, 12s 0d; John Liddell ther, and his wyfe, 12s 0d; and Alexander Kirktoune ther, and his wyfe, 12s 0d.

CRAIGDOUNE

George Leask, tennent ther, and his wyfe, 12s 0d; Alexander Smith, his servant, 13s 2d; Alexander Davidson, in Muirbray, and his wyfe, 12s 0d; Arthur Meason ther, and his wyfe, 12s 0d; George Davidson ther, and his wyfe, 12s 0d; John Huntur, at Bridgend, and his wyfe, 12s 0d; Robert Birnie, in Mossheid of Tarves, and his wyfe, 12s 0d; Robert Scrogie ther, 6s 0d; John Rhynie ther, elder, and his wyfe, 12s 0d; and John Rhynie, younger, and his wyfe, 12s 0d.

John Ritchie, cottar in Breklie, and his wyfe, 12s 0d; Marjorie Charles ther, 6s 0d;Andrew Hardie, taillior ther, his wyfe and his sone and his daughter in familia, £ 1. 4s 0d; Robert Wishart, cottar ther, and his wyfe, 12s 0d;James Duguid, in Preymuir, wyver, and his wyfe, 18s 0d; William and Alexander Duguids, his sons in familia, 12s 0d; Robert Maison, wyver, ther, his wyfe and chyld, and his mother in familia, £ 1. 12s 0d; William Kenet, cottar, 6s 0d; Elspeth Wilkine, widow, 6s 0d; Patrick Crichtoun, and his wyfe, 12s 0d; Andrew Lamb ther, and his wyfe, 12s 0d; William Seatoun, and his wyfe, 12s 0d; and Jean Ferqiour, his servant, 0s 0d.

John Duiguid, wyver, for his own, his wyfe, and daughter in familia, £ 1. 4s 0d; Alexander Chyne, shoemaker, and his wyfe, 18s 0d; John Wright, in Tarves, for his valuatione of waller rent in the pariochen of Aboyne, is lyable in £ 1. 0s 0d, with his oun, his wyfe and daughter in familia, £ 1. 18s 0d; James Chrystie, their servant, 9s 10d; Helen Duiguid, 10s 8d; James Moir, smith in Tarves, and his wife, 18s 0d; William Chalmers, his aprentice, 12s 0d; Andrew Grig, his servant, 13s 0d; and Isobell Mile, servant, 10s 0d.

Alexander Black, taylor, and his wife, 18s 0d; John Gray, merchant in Tarves, for his free stock, being under 500 merks, poll is one merk, and the generall poll is 19s 4d; William Mitchell, merchant ther, for his free stock and generall poll, 13s 4d, for himself and wife, 12s 0d; Alexander Mitchell, his servant, 9s 0d; Agnes Couper, 9s 0d; Mr William Greig, schoolmaster in Tarves, and his wyfe, 12s 0d; Margaret Strachan, his mother in familia, 6s 0d; Mr John Broun, Doctor, of Tarves, 6s 0d; Alexander Jack, servant, 14s 0d; Margaret Sangster, 10s 6d; and Isobell Jack, chyld keeper, 8s 0d;

James Duiguid, merchant in Tarves, his free stock being above 500 merks, is lyeable for £ 2. 10s. 0d, with the generall poll for himself, wyfe, and three children in familia, is £ 4. 0s 0d; Margaret Duguid, his servant, 7s 6d; Robert Fiddes, merchant in Tarves, his free stock being above 500 merks, is lyable in £ 2. 10s 0d of poll, and the generall poll for himselfe, his wyfe, and fyve children, £ 4. 12s 0d; Gilbert Midletoun, merchant ther, his free stock being above 500 merks, is lyable in the poll of £ 2. 10s 0d, with his own and his wyfes generall poll, £ 3. 2s 0d; Robert Ritchie, shoemaker ther, and his wyfe, 18s 0d; Alexander Davidson ther, and his wyfe, 12s 0d; William Steiven, and his wyfe, 12s 0d; John Smith, shoemaker ther, and his wyfe, 18s 0d; and John Gammock ther, and his wyfe, 12s 0d

Elspeth Smith, widow in Tarves, Mr William and Mr Alexander Laus, her sones, 18s 0d; Robert Rainie, servant, 10s 4d; Isobell Smith, servant, 9s 0d; Patrick Charles ther, and wyfe, 12s 0d; Margaret Forbes, servant, 9s 0d; James Midletoun, nottar publict in Tarves, his poll is £ 4 and the generall poll for himselfe, wyfe, daughter, and Isobell England in familia, is £ 5. 4s 0d; Andrew Gray ther, his wyfe, and sone in familia, 18s 0d; William Edmond, in Tarvis, and his wyfe, 12s 0d; and David Mureson ther, and his wyfe, 12s 0d.

SUAILL OF TILLELT

Helen Walker ther, 6s 0d; James Simsone, her man servant, 14s 8d; Margaret Gray ther, 10s 8d.

WALK MILNE OF RAKSTOUNE

John Milne, waker ther, for his oun, his wyfe, and sone, in familia, £ 1. 4s 0d; William Steiven, indweller in Tarves, and his wyfe, 12s 0d; Margaret Harvie, his mother, 6s 0d; and Margaret Couper, widow, in Tarves, 6s 0d.

The valuation of the lands of Achorthes, belonging to John Forbes, was put at £ 200, of which the "hundreth pairt " - £ 2. 0s 0d - was "peyable by the tennents." This is how the charges were allocated:

'TENENTS' IN THE LANDS OF ACHORTHES

Alexander Auld, in Achorthes, his proportione of the valuatione, 11s 2d; John Scroggie, in Caulsey Greens, 9s 0d; James Archbald, in Kelliebray, 3s 0d; Alexander Cobler, in Achorthes, 2s 2d; James Hardie ther, 2s 2d; Thomas Gormack ther, 2s 2d; George Duiguid ther, 2s 2d; The Aires* of umquhill ** Isobell Crichtoun, 2s 2d; Alexander Chrystie ther, 2s 2d; John Benzie ther, 2s 2d; and James Barkley ther, 1s 8d.

The general poll was paid as follows:

The said John Forbes his poll is £ 9, and the generall poll for himselfe and lady is £ 9. 12s 0d; Item, seven children in familia, £ 2. 2s 0d; John Scroggie, servant, 15s 0d; James Leith, 12s 8d; Robert Norvell, servant, 12s 8d; John Knox, servant, 10s 8d; Christian Walker, 11s 4d; Margaret Ritchie, servant, 11s 4d; Barbra Walker, servant, 8s 8d; Anna Seaton, liferentrix of the Lands of Achorthes, is pollable in the soume of £ 3, as the third pairt of her deceast husbands poll, and the generall poll of 6s for herselfe, and 6s for her daughter in familia, £ 3. 12s 0d; Agnes Glenny, her servant, 8s 8d; Margaret Bartlet, servant, 7s 8d.

CORSHILL

Alexander Auld, tennent ther, 6s 0d; His wyfe and sone, in familia, 12s 0d; and John Scroggie, in Calsey Greens, for his own and his wyfes generall poll, is 12s 0d.

italic *Aires* - heirs; ** **unquhill** - deceased, late.

ACHORTHES

Alexander Cobler, taillior ther, for himselfe, his wyfe, and sone in familia, £ 1. 4s 0d; James Hardy, smith ther, and his mother, 18s 0d; Thomas Gormack, gardener, and his wyfe, 18s 0d; George Duiguid, wyver, and his boy, 18s 0d; Alexander Chrystie ther, and his wife, 12s 0d; John Bennie ther, and his wyfe, 12s 0d; James Barkley, and his wyfe, 12s 0d; James Godsman, shoemaker ther, for himselfe, trade, his wyfe and boy, £ 1. 4s 0d; Alexander Rae, taillior ther, and his wyfe, 18s 0d; William Henderson, taylor, and his wyfe, 18s 0d; Isobell Henderson in Achorthes, and her sone, 12s 0d; James Ritchie ther, 6s 0d; Helen and Christian Wilsons, and Lilias Gray, 18s 0d; William Robertson, in Achorthes, 6s 0d; Isobell Gray, widow, 6s 0d; John Broun, and his wyfe, 12s 0d; and Alexander Dyce, and his wyfe, 12s 0d.

KELLEBRAE

James Archbald, tennent ther, for his own and his wyfes generall poll, 12s 0d; her servant lass 7s 0d.

The lands belonging to Sir Alexander Forbes of Tolquhon were valued at £ 1500, of which the tenants had to find £ 15. 0s 0d. It was to be paid as follows:

15s 6d - by Robert Reid of Meikle Ythsie; 10s 8d - by Peter Broun of Litle Ythsie; 10s 4d each - by Robert Forbes, Mill of Ythsie, Robert Milne, Meikle Ythsie, Alexander Byres of Meikle Ythsie, Thomas Byres and Alexander Glenny in Newseat of Tolquhon, George Gavin in Wester Kilnary, James Man in Over Kilmary, Alexander Gray in Oldtoune, William Moir in Mossie, James Smith in Gatesyde, John Gavin at the Mill of Frechell, Patrick Smith in New Balgow, John Petrie in Hattonslap, Walter Breichen in Kirkfoord, William Gavin in Dalforkie, John Breichen in Tullofoord, William Burr in Flobbets, John Murdo in Nether Kirktoune, William Findlay in Over Kirktoune, and Thomas Wilsone in Bairtholchaple.

7s 0d each - by John Hunter in Silvermoss, and Gavin Huntar in Old Balgow; 5s 2d each - by Elspeth Broun in Boghouse, Patrick Glenny in Midleboghouse, Robert Smith in Overboghouse, Arthur Milne at the Mill of Tolquhon, William Ritchie in Brayside, Robert Gavin in Raitshill, and Robert Steiven in Gairdseall; 3s 6d each - by John Sangster in Leverockley, John Cocker in Guthecairn, and John Kellie in Chaplecross; 3s 4d each - by Andrew Ogilvie in Angellwell and John Brichen in Rossocklo.

And this is how the Forbes household was expected to raise the tax on Tolquhon:

Sir Alexander Forbes, £ 24 6s 0d; Mrs Elizabeth Forbes in familia, £ 3. 6. 0d; James Man, servant, £ 1. 6s 0d; James Broun, servant, £ 1. 1s 0d; Alexander Barkley, 16s 0d; Charles Chessor, 16s 0d; his wyfe, 6s 0d; John Kennet, 10s 8d; Marjorie Sutherland, 11s 4d; Barbra Broddie, 11s 4d; William Pape, 16s 0d; William Burrell, gardner, and his wife, 18s 0d; Alexander Forsyth, 6s 0d; Jean Duguid, 9s 0d; William Youngson, cottar, and his wife, 12s 0d; Isobell Walker, daughter to James Walker, 6s 0d; and James Walker, cottar, and his wife, 12s 0d.

LITLE YTHSIE

Patrick Broun, tennent ther, and his wife, 12s 0d; William and Elspet Brounes, his children, 12s 0d; Andrew Duguid, 9s 6d; James Auchinleck, 9s 6d; William Murker, 9s 6d; Bessie Cook, 10s 8d; George Gray, cottar, and his wife, 12s 0d; William Duiged, weaver ther, for his trade, his oun, his wife and daughters generall poll, £ 1. 4s 0d; William Lovie, and his wife, 12s 0d; Patrick Murkar, and his wife, 12s 0d; Alexander Broun ther, and his wife, 12s 0d; Isobell Gibb ther, and his daughter, 12s 0d; and Barbra Gray, cottar woman, 6s 0d.

MEIKLE YTHSIE

Gilbert Milne, tennent ther, and his wife, 12s 0d; John, Jannet and Elspeth Milnes, his daughters in familia, 18s 0d; Alexander Scott, 11s 6d; Isobell Murkar, cottar, 6s 0d; Margaret Milne, cottar woman, 6s 0d; Alexander Byres, tennent, and his wife, 12s 0d; John Broggan, 10s 2d; Agnes Boddy, 10s 6d; James Brydie, cottar, and his wife and daughter, 18s 0d; Andrew Gibb, cottar, and his wife, 12s 0d; James Chalmers, cottar, and his wife, 12s 0d; Robert Reid, tennent ther, and his wife, 12s 0d; George Laurie, his servant, 14s 8d; William Wallace, 10s 6d; John Auld, 10s 2d; James Caillie, 10s 2d; John Craig, cottar, and his wyfe, 12s 0d; John Edward and his wyfe, 12s 0d; and George Davidson, in Reidfoords, and his wyfe, 12s 0d.

MILL OF YTHSIE

Robert Forbes, tennent ther, he classing himself as a gentleman, his poll is £ 3. 6s 0d; Item, his wife and daughter, 12s 0d; John Rae, his servant, 13s 8d; Isobell Godsman, 10s 6d; and Margaret Ross, 10s 6d.

BOGHOUSE OF TOLQUHON

Elspeth Broun, tennent ther, 6s 0d; Robert Smith, her servant, 9s 8d; Margaret Shirrif, 6s 0d; Christian Murker, 9s 4d; and John Smith, tradesman, and his wyfe, 18s 0d.

NEWSEAT OF TOLQUHON

Thomas Byres, teennent ther, and his wyfe, 12s 0d; William Byres, his sone in familia, 6s 0d; Alexander Syme, 15s 0d; James Riddell, 11s 4d; Jean Muireson, 10s 8d; William Breichen ther, and his wyfe, 12s 0d; Alexander Forsyth ther, and his wyfe, 12s 0d; John Midletoun, and his wyfe, 12s 0d; Alexander Glenny, tennent ther, and his wyfe, 12s 0d; James Umphray, his servant, 15s 0d; James Dyce, 7s 10d; William Essells (no trade), and his wyfe, 12s 0d; Isobell and Margaret Grays, cottar women, 12s 0d; Margaret and Marjory Grays, cottar women, 12s 0d; and Alexander Murray ther, his soun, his wyfe and daughter in familia, 18s 0d.

MIDLE BOGHOUSE

Patrick Glenny, tennent, and his wyfe, 12s 0d; James and Isobell Glennies, his children, 12s 0d; James Beaton, 12s 8d; George Duiguid, for no trade but for his and wyfes generall poll, 12s 0d; and Jean Jack, servant, 6s 0d.

OVER BOGHOUSE

Robert Smith, tennent ther, and his wife, 12s 0d; James Smith, his sone in familia, 6s 0d.

MILL OF TOLQUHON

Arthur Milne, tennent ther, and his wyfe, 12s 0d; Andrew Vass, his servant, 14s 0d; and William Milne, 10s 8d.

BRAESYDE

William Ritchie, tennent ther, and his wyfe, 12s 0d; Elizabeth Reid, his sister-in-law, 6s 0d; Isobell Chrystie, 6s 8d; and John Porter ther, and his wife, of generall poll, 12s 0d.

RAITSHILL

Robert Gavin, tennent ther, and his wyfe, 12s 0d; Robert Forsyth ther, and his wife, 12s 0d; and Isobell Forsyth, his daughter in familia, 6s 0d.

WESTER KILNARY

George Gavin, tennent ther, and his wyfe, 12s 0d; Robert, Isobell and Elspeth Gavins, children, 18s 0d; John Porter, for fee and generall poll, 10s 8d; Isobell Symer, 10s 0d; William Gavin, shoemaker, and his wyfe, 18s 0d; and Isobell Yuill, cottar woman, 6s 0d.

CAIRDSEALL

Robert Steiven, tennent ther, and his wyfe, 12s 0d; John Steiven, his sone, 6s 0d; James Chalmers, shoemaker, and his wife, 18s 0d; Alexander Austin, subtennent to James Man in Over Kilnary, and his wife, 12s 0d; Alexander Hill, wyver, and his wife, 18s 0d; George Simmer (no trade), and his wife, 12s 0d; James Wyne (no trade), and his wife, 12s 0d; Margaret Wyne, his daughter in familia, 6s 0d;James Hill, servant to James Man, 14s 8d; and James Wyne, younger, servant to him, 10s 0d.

GATESIDE OF FUCHELL

James Smith, tennent ther, and his wife, 12s 0d; William Grumma, his servant, 14s 8d; John Gordon, servant, 8s 6d; John Mitchell, shoemaker ther, and his wife, 18s 0d; Janet Granna, cottar woman, 6s 0d; James Lamb, cottar, and his wife, 12s 0d; and Elspeth and Elizabeth Smiths, their daughters, 12s 0d.

SILVERMOSS

John Huntar, tennent ther, a tradesman, and his wife, 18s 0d; John and Margrat Huntars, children, 12s 0d; and Patrick Troup, cottar, and his wife, 12s 0d.

MILLTOUN OF FUCHELL

John Gavin, tennent ther, and his wife, 12s 0d; John Scoutie, servant, 11s 6d; George Breichen, 12s 4d; Janet Salter, 8s 6d; James Dickson, miller, and his wife, 18s 0d; John Pirie, cottar, and his wife, 12s 0d; George Henderson, taylor, and his wife, 18s 0d; Alexander Broun, cottar, and his wife, 12s 0d; Alexander Sime, cottar, and his wife, 12s 0d; William Rainie, cottar, his wife, and two daughters, £ 1. 4s 0d; Isobell Froyne, 6s 0d; and James Walker, cottar, and his wife, 12s 0d.

NEW BALGOVE

Patrick Smith, tennent ther, and his wife, 12s 0d; George Steivensone, his servant, 12s 0d; Barbara Chrystie, 9s 0d; George Clerk, wyver, and his wife, 18s 0d; Robert Brebner, and his wife, 12s 0d; and James Duguid, and his wife, 12s 0d.

OLD BALGOVE

Gavin Hunter, tennent ther, and his wife, 12s 0d; John Rainie, his servant, 9s 10d; Elspeth Allardyce, 9s 10d; and George Troup, cottar, and his wife, 12s 0d.

ANGELWELL

Andrew Ogilvie ther, and his wife, 12s 0d; James Breichen in Rosole, and his wife, 12s 0d; Margaret Breichen, his daughter, 6s 0d; and Alexander Webster, cottar, and his wife, 12s 0d.

LEVEROCKLYES

John Sangster, tennent ther, and his wife, 12s 0d.

MOSSYDS

William Moir, tennent ther, and his wife, 12s 0d; Isobell Moir, his daughter 6s 0d; John Abernethie, 9s 6d; Alexander Sangster, cottar, and his wyfe, 12s 0d; Andrew Watt and Barbara Shirris, 12s 0d; and Isobel Hay and Helen Reidheid, cottars, 12s 0d.

OLD TOUNE OF FOCHELL

Alexander Gray, tennent ther, and his mother, with three sisters in familia, £ 1. 10s 0d; Alexander Thomson ther, and his wife, 12s 0d; David Beany there, and his wife, 12s 0d; John Couie there, and his mother in familia, 12s 0d; Isobell Rae, grasswoman, 6s 0d; John Mitchell and his wife, 12s 0d; Alexander Burnet, ther and his wife, 12s 0d; and George Walker, wyver in Reidmoss, and George Walker, his son in familia, £ 1. 4s 0d.

HALTOUN SLAPP

James Peirie, tennent ther, and his wyfe, with two children in familia, £ 1. 4s 0d; George Salter, cottar, and his wyfe, 12s 0d; Elspeth Swap, cottar woman, 6s 0d; and Margaret Taylor, cottar, and her daughter, 12s 0d.

KIRKFOORD

Walter Breichen ther, and his wyfe, 12s 0d; Thomas Fraser ther, his wife, and two daughters, £ 1. 4s 0d; James Webster, cottar, and his wyfe, 12s 0d; and Jean Wood, cottar woman, 6s 0d.

DALFORKIE

William Gow ther, and his wyfe, 12s 0d; Jean Gow, his sister, 6s 0d; George Beanie, 14s 0d; George Knolls, 10s 2d; George McKie, cottar, and his wyfe, 12s 0d; Marjorie Troup, cottar woman, 6s 0d; Andrew Cockar, wyver, and his wife, 18s 0d; and George Greive, cottar, and his wyfe, 12s 0d.

FULLFOORD

John Breichen, tennent ther, his wyfe and two daughters in familia, £ 1. 4s 0d; John Mitchell, 9s 0d; Helen Ferguson, grasswoman, and her two daughters in familia, 18s 0d; John Raynie , shoemaker, his wyfe and sone in familia, £ 1. 4s 0d; George Raynie, cottar, and his wife, 12s 0d; and James Catto, and his wyfe, with his daughter, 18s 0d.

CUTHER CAIRNE

James Cockar, tennent ther, and his wyfe, and Isobell Cockar, his daughter, and William Wilsone, sone-in-law, £ 1. 4s 0d; James Taylor, 10s 6d; and Isobell Kennet, cottar woman, 6s 0d.

SLOBATTS

William Burr, tennent ther, and his wyfe, 12s 0d; Robert Burr, elder, ther, and his wyfe, with three children in familia, £ 1. 10s 0d; John Burr ther, and his wyfe, 12s 0d; Robert Burr, younger, ther, and his wyfe, 12s 0d; John Edward, cottar, and his wyfe, 12s 0d; and Isobell Smith, cottar, 6s 0d.

NETHER KIRKTOUNE

John Murdo, tennent ther, and his wyfe, 12s 0d; William Bruce, his servant, 13s 6d; George Brandie, 10s 0d; Isobell Auld, 10s 8d; Alexander Euen, wyver, and his wyfe, 18s 0d; and James Steiven, and his wyfe, 12s 0d.

OVER KIRKTOUNE

William Findlay, tennent ther, and his wyfe, 12s 0d; William Haregare ther, and his wyfe, 12s 0d; Agnes Murdo, their daughter-in-law, 6s 0d; William Sinclair, cottar, and his wyfe, 12s 0d; and Helen McKie, cottar woman, 6s 0d.

BARTHOLCHAPLE

Thomas Wilson, tennent ther, and his wyfe, 12s 0d; John Thomson, 12s 0d; John Euen, 9s 2d; Christian Suttor, cottar woman, 6s 0d; William Scott, cottar, and his wyfe, 12s 0d; Isobell Ferguson, cottar woman, 12s 0d; Andrew Scott, cottar, and his wyfe, 12s 0d; Isobell Scott, his daughter, 6s 0d; John Kellie, in Chappell Croft, and his wyfe, 12s 0d; and Margaret Kellie, his daughter, 6s 0d.

Mr George Anderson, minister at Tarves, is pollable in £ 3, and the generall poll for himselfe, his wyffe, James, William, Robert, Gilbert, Margaret, Anna and Elspeth Andersons, his children in familia, in all is £ 5. 14s 0d; Isobell Midletoun, relict of the deceast Mr Alexander Garden, minister at the Kirk of Forge, is lyable for the third pairt of her husbands poll, which (if allyve) wold have been £ 3, and the generall poll of 6s, is £ 1. 6s 0d; James Lesslie, his servant, 14s 0d; Isobell Smith, servant, 11s 0d; and Christian Barkley, 10s 3d.

The lands of George Gray of Shivas were valued at £ 600, and the hundredth part for which tenants were liable was apportioned as follows:

£ 2 - John Strachan and John Stewart, in the Mayns of Skilmathilla; £ 1 each - Imprimis, Andrew Gray, tennent in Quilraxe; Thomas Gray, tennent in Old Mill of Shives; Thomas Strachan, in New Milne of Shives; and George Smith and Robert Forbes in Newseat.

The bill faced by the Shivas household was allocated thus:
The said George Gray of Shives, his valwatione being above £500, his poll is £ 12 and the generall poll for himself and wyfe, is £ 12. 12s 0d; George Gray, major, 14s 0d; George Gray, minor, 14s 0d; Christian Hatt, 10s 8d; Andrew Paull, gardner, and his wyfe, 18s 0d; Gilbert Murdo, cottar, and his wyfe, 12s 0d; James Cruickshank, and his wyfe, 12s 0d; William Reid, and his wyfe, 12s 0d; George Saint, and his wyfe, 12s 0d; David Vass, and his wyfe, 12s 0d; Alexander Kirktoun, smith, 12s 0d; Alexander Walker, and his wyfe, 12s 0d; Isobell Boghouse, cottar woman, 6s 0d; Robert Boghouse, cottar, and his wyfe, 12s 0d; George Cruickshank, and his wyfe, 12s 0d; George Maitland, and his wyfe, 12s 0d; and John Sangster, and his wyfe, with their daughter, 18s 0d.

SKILMATHILLIE

John Strachan, tennent ther, and his wyfe, with his daughter in familia, 18s 0d; Ane servant man, 10s 0d; and George Stewart, tennent ther, and his wyfe, 12s 0d.

OLD MILL OF SHIVES

Thomas Strachan, tennent ther, and his wyfe, 12s 0d; Helen Arthur, 11s 0d; John Walker ther, his wife, and Barbra Watson, his sister-in-law, 18s 0d; Janet Thomsone, 9s 4d; and George Davidson, and his wyfe, 12s 0d.

QUILRAXE

Andrew Gray, tennent ther, 6s 0d; George Massie, his servant, 11s 0d; Jean Massie, his servant, 10s 0d; Anna Smith, his servant, 10s 0d; George Cow, and his wyfe, 10s 0d; Barbra Stephan, cottar woman, 6s 0d; John Milne, and his wyfe, 12s 0d; James Gibb, and his wyfe, 12s 0d; John Irving, subtennent ther, and his wyfe, 12s 0d; George Thomsone ther, and his wyfe, 12s 0d; James Gordon, 6s 0d; and Beatrix Sim, cottar woman, 6s 0d.

MILL OF SHIVES

Thomas Gray, tennent ther, and his wyfe, 12s 0d; William Hay, his servant, 16s 0d; Robert Wyshart, 12s 6d; Isobell Norrie, 10s 0d; Lucriss Hay, 10s 0d; Barbra Massie, 8s 0d; William Gray, 8s 5d; William Gordon, 8s 5d; Gavin Hardie, miller, and his wife, 12s 0d; William Brogan, and his wife, 12s 0d; and John Hatt, and his wyfe, 12s 0d.

NEWSEAT OF SHIVES

Robert Forbes, tennent ther, and his wyfe, 12s 0d; his servant, 10s 2d; Gilbert Edward and his wife, 12s 0d; George Anderson, and his wyfe, 12s 0d; George Smith, tennent ther, and his wyfe, 12s 0d; Alexander Home, his servant, 8s 0d; and George Webster, wyver, and his wyfe, 18s 0d.

BROADWARD OF SHIVES

James Reid, tennent ther, and his wyfe, 12s 0d; Alexander Reid, his brother, 6s 0d; and James Fraser, 9s 6d.

James Keith of Tillegonie, King's Commissioner for collecting the poll tax in Tarves, had his lands valued at £ 300, and the "hundreth pairt " was found as follows:

14s 0d - William Cassie in Over Tilegonie; 8s 0d - William Webster in Overwoodhill; 4s 0d each -James Leg at the Mill of Tilgonie, John Wilson in Netherwoodhill, John Muireson, tennent ther, Patrick Lesslie in Montylay, and Adam Lea in Sutherley; 3s 0d - John Fraser in Earlesfoord; 2s 0d each - James Meason and John McKie in Netherwoodhill, George Milne and Alexander Gordon in Midlepleugh, and William Smith and James Fraser in Wedderbyres; 1s 0d - Donald Urquhart in Netherwoodhill.

The laird's own household paid the tax thus:
The Laird of Tillegonie, his valuatione in the said parioch being above £ 200, is lyable for £ 9 of poll, and the general poll, £ 9. 6s 0d; his ladys generall poll, 6s 0d; His seven children in familia, viz James, William, Anna, Isobell, Margaret, Jean and Jannet Keiths, £ 2. 2s 0d; John Brebner, his servant, 11s 0d; William Smith, 11s 0d; Francis Watt, 15s 0d; William Hendry, 10s 0d; John Rainie, 7s 8d; Alexander Gordon, 8s 0d; George Webster, 8s 0d; Jean Milne, 11s 0d;Christian Hay, 10s 6d; Isobell McIntoch, 10s 0d; James Duncan, gardner ther, and his wyfe, 18s 0d; James Duncan, his son, 6s 0d; Jean Duncan, 8s 0d; and Margaret Hay 6s 0d.

MONTGLAY

Patrick Leask ther, his wyfe, and daughter, 18s 0d; Adam Leask, in Sacherlye, and his wyfe, 12s 0d; William Cassie, tennent in Over Tilegonie, 6s 0d; His wyfe, and James Cassie, his sone, 12s 0d; and William Cassie, ane other sone, packman, 12s 0d.

UNDERWASLES

Patrick Rainie, tenent ther, and his wyfe, 12s 0d; William Rainie, taillyor, 12s 0d; Isobell Rainie, 8s 4d; and James Leg, in Milne of Tilegoneie, and his wyfe, 12s 0d.

EARLESFOORD

John Fraser, tennent ther, and his wyfe, 12s 0d; and ane woman servant, 8s 4d.

OVER WOODHILL

William Webster, tenent ther, and his wyfe, 12s 0d; Alexander Beinie, 13s 0d; Marjorie Manson, cottar woman ther, and William Clerk, her sone, taillior, 18s 0d; and George Mitchill, and his wyfe, 12s 0d.

NETHER WOODHILL

John Wilsone, tennent ther, and his wyfe, 12s 0d; James Mansone, tennent ther, and his wyfe, 12s 0d; James Massone, in Midpleugh, and his wyfe, 12s 0d; Alexander Gordon, tennent ther, and his wyfe, 12s 0d; John McKie ther, and his wyfe and daughter, 18s 0d; Donald Urquhart, and his wyfe, 12s 0d; and George McKie ther, and his wyfe, 12s 0d.

WEDDERBYRES

John Young, tennent and wyver ther, his oun and his wyfes generall poll is 18s 0d; Jean Young, his daughter in familia, 6s 0d; William Smith ther, and his wyfe, 12s 0d; James Fraser, pyper ther, and his wyfe, 18s 0d; George Cranathie ther, 6s 0d; Elspeth Smith, 6s 0d; George Webster, and his wyfe, 12s 0d; and Margaret Cobler ther, 6s 0d.

The £ 6. 0s 0d representing the "hundreth pairt " of the valuation of the lands of Cairnbrogie was to be paid in this way:

17s 4d each - Patrick Maitland in Newplace of Cairnbrogie, and Robert Glennie and William McKie in Old Cairnbrogie; 17s 2d each - George Johnstoun in New Cairnbrogie, and Kathrine Couper and John Craigheid in Old Cairnbrogie; 8s 6d - Alexander Smith in Smidiehill; 8s 0d - John Leith, at the Mill of Cairnbrogie.

NEW CAIRNBROGIE

George Johnstoun, tennent ther, his wyfe and daughter, 18s 0d; Isobell Johnstoun, his sister, 6s 0d; John Duncan, 13s 4d; William Duncan 9s 8d; Isobell Johnstoun, 10s 8d; and John Archbald, cottar, and his wyfe, 12s 0d.

OLD CAIRNBROGIE

Kathrine Couper, tennent ther, 6s 0d; Robert Steiven, 14s 0d; Elspeth Forbes, 10s 0d; Patrick Millne, subtennent, wright, and his wyfe, 18s 0d; George Craighead, and his wyfe, 12s 0d; James Henderson, cottar, and his wyfe, 12s 0d; John Craighead, tennent, and his wyfe, 12s 0d; John Drummond, and his wyfe, 12s 0d; William Gray, tennent, and his wyfe, 12s 0d; Isobell Kirktoun, 10s 0d; Beatrix Gormock, 10s 0d; James Walker, 9s 0d; Margaret McKie, 9s 0d; William Ritchie, shoemaker, and his wyfe, 18s 0d; and William Archbald, cobler, and his wyfe, 18s 0d; Robert Glenny, tennent and wyver, and his wyfe, 18s 0d; William McKie, tennent ther, and his wyfe, 12s 0d; John Leith, at the Milne of Cairnbrogie, his oun and his wyfs generall poll, 12s 0d; George Leith, his servant, 11s 0d; and William Pirie, pickman, and his wyfe, 18s 0d.

SMIDEHILL

Alexander Smith, tennent ther, his father and brother in familia, 18s 0d; Patrick Aitken in Sunnysyde, and his wife, 12s 0d.

NEWPLACE OF CAIRNBROGIE

Patrick Maitland, tennent ther, and his wife, 12s 0d; John and Margrat Maitlands, his children, 12s 0d; William Shuon, 16s 0d; William Scorgack, 16s 0d; James Glennie, 12s 8d; James Thomsone, 7s 6d; Agnes Kirktoune, 11s 4d; Isobell Walker, 10s 8d; William Young, cottar, and his wyfe, 12s 0d;Jean Thomson, cottar woman, 6s 0d; Elspeth Gordon, cottar woman, 6s 0d; Margaret King ther, and her daughter, 12s 0d; Isobell Thomson, cottar woman, 6s 0d; Patrick Charles, taylor, and his wyfe, 18s 0d; William Anderson, cottar, and his wyfe, 12s 0d; William Walker, cottar, and his wyfe, 12s 0d; Isobell Kirktoun, cottar woman, 6s 0d; James Maitland, and his wyfe, 12s 0d; Thomas Webster, cottar, and his wyfe, 12s 0d; George Walker, wyver, and his wyfe, 18s 0d; James Steivenson, tinker, and his wyfe, 18s 0d; Andrew Brebner, cottar, 6s 0d; and Elizabeth Hepburne, 6s 0d.

" Suma of the paroch of Tarves amounts to fyve hundreth and fourtein punds, eighteen shillings and nyne pennies..£ 514. 18s 9d"

In this 1807 map of Aberdeenshire, the North Sea is described as the 'British Ocean'. Tarves is 20 miles North of Aberdeen.

Illustration: author's collection

Chapter 8

Witches, Warlocks
and Hangmen

H E did not break until roused from a fitful sleep by the clatter of nails being driven into the timber of the scaffold outside his cell window. "In the course of the night he was terribly agitated," said *Aberdeenshire's Black Kalendar.* "The noise seemed to shake his very soul."

The author of this historical catalogue of public hangings and floggings in Aberdeen was commenting on the last hours of 20-year-old William Allan, son of a Tarves crofter. The date was Friday, 10 February, 1826. Allan had murdered a cattle drover for the 36 shillings with which he was returning to his home in Sutherland from a cattle sale in the south.

The encounter which led to this appointment with the hangman occurred on the road south of Aberdeen where Allan met elderly Alexander Mackay on his long hike towards the Highlands. Allan, who had married just a year earlier and moved to a croft a few miles away at Monquhitter, travelled with Mackay to Daviot where they spent the night at an inn. Though the Highlander became suspicious of Allan's intentions, he was a simple soul and was persuaded next morning to turn back with Allan to visit a fair at Tarves, with the promise of a night's lodging at his father's Tarves croft. But on a desolate footpath at the Den of Rothie, near Fyvie, Allan felled Mackay with a leaded whip, striking him repeatedly until he had fractured his skull and broken one of his ribs.

Allan snatched his victim's purse and made off over the moors, leaving Mackay for dead. But the drover was still alive and managed to crawl to the Lewes of Fyvie where he lay at an inn for two weeks before succumbing to his injuries. During that interval he had been able to relate the story of the attack and gave an accurate description of his assailant and his dress. The fugitive was arrested while feeding cattle on a moss at his croft and was brought to Fyvie where he was identified by the dying man.

The *Black Kalendar* informs us that when Allan was sentenced in Aberdeen he "became quite composed, sat down with a smile on his face and conversed cheerfully with the officer beside him." Allan later confessed to the crime but showed no signs of repentance. Three weeks before his date with the hangman an attempt to escape was foiled by his jailers.

"Except when visited by his wife and sisters," the *Kalendar* says, "he scarcely seemed to manifest any deep feeling of his situation. On the day immediately preceding his execution his heart was so far softened that he expressed sorrow for his crime and requested that the clergymen would not leave him but administer religious consolation to him through the night."

Allan dozed off but was wakened by the noise of the tradesmen erecting the scaffold. "In the course of the night he was terribly agitated," the *Kalendar* adds. "The noise made by the workmen employed in erecting the scaffold seemed to shake his very soul. When his arms were pinioned, previous to his being led down to the Old Court House, he fainted away, and again when he reached the bottom of the stair. He sat in a chair manifesting great emotion while the 51st Psalm was sung, in which he joined. On being brought out he fainted away while the Rev Mr Thom was praying. At about eight minutes from two the drop fell and he died with very little struggle. His body was conveyed to the Marishal College for dissection."

In a closely-knit parish like Tarves, where serious crime was comparatively rare, the hanging of William Allan would have been a sensation and if the community followed the custom of the times it is likely that a number of the more prurient among its parishioners travelled to Aberdeen to witness the execution. Barbaric though the practice appears to us today, it was common then for spectators to turn out in their thousands to watch or to shout and jeer as a man or woman died on the gallows.

Public executions in Aberdeenshire were normally carried out in the Castlegate or in the courtyard of the Old City Chambers in Lodge Walk, Aberdeen. Huge, noisy crowds gathered to leer or jeer, or to partake in raucous celebration which reached fever-pitch as the moment of the 'drop' approached. As the burial of executed criminals was considered a desecration of sacred ground, relatives were permitted, after a period of time, to cut down the body and take it out to sea for burial. Sometimes a bloated corpse, washed ashore and picked up by beachcombers, would be delivered, for a few shillings, to the surgeons at Kings College, supposedly in the interests of advancing medical knowledge.

It was not, of course, necessary in those days to have committed murder to end up on the scaffold. The luckless were consigned to an early meeting with their Maker for lesser crimes like sheep-stealing, wife-beating or even petty theft. Banishment for life, transportation and public whipping through the city's streets were meted out for offences which would today bring, at most, a custodial sentence. In 1785, for instance, a vagrant, John McDonald, was charged with two acts of wilful fire-raising in Aberdeenshire by burning down the stacks, yards and houses of two farmers. He was arrested when seen near one of the houses with a burning peat "which he pretended to have procured to light a tobacco pipe but it appeared he had never used it for that purpose." Though the accused was clearly mentally handicapped, he was sentenced to death. It was recorded that he believed if he ate enough meat the hanging would not kill him. During the period when an attending clergyman was employed with him in devotional exercises, McDonald insisted: "Och, never mind your prayers - hand up the shibbery!"* McDonald denied his crime with his last breath.

In 1770 Christian Spence, wife of John Gray in Pitmedden, and her son James were found guilty of setting fire to a "cotton yarn " belonging to a neighbour, John Lessel. The *Black Kalendar* relates that the Advocate-Depute restricted the punishment because of mitigating circumstances. Nevertheless, the two prisoners were carried through Aberdeen in a cart, with ropes about their necks and the hangman in attendance. James Gray was then banished from Scotland for life while his mother was imprisoned until "she should find caution to keep the peace and his Majesty's lieges harmless and skaithless for three years."

Banishment for life was also the lot in March 1786 of Margaret Walker "for keeping a house of bad fame" and Jean Watt for stealing a duffle cloak and selling it. But the two Aberdeen women did not go down without leaving their mark on the magistrates.

After the guilty verdict, Walker - better known to the citizens as 'Lucky Walker' - was brought out and stood for an hour at the pillory atop the Tolbooth stair, attended by the hangman and bearing on her breast a placard identifying her as an "Infamous Bawd and Receipt of Theft."

While standing there in full view of the citizenry, Walker relieved her situation by abusing the magistrates who had imposed sentence and the town's clergymen, Abercrombie, Hogg and Shaw, who had been her enemies and had brought her to court. Much to the delight of the onlookers who were there to be entertained, she said of the magistrates:

> "It's ill their pairt to use me this way - for there is no ane o' them that
> hae's na been well entertain'd in my house, wi' a'thing that they
> wantit, except Provost Cruden - and I will except him."

After her pillorying, Walker was drummed through the town and banished the city and liberties for life, along with Jean Watt who had stolen the cloak.

Two months later, at the same court, Agnes Simpson was tried for the murder of her child, an eight-months-old infant. Doctors reported that she was insane and was incapable of conducting her own defence. The court deserted the case against her but ten years later she was found guilty of having drowned a second child.

She was again declared to be insane and was ordered into perpetual confinement in the prison at Banff. There, she bore a child to one of the jailers who was charged with having subsequently murdered it. He was acquitted. Agnes Simpson was a witness at his trial!

shibbery - meat

Thomas Rany and his wife were borne through the streets of Aberdeen, bound together in a cart, with paper crowns on their heads proclaiming: "for thift and ressett of thift", and were "perpetuallie baneist this burgh." Vandals who broke church windows in Old Aberdeen were "bound to the cross for 24 hours and bridled thereat", while their parents or masters made good the damage. An incident of merry-making by young people caused the Presbytery of Aberdeen to issue this edict:

> "If any man or woman be convict in the lyk monstrous behaviour in tym cumming, to wit, either men dansin in women's apparel, or women in men's apparel, or yett if women be fand dansin publiclie through the strettis maskit and disgsit in sic a wanton and unchaste form in companie with men, the doers sall pay a pecunial penaltie to the puir, and also mak their public repentance on the stuill, and for the second fault sal make it in sackcloth. "

There was no way out for Oldmeldrum hawker John Booth in 1857, charged with the murder of Jean Barclay during a family fracas in the village. Booth was said to travel the country with a box of hardware and had been on a drinking bout with cronies at a local hostelry when allusions were made to the infidelity of his wife. Booth staggered home, dragged his wife from bed and stabbed her with a spring-backed clasp-knife.

The wife, a stout active woman in her mid-thirties, broke free and ran to the house of her father who kept a small shop in the village. Booth followed and finding the door closed, burst it open. His 70-year-old mother-in-law ran past him to seek assistance in the street but was savagely attacked and fell, dying of stab wounds.

Booth gave himself up to the local policeman but it is scarcely surprising, in the judicial climate of the time, that the sentence of the court was that:

> "You, the said John Booth, to be taken from the bar to the prison of Aberdeen, there to be detained and fed on bread and water, until Wednesday 21st of October, and upon that day, between the hours of eight and ten o'clock, to be taken to the common place of execution, and there by the hands of the common hangman, to be hanged by the neck until dead and your body to be buried within the precincts of the prison; and may God Almighty have mercy on your soul."

Among those who escaped the hangman at the eleventh hour were James Robertson and Alexander Hay, sentenced to hang for stealing 36 sheep at Strichen and selling them to the minister at Dyce. They were described as "persons of bad and broken fame, thieves and receptors of theft." Before the day set for their execution, however, their sentence was commuted to banishment for life. Also banished, in 1756, was Christian Clark who was tried on a comprehensive indictment of "bringing forth two bastards, keeping a disorderly house, entertaining men by night and day, and sailors upon Sundays, and being by habit and repute a harlot and a loose woman, and keeping a bawdy house." She was also warned that if she was still in Aberdeeshire after a month she would be publicly whipped at the market cross by the common hangman and again banished. Farmer John Hutcheon was charged with housebreaking, including the theft of a gold watch, £50 and five head of cattle. He was hanged on 28th June 1764.

There were constant reminders in medieval and later ages of man's inhumanity to man as ignorance and superstition bred unimaginable levels of cruelty in the serene county we know today as Aberdeenshire.

Witchcraft flourished, with relentless persecution, torture and death commonplace in the North-East. During the period between 1450 and 1750, it is estimated that upwards of 17,000 witches perished in Scotland, usually by burning, while thousands more were banished or subjected to hideous abuse.

In Aberdeenshire, particularly in the most backward rural parishes, an almost uncontrollable epidemic of witch-hunting broke out at the end of the 16th century after issue by the Privy Council of standing commissions to local authorities to round up witches and put them on trial.

According to the archives of the local Dean of Guild, one man and 23 women were burned for witchcraft in Aberdeen in 1597 alone. Most were arrested and brought in from the surrounding countryside. One of the most notorious cases was described by Gavin Turreff in *Antiquarian Gleanings from Aberdeenshire Records* (1871). He wrote:

> "Public curiosity seems to have grown with the increased frequency of these exhibitions, as one of the items of the expense was 'for careing of four sparris* to withstand the press of the people, quhairof** there was tua broken."

The charge, extracted from the original record and couched in its language, was:

> "Upon Hallowein last bypast, at twelff houris or thairby, Thomas Leyis, accompaneit with Jannett Wischert, Isobel Coker, Isobell Monteithe and Kathren Mitchell, relict (widow) of umquhill (late) Charles Dun, litster (dyer), sorceraris and witches, with ane gryt number of ither witches, cam to the mercat and fish cross of Aberdene, under the conduct and gyding of the dewill, present with you all in company, playing before you on his kynd of instruments.

> "Ye all dansit about baythe the said crosse and the meill mercate ane lang space of tym; thow, the said Thomas, was foremost and led the ring, and dang (hit) the said Kathren Mitchell because she spoilt your dans, and ran nocht sa fast about as the rest. Testifeit by the said Kathren Mitchell, qua (who) was present with thee at the tym foresaid, dansin wi the dewill."

The court sitting, in Aberdeen's then dreaded Tolbooth, was chaired by Provost Alexander Rutherford, with Bailies Alexander Cullen and Alexander Jaffray, and 21 jurors.

* ***sparris*** - *barriers* ; ***quhairof*** - *whereof*

The record states:

> "Thomas Leyis, son of John Leyis, stabler in Aberdeen, was accusit
> as a common notorious witch, in using of witchcraft and sorcerie
> these dyvers years bygane, being deneyit be the said Thomas, was
> referrit to the knauledge of the assis (assembly). The haill (whole)
> assis convicts and fyllis Thomas Leyis in the first poynt, that he
> was the ringleader of the dance on Hallowein last about the croce,
> and in either speciall poynts, and as a notorious witche be oppen
> voce and common fame."

Janet Wishart, who was apparently Thomas Leys' mother, was accused of
"casting the evil eye", of causing 12 hens to drop dead at her feet, and of
bringing ruin to a family by casting a spell on them "using nine grains of wheat
and a twig of rowan." She was also said to have caused cows to give poison
instead of milk and to have dismembered bodies hanging on the gallows at
Aberdeen.

It seems that all but Kathren Mitchell were condemned, for the town's accounts
detail the expenses incurred in burning them:

Thomas Leyis

For peattis, tar barrelis, fir and coallis to burn the said Thomas, and to John Justice for his fie in executing him	£ 2. 13. 4

Janet Wischert and Isobel Cocker

For twenty loads of peattis to burn them	£ 2	0.	0
Ane boll of coillis		1.	4. 0
Four tar barrellis		1.	6. 8
Fir and win barrellis			16. 8
A staik, and dressing of it			16. 0
Four fadomes of towis (rope)		4.	0. 0
Careing the peattis, coallis			13. 4
To John Justice for their execution			13. 4

For trailling Monteithe through the streits of the toun in ane cart, quha (who) hangit herself in prison, and eirding (burying) her	10. 0.

A grisly business indeed, but William Dunn, the Dean of Guild, seems to have
profited greatly from it. So grateful were the Provost and town council, in fact,
that they presented him with the princely sum of £ 47. 3s 4d in recognition of
his dedication to duty as well as his "extraordinarie takin panis in the burning
of the gryt numer of the witches brunt this year." The award, they added, was to
"incurage ithers to travel also diligentlie in the discharge of thair office."

Gilbert Barnes was paid the huge sum of £ 50. 13s 4d for "sustentatioun of the witches in prison from the 16th of Marche to the 23rd of May nixt" while blacksmith Alex Reid earned £ 1. 12s for making "two pair of sheckills to the witches in the stephill" and Thomas Dickson was paid £ 1. 10s "in recompence of his halbert broken at the execution of the witches." John Justice was paid an additional fee of £ 1. 6s 8d for "burning upon the cheik of four several persons suspect of witchcraft and banischet" and Alex Home earned £ 2. 6s 8d for "mackin off joggis, stepills and lockis to the witches."

A barrow "to carie ye cripple witches" cost 6s and, perhaps oddest and most lucrative of all, Alex Ramsay collected an incredible £ 142. 3s 4d for "interteining ye witches"! What kind of entertainment, one wonders, would condemned witches require? Andrew Clerk received £ 6. 13s 4d for "his pains in wrytting ye dittays on ye witches and sitting as clerk in ye commission".

Walking the bustling streets of the modern city today, it is almost impossible to conceive that crimes as awful as these were committed there. There is no doubt, however, that witch-hunting and the subsequent trials and public executions created rich pickings for the unscrupulous - from doctors to clergymen, torturers to carpenters and scribes, even the innkeepers who relished the lucrative trade brought by the huge crowds who came to revel.

The witch hunt was persistent throughout Aberdeenshire, affecting the lives of all. The lesser crime of 'charming' (dealing in spells) was also a target for religious fanatics seeking to cleanse that dismal landscape of Satan's influence. The Ellon Presbytery archives abound with references to the practice. These are but a handful from the Rev William Mair's extensive research:

● 1599 Janet Davidson complained she had been slandered as a witch. Witnesses stated that their cattle had never prospered since Davidson came to dwell beside them. It was said she could "caus a sick bairn to gang as she pleased" (either die or recover). The leaves of the record are so wasted at this point that the outcome of the hearing at Ellon is lost to us.

● 1600 James Annand and John Johnston of Archedlaw, were accused of slandering Helen Gibb as a witch. Johnston claimed that during the night Gibb came and sat down at his door to practice witchcraft, and said he could prove she had "bocht her lyff befoir " - made a bargain with the devil to get more years added on to her life. The case came up at five meetings of the Presbytery and witnesses were heard from Dugalheid, Shethin, Raakistoun and Auchedly. It was alleged by Johnston that Gibb "cam betwixt his durris (doors) befoir he raiss from his bed with hir hair amang hir eis (eyes) and maid watter" (urinated). In the end, Johnston was found guilty of slander and sentenced to one Sunday on the penitence stool, to crave Gibb's pardon and to pay 26s 8d - a not inconsiderable sum at the time.

● 1602 Barbara Leslie and her son George Rennie, with his wife Marjory Smith, were sentenced to repentance for "admitting of a begar wyf to charm the said George for the fevers."

● 1607 Another member of the Auchedly family of Johnstons - Alexander - was accused of having sent for Malie Wysack, a Methlick witch, to cure his son John. An attempt was made to arrest Wysack and hand her over to the Sheriff but she had fled the area and the case against Johnston was deserted.

● 1610 A group of 13 women and five men, all farm servants from Cairnbrogie, Tarves, were reported to the Bishop of Aberdeen for "superstitioun and idolatry in passing in pilgrimage to the Chapell of Meldrum and the well callit Lady Well of Park." An investigation established that one party had washed a sick child in the well waters and all had drank from it. The wrath of the Bishop - if he expressed it - may rest in pages long since disappeared from the record.

● 1625 Blacksmith Thomas Smyth was ordained to pay 10 merks and "mak repentance sax Sundayis in sackcloth, bairfuitt and bairlegit." He was also given the salutary warning "not to use ye lyk charming in tyme cuming under ye paine to be persewit of his lyif as ane witch." Smyth had been employed by Patrick Couper and his daughter Barbara in Monkshill to charm " thair bairne that wes seik." They, too, had to make repentance in church. It was Smyth's practice to lay the naked child on his anvil which he struck three times with his great forehammer while calling out :

    " Ather pair (worsen) or mend in the name of Father, Soin and Halie
      gaist, in God's name."

● 1662 Sackcloth retribution was also meted out to Robert Forbes in Tilliegonie who admitted having been "ane User of Charms this dyvers yeirs bygane and humblie and penitentlie confessed ye greatness of ye sin."

● 1666 George Shires was obliged to do penance for charming cattle! He admitted burying a sick cow, changing a byre door and applying a cure, and setting apart a piece of ground for burying other cattle that succumbed.

● 1709 The ministers of Methlick and Tarves were appointed to investigate a case of charming said to have been practised by George Ogilvie in Tarves. Ogilvie said that "labouring under a pain in his head, he went to see Alex Simpson, who stroke upon his head and did tye it, using these words audibly - Lord bless the work of my hands."

Simpson denied that he had indulged in any form of charming. Ogilvie was ordered to publicly acknowledge his guilt and the two ministers went on to denounce the practice of charming from their pulpits,warning of exemplary censure by the Church.

Today, there is an inclination to shudder at the power exerted by the Church on one hand and the law on the other over the lives of these simple crofter folk who already had more than enough on their hands as they sought to wrest a living from cruel ground. Theirs was truly a peculiar brand of wretchedness, an uncompromising serfdom, with fetters that came down from feudal days.

Chapter 9

The Tarves Kidnapper

IN the mid 18th century, Aberdeen and its neighbouring countryside was plagued by a trade in human beings which smacked, though rather more nastily than the legend, of the activities of the Pied Piper of Hamlin. The kidnapping of children from town streets and the countryside was rife between 1740 and 1746 - a barbarous traffic which thrived on the theft or enticement of youngsters from their homes and selling them into slavery in the North American plantations.

One of the leading individuals engaged in this nefarious pursuit was Aberdeen merchant and Tarves farmer, Bailie William Fordyce of Auquhorthies. Along with Aberdeen's Deputy Town Clerk, Walter Cochrane, Bailies William Davidson and James Jopp, Alexander Mitchell of Colpna, and a town merchant known as 'Bonny John' Burnett, he made illicit use of Aberdeen ships engaged in a burgeoning Transatlantic trade. Not content with their legitimate gains from this business, they organised a system of ensnaring children, especially those from the countryside who were more easily impressed by what was supposedly to be had in the town. It is estimated that in five years more than 600 children were entrapped and sold into a slavery from which few ever returned.

For an account of this trade, which was also carried out at other British ports, the author is unaware of a better source than Gavin Turreff's *Antiquarian Gleanings*, published in 1871 and based on earlier publications by the Spalding Club.

Turreff says:

> "The extent, the misery and the horrors of this ignominious trade, and the reckless manner in which it was pursued, might surpass belief were they not too clearly established by testimony which it is impossible to doubt."

Groups were openly formed for carrying it on, he says, and ships left the port with "crowds of unhappy beings, of whom hardly one ever returned to his native land." The individuals engaged in the guilty commerce were men of note like Bailie Fordyce, whose methods of entrapping victims were as varied as they were infamous.

Turreff:

> "Every art of deceit and seduction was employed; agents, drummers, pipers and recruiting sergeants were dispersed throughout the town and shire to assail the unwary with bribes, alluring promises, intoxication, and still more disgraceful temptations. Parties of men patrolled the streets of the burgh like press-gangs, and, by open violence, seized on such boys as seemed fit for their purpose. The inhabitants of the neighbourhood dared not send their children into the town and even trembled lest they should be snatched away from their homes. For in all parts of the county emissaries were abroad; in the dead of night children were taken by force from the beds where they slept; and remote valleys distant from the city were infested by ruffians who hunted their prey as beasts of the chase."

Such were the scarcities and depravities of the time that the poor were sometimes induced to part with their own offspring, and the account books of those operating the trade include entries like: "To Robert Ross for listing his son, one shilling", and "To MacLean, for listing his brother, Donald, one shilling and sixpence."

According to Turreff, the individuals kidnapped were of every character, sex and age, including men and women as well as youths and boys not more than six years old.

> "Once in the possession of their oppressors, they were driven in flocks through the town like sheep, under the care of a keeper armed with a whip; or they were shut up in a barn in Rennie's Wynd, off the Green, where a piper was hired to play to them, while they were freely supplied with cards in order to divert their thoughts from any attempt to escape. Nay, so unblushingly was this infamous commerce practised that, when other receptacles overflowed, the public work-house was used as a place of incarceration; and when this, too, failed, the tolbooth or common prison was appropriated, and numbers of individuals were detained in it for weeks together."

Lord Dreghorn, who was later to be counsel in the case by which the trade was exposed, described how parents and other relatives flocked to Aberdeen hoping to effect the release of their kidnapped children - hopes which they would never have entertained had they known that the deputy town clerk and several of the bailies were determined to thwart them.

> "No solicitations or entreaties availed, and those who seemed too importunate were threatened themselves with banishment, imprisonment and other distress. Nothing more piteous and moving can well be figured than to see fathers and mothers running frantic through the streets, crowding to the doors and windows of the houses where their children were incarcerated, and there giving them their blessing, taking farewell of them for ever, and departing in anguish, imprecating curses upon those who were authors of their misery."

The colonial conditions faced by those who had been shanghaied were truly miserable. They were sold to planters for terms of five to seven years and were treated harshly and cruelly, whipped at the pleasure of their masters. If they deserted for more than 30 days, a full year was added to their slavery term. Many took their own lives.

It is scarcely credible to us today that such a trade could have flourished so openly - indeed, operated at all - and that redress was neither sought nor obtained, but Turreff reminds us that Scotland was at that time barely civilised. The lower orders, upon whom these injuries were inflicted, were as ignorant of their rights as they were powerless to assert them. Many who sought the restoration of their children were so terrified by threats of banishment or imprisonment that they abandoned their attempts. The kidnappers, by virtue of their positions in society, were too powerful to be taken to task. Indeed, one agonised father who sought to raise an action with the Lords of Session could not find a sheriff's officer in Aberdeen who would summon the defendants.

Retribution was not exacted for almost 20 years - and even then it was a puny punishment for the promoters of such a horrid trade. Among the youngsters carried off in 1741 had been one named Peter Williamson, from Aboyne, a "rough, ragged, long, stourie, clever boy", who was lured aboard a vessel in Aberdeen harbour, which was soon to sail for Philadelphia. After a life of astonishing adventures and several reversals of fortune, he was discharged from the Army at Plymouth in 1758, on account of wounds, and with six shillings in his pocket set out on his long journey home. He lingered for a time at York where he published a tract entitled *French and Indian Cruelty, exemplified in the Life and various Vicissitudes of Fortune of Peter Williamson, who was carried off from Aberdeen in his Infancy, and sold as a Slave in Pennsylvania.*

Such was the impact of the tract and the extent of its sales that Williamson, now well-funded, headed North to re-join his family and to seek revenge for the wrongs he had endured. To broaden the pamphlet's sales still further, he roamed the streets of Aberdeen in the dress and arms of an American Indian, lecturing appreciative audiences about the brutality of life on the plantations. His exposure of the kidnapping trade, however, incurred the wrath of the magistrates who, adopting the dual roles of accuser and condemner, charged him with having issued "a scurrillous and infamous libel on the Corporation of the City of Aberdeen and whole members thereof." He was convicted. The offending pages of the pamphlet were ordered to be torn out and burned at the

Market Cross by the common hangman, and Williamson was jailed, fined ten shillings and then banished from the city. He was not to be dismissed so easily, however and at Edinburgh in 1762 he raised an action against the Aberdeen bailies, being awarded £ 100 damages, as well as costs assessed at £ 80, the defendants being personally liable for payment.

The magistrates evaded the court decree and paid no part of the sums from their own pockets. Instead, the devious group persuaded Lord Findlater, patron of the town and Lord High Admiral of Scotland, to pay the costs by using funds from the salvage money accruing from wrecked vessels!

Williamson proceeded to raise an action against Bailie Fordyce of Auquhorthies and others in December 1768, being awarded damages of £ 200 and costs of one hundred guineas. Every possible ruse was employed by the defendants to evade the sentence, culminating in a farcical arbitration by the Sheriff-Substitute of Aberdeenshire. They entered into a conspiracy to intoxicate the arbiter and procure his signature to a decision in their favour!

Gavin Turreff describes how the arbiter responded to the ploy:

> "On the day preceding that on which he gave his interlocutor he was busy at hot punch about eleven o'clock forenoon; having become very drunk at two o'clock, he sat down to dinner, after which he sat close drinking, as is the phrase in that part of the country, *helter-skelter* - that is copiously and alternately - of different liquors, til eleven o'clock at night, when being dead drunk, he was conveyed home by his two maid-servants. On the morrow, shortly after nine o'clock, a large doze of spirits, white wine and punch was administered to him, with cooling draughts of porter from time to time. After dinner, he and two others, sat down to Ombre (cards), drinking at the same time, *helter-skelter,* a bottle and a half of Malaga, a mug of porter, two bottles of claret, a mutchkin and a half of rum made into punch. After these potations, the learned Sheriff gravely pronounced judgment, and retired to bed, where he lay all the next day (being Sunday) dead drunk and speechless."

Though Bailie Fordyce and his criminal cronies were successful in securing a favourable opinion from the Sheriff, the judgment was later set aside by the Supreme Court. Whether Fordyce ever satisfied that court is not known, for he vanishes from record soon afterwards. Tarves banker, shorthorn breeder and local historian Duthie Webster recorded some 50 years ago the widespread acceptance of a tale that the Tarves kidnapper had vanished in rather mysterious circumstances:

> "He came home much disturbed one evening, and was reported to have died during the night. He was buried in a few days but the local story is that he really fled the country, the coffin being weighted down with stones. The information had come out that he was involved in the rascally business of selling boys to the West Indies, ostensibly as apprentices, but practically into slavery - not much wonder that he suddenly disappeared."

The multi-talented Williamson made his home in Edinburgh where he was a banker and vintner, later becoming a publisher and producing Edinburgh's first directory. He also served as a postmaster, being credited with establishing the penny post in the Scottish capital.

Among those who gave evidence during Williamson's protracted lawsuits against the magistrates was William Jamieson, an Oldmeldrum crofter whose land belonged to the Earl of Aberdeen's estates. William's 10-year-old son John disappeared in the Spring of 1741 and was seen on the road to Aberdeen with two other boys and the man-servant of a notorious Aberdeen merchant, "Bonny John" Burnett. William confronted Burnett in the city but was refused access to his son, by then imprisoned in a barn near the harbour. Jamieson was advised by townspeople to whom he related his plight that there was little point in applying to the magistrates to have his son liberated since some of them "had a hand in these doings as well as John Burnett."

The Earl of Aberdeen intervened to secure a bond from Burnett that he would return the youngster to his parents, under a penalty of £ 50 sterling. Young Jamieson had sailed for Maryland, however, and was never again seen by his family. His father went on to serve some years in the Army, ultimately returning to find that Burnett had been declared bankrupt and had, like fellow kidnapper Fordyce, fled the country.

Chapter 10

Penury and Parsimony

T HOSE who recognised a need for change found it a more benign time. For others, change - and pain - lurked in the wings. In the Aberdeenshire parishes, stubborn tradition and the customs of bygone times persisted on the land. The parsimony of some who laid claim to the land bred penury in the multitude who tilled it. Greed erected barriers to change.

Beyond that unbending scene, however, it was the Age of Enlightenment - the great cultural and intellectual awakening that swept Europe in the middle years of the 18th century. While Tarves and Methlick cottars hacked at untamed soil, philosophers elsewhere proclaimed that nothing in the world was beyond improvement. Anything that failed to enhance human happiness could not be justified, they declared. Human dignity and free-will were re-discovered as the dead hands of tradition and superstition were wrenched away. But the Tarvesians and their kin were as blind men, heedless of the signposts to change.

Philosophy and literature flourished in the wider world. In Scotland, David Hume, Thomas Carlyle, Sydney Smith, Sir Walter Scott and Robert Burns were all products of the period. James Boswell, biographer of Dr Johnson, Tobias Smollett, and James Watt who harnessed the power of steam, were of that remarkable age, too. Scottish inventors, engineers and physicians led the world. Britain became the workshop of the world as the Industrial Revolution spread throughout the nation.

Though it was not yet apparent in the North-East corner of Scotland, man's relationship with the soil was changing for ever, too. Encouraged by Acts of Parliament, the enclosure system was starting to transform the face of English farming, open farms making way for enclosed fields, and agricultural techniques undergoing a revolution of their own. Farming would now be practised on a grander scale, gaining the benefits that would accrue from mechanisation, extensive land drainage and the first tentative experiments in stock-breeding.

A machine developed by English farmer-inventor Jethro Tull in far-away Berkshire was changing the agricultural practices of centuries. No longer would there be a need to manually scatter seed, with all the waste and tedium that the procedure entailed. For Tull had made a seed-sowing machine which delivered the seeds to the soil in straight even lines. The invention was anathema to some, particularly to farm labourers who feared that the machine would put their jobs in jeopardy. Some even went on strike as a protest against its introduction. It would be many years, however, before Tull's invention revolutionised traditional farming practices in backward Tarves.

Employing Tull's straight-line drilling of wheat and roots, which allowed a horse-drawn hoe to cultivate the space between the rows, meant that the soil could be constantly tilled. Seed drills were appearing on farms in England and in parts of the Scottish Lowlands. So, too, was the Rotherham triangular plough. Large teams of oxen were being replaced by pairs of horses. Farmers were responding to increasingly diverse demands from the market-place. For, as industry developed, so did the need for raw materials - hides for leather goods, bones for glue, animal fats for soap. Only by turning to labour-saving devices could market demands be met.

In 1707 Scotland had joined with England in the Treaty of Union. A crucial factor in winning over Scottish opinion was an undertaking by the London Parliament to safeguard the privileges of the Presbyterian Church and the Scottish legal system. With Scotland virtually bankrupt after its disastrous attempt to colonise the Darien Peninsula, the Union with England gave a badly needed boost to the country's economy, as well as removing the threat of further wars between the two nations.

With the Treaty of Union, however, Scotland had to accept a Hanoverian succession to the throne. Jacobite loyalties persisted in the Highlands, though support for their cause was only lukewarm in North-East Scotland. James Edward Stuart, son of the deposed James II, was regarded by some as Scotland's king. The 'Old Pretender', as he was known by the Hanoverians, made unsuccessful attempts to regain the throne. In 1708 he got only as far as the Firth of Forth. In 1715, he persuaded the Earl of Mar - known as 'Bobbing John' because of his political vacillation - to raise an army of Highlanders, but the rising ended inconclusively. The disillusioned 'Old Pretender' fled to France, leaving the Highlanders to fend for themselves.

Hardship was never far from the braes and hollows of Tarves. The rural population was on the decline. Between 1750 and 1790, alone, the number of people residing in the parish had dropped by almost 700 to under 1700. Similar depopulation was recorded at Methlick and Udny. Nevertheless, the struggle with soil and season went inexorably on. Though the sweeping improvements in agricultural methods now being effected in the more enlightened South had not yet reached these parishes, a few of the major landowners had made a start to enclosing the land, using lime in their fields and introducing a strict scientifically-based rotation of crops. Leading the way, at Monymusk on nearby Donside, was the visionary Sir Archibald Grant, who was experimenting with new methods of farming before disseminating them more widely. He created new roads on his estates, enclosed his fields and sheltered them with huge numbers of trees. Clover, ryegrass and turnips were grown experimentally as cattle feed and new crop rotations were introduced. Sir Archibald produced a pamphlet, widely circulated among his tenants, explaining how they could be better farmers, and offering financial assistance with improvements to their land and implements.

By the middle years of the 18th century, Formartine farmers had become obliged to hire servants for the whole harvest since it was increasingly difficult to procure day labourers. They had themselves largely to blame.The Methlick minister, the Rev Alexander Knolls, was quite specific about the reasons for the dearth of men and the steady drift of manpower away from the land:

> "The rents are much raised upon the farmers, who do all they can to make their subtenants pay the additional rent. Servants wages are so high that people who need them must put up with fewer than formerly. The number of manufactures and manufacturers is so much increased, as to draw a great many hands from the country into towns, so that servants for agriculture are scarce. And for some time past the cottagers have gone to towns, having found their immediate masters rather too hard upon them."

At that time a farm labourer could expect to earn about £ 6 a year, though a woman received only about £ 2. 10s. There was scant provision for equality of the sexes then! When hired as a day labourer for the harvest, a man would be paid £1. 10s for the duration, though women only received between 16s 8d and 18s 4d. They were all fed at the house where the harvest was being gathered in.

It is scarcely surprising that the peasantry exhibited little enthusiasm for change or improvement. The casting and drying of peats and turf and transporting these back to the smallholding, the laird, the minister and anyone else to whom they were in ancient bondage, employed the servants and horses during much of the summer - a formidable obstacle to improving their own stubborn acres.

The Rev John Rose, Udny, wrote at the time:

> "The old mode of farming prevails. Each year they manure with the dung of their cattle one third of what is called infield ground, in which bear (barley) is sown; then follow two successive crops of oats, by which means the ground is never cleared of weeds. They fold their cattle on the outfields and take three or four successive crops of oats. Much more grain is produced in the parish than is annually consumed in it. The farms are universally thirled to a mill and obliged to pay, some the 11th or 12th, many the 16th or 20th part of the produce to the tacksman of the mill, whether the corns are carried to the mill or not. The people are sober, industrious, and seemingly.contented with their situation; yet there are many things which would contribute to better their circumstances. In particular, the taking off the duty on coals, by which they could supply themselves with fuel, with much less labour and expense, and be able to employ the summer in bringing lime, and enclosing their fields; whereas at present the summer is wasted in procuring peats and turf.

"The high duties on malt and leather fall heavy on those who have large families. If the proprietors of estates, instead of taking grassums* at the end of 19 years, by which their tenants are impoverished, would ask a moderate rise in rent, give them long leases, encouragement for building tolerable houses and inclosing their ground, abolish the multures at mills, so that payment could only be exacted for work, and oblige the tenants to sublet their ground to subtenants for a certain number of years, and if the public roads, which are exceedingly bad, were under better management, and kept in proper repair, the situation of all ranks would be considerably improved."

A far-sighted man, Mr Rose, with a profound concern for the welfare of his parishioners - but it would be many years before the long-ingrained greed that afflicted the countryside gave way to commonsense and fair play.

His colleague, Mr Knolls at Methlick, observed:

"The price of every article of provisions is doubled within 40 years past. The people are very diligent and industrious. The manufacture carried on here is that of knitting stockings, in which persons of every age and sex are employed when other work does not interfere; this enables them to live tolerably well, and to pay their rents.

"They are generally frugal, more expensive in dress than in diet. They are also a social people : there may be sometimes 60, 70, and sometimes 100 at a wedding to the expense of which the guests contribute, by sending some milk, butter, cheese and poultry and some send stone plates and stone jugs."

Privation had not yet become a stranger to the 'poor man's land.' The crop in 1782 was a disaster and the amount of meal produced perilously small. The Laird of Shivas, Hugh Forbes, and his wife, Christian Garden, provided work and food for their starving Tarves tenants by employing them in clearing boulders from their fields. Mr Knolls commented:

"Had it not been for what Government allowed at a low price, part in meal, part in peas, there had been a great scarcity; and besides it was happy for the poor that flour that year was cheap, for the poorer sort did at that time use flour-bread, otherwise they would have been in danger of perishing. Since that time, more potatoes are planted and more turnips sown than formerly.

Commenting on the threatened famine conditions during 1782 and 1783, the Rev John Rose, Udny, wrote:

"The crop, from want of sunshine to ripen it, and by intense frost and snow, which came on before it could be cut down, was exceedingly deficient. The inhabitants of this parish bought bear and pease imported at Aberdeen, by which, with their own scanty crop, they supported themselves. The church session purchased some meal and grain, which they caused make into meal; this was sold in small quantities to the

* **grassums** - bribes

poorest of the parishioners. Thirty bolls of meal, and 2 bolls of pease, granted by Government in 1783, proved a useful and seasonable supply to many, so that no person died for want, but many of the farmers were considerably impoverished by these two deficient crops."

Yet, Formartine folk were in some senses better off than they had ever been. At the turn of the 17th/18th centuries there had been scarcely a cart in the parishes. Now, almost everyone had a cart of sorts. A carpenter was earning 1s a day, a tailor 6d with his victuals, and a mason 1s 6d.

Butter made on the farms and crofts was earning a county-wide reputation, fetching 8d a pound at the Aberdeen market. Cheese was sold at 4s to 5s a stone. Cows generally yielded about eight pints a day. One farmer - clearly considered by Tarves folk to be extremely affluent - kept 14 large cows, the milk of which, after the cream had been taken off, was sent every day to Aberdeen where it sold for "1d the Scotch pint." The price of a hen or duck ranged between 8d and 10d and eggs sold at between 3d and 4d a dozen.

Virtually everyone in that countryside - men, women and children - was a knitter of stockings. Merchants or their representatives from Aberdeen traded with the Tarves wives every two weeks at a well-known ale-house at Raitshill, handing over the wool for knitting and collecting the latest batches of finished stockings. The wives were treated to hot ale, a practice whose notoriety led to the charge, brandished in many a household, that the nearest road to every place was past the ale-house at Raitshill!

The farm worker's daily fare was a choice from oat-meal, cabbage, kail, whey and milk from the cow. The ubiquitous oat-meal was made into brose of various kinds. There was water brose - dry meal, stirred with boiling water, milk poured on and supped with an old horn spoon; or ale brose - made with boiling home brew rather than water; kail brose - made with the hot "*bree*" from the kail pot; and cabbage brose (made in a similar way). Brose was the mainstay of every meal, supplemented by oat-cakes and cheese as well as milk and potatoes. In season, herrings would be bought from itinerant fishwives who carried their creels on their backs all the way from Collieston on the east coast.

The 18th century farm labourer, who did not have land of his own, sold his services to the most generous bidder at the Whitsunday and Martinmas feeing markets. Sometimes he would strike a mutual accord with his hirer and stay for a year or two, though obliged to endure a brutalising existence in outbuildings or in the truly basic bothies which housed itinerant workers in that bare landscape. When married, he would be engaged as a cottar and acquire the use of a cottar house - though this was a dubious benefit when measured against his loss of freedom to move at will and the imposition of a new brand of servitude. Mr Rose affords us some clues about how the married cottar man could expect to survive:

"He has a boll's sowing or two from the tenant; it is plowed to him; his cow kept in summer with the farmer's cattle; and the straw of his corn from his croft maintains the cow during winter. He has liberty to cast turf for himself and sometimes a few peats. He works to the farmer in harvest, attends the plough during winter and spring, at which time he either receives his victuals in the farmer's house or has allowed him two pecks of oat-meal a week.

"What time he has to spare in summer, from Whitsunday to harvest, he works for day's wages to different persons. His wife and children weave stockings until the boys are fit for herding cattle. What is thus earned, if he and his wife are industrious, and his family keep in health, maintains them in a sober way."

Even if he had the use of a house, the cottar faced an ever-present threat that having improved it, he could have it taken away from him. He would possess it only from year to year and it was the practice rather than the exception that when Term time came round the cottar had to load his few pathetic possessions on to a farm cart and take to the road again in search of more lucrative work or a more amenable master.

It was an iniquitous system, encouraged by unscrupulous farmers. In his engaging folk history of the Scottish farm touns - *The Ballad and the Plough* - Tarves's David Kerr Cameron captures the cruelty of that time:

"The cottar folk travelled light. Few travelled hopefully, for the years had taught them better, but in time the May 'flitting' became an addiction, a rooted custom of a rootless society. It may even have been a kind of protest against the tied-cottage tyranny of that time that made a married farm servant - a skilled grieve, ploughman, bailie or orra man - give his wife and children as hostages to fortune. Where a single bothy lad with a mother's house to go home to if it came to it, could tell a miserly or tyrannical farmer what he thought of him and fare little the worse for it, the cottar with his family to think of could hardly afford to. This fact set him at a permanent disadvantage in the feeing market, too, and he was often viciously exploited. Many of today's farming dynasties were shamefully founded on the wealth that came from squeezing such men into penury."

Crude and rude though bothy life most certainly was, Cameron identifies a kind of saving grace in the songs and the music they spawned:

"One fine thing did come out of them: the bothy ballads - that ringing psalmology of the ills of the countryside, a running commentary on the lives of its people. The ballads named names with a fearlessness that latter-day chroniclers would envy; the hard routine of specific farms is forthrightly recorded and unscrupulous farmers given their scoundrelly characters. They give advice, these ballads, on how to keep clear of bad fees on market day, encouragement to lasses but lately forsaken and maids as yet unmolested. Enshrined in their untutored lines is a whole history; now they are almost our only link with the real quality of that life of the farm touns."

Chapter 11

Fire and Brimstone

BE it in sunshine or blizzard, generations of Tarvesians, after six days of back-breaking toil in the fields, trudged on the Sabbath from their crofts to the dilapidated kirk on the hill to digest their weekly potion of fire and brimstone, delivered by Presbyterian ministers who were specialists in Hell, Damnation and the Wages of Sin.

A word portrait of the 18th century Sabbath in these parts was penned by that most meticulous of researchers, the Rev Thomas Mair, whose *Extracts from the Records of the Presbytery of Ellon* have proved such an invaluable source in the writing of this book. In the piquancy of his narrative and the detail of his research, he re-created the rural North-East holy day as few others could.

Thomas Mair wrote:

> "Owing to the state of the roads, no wheeled vehicles drove to or from the church, but on the coming out of the congregation a considerable stud of horses, in riding graith and held by serving men, had figured on the village square or green, the horns on the side-saddles of the ladies showing deer-like in the crowd. An interesting spectacle for the common people had been the mounting and riding off of the gentry, and many had lingered to witness it ere trudging off to their far-scattered places of abode, and cocked their ears to gather in some piece of badinage from the august surroundings of the 'louping-on' seat.

> "How far it was the fashion for the ladies to ride on palfreys of their own, or on pillions behind their spurred and booted lords cannot be said here - there are instances of both ways."

The spectacle of the gentry's departure was not the sole reason for some to dawdle by the wayside. For more than a few, the long arid sermon in a comfortless kirk bred a thirst which could be quenched in the nearby hostelry.

Mair:

> "But who are these ruddy-faced parishioners who yet linger on the scene, though their homes be miles to landward - and though they look towards and even take some steps along the road they ought to tread, yet, like Lot's wife, turn and look back? Their unspoken hesitation, though mystifying to a stranger, is eloquent to one another, and as they sidle towards one or other of the abundant taverns or change-houses of the village and disappear there, the question is answered."

Mair's surmise of the goings-on at the tavern is poignant, yet bordering on the comical:

> "Remembrances of the chappin jug and barley-bree, acting on the tissues of the brain, have made them loth to depart without a tasting. On occasions, the landward man is attended by an able-bodied spouse - she may have tarried to look after him, but it was not difficult to coax her generous lips into a kiss of welcome with the foaming bicker.

> "As afternoon wears on, the 'howf' and taverns give forth increasing tokens that they are the abodes of lively human habitation, as the revellers mellow and develop their natural proclivities - the assiduous ale-bibber, the 'fine drunken boddy' or the 'blusterin' blellum."

For some there would be repercussions:

> "Well for them all if they suspend their carousals and take the road, ere yet they give cause for their names being enrolled in the books of Session or Presbytery - a couple of elders (not altogether immaculate themselves) may be listening to the waxing clamour round the corner, and laying their heads together. Should a delation ensue, there are weary days in store for these stragglers from rectitude - trudging to the meeting place of Session or Presbytery, good, bad and indifferent of them, and awaiting perhaps the great part of a day, either as panels or witnesses. But, apart from the harassing number of appearances that had to be made before them, it cannot be said that the Presbytery were other than merciful and even long-suffering judges - their punishments were severe only as being so grotesque."

In those far-off days, much of the Sabbath was spent in the kirk or the kirkyard and, for many, in the hostelries of the village. There was a tacit understanding, says Mair, that the people could not sit out the long service without a withdrawal for a time. So, after the first portion of the service, there came to be a continual going out and coming in - with scant regard for a suitable interval. A great proportion of the congregation would be in the kirkyard in clusters, and the neighbouring public house or houses would be thronged with as many as could be supplied.

Mair:

> "In the earlier days of the Presbytery, the Communion Sunday was not held more sacred than others from the quarrels and bloodshed so liable to break out - and the protraction of the service over the whole day, while meantime the people had to eat, and also to drink, had conduced to this; but that toned down with time.

> "For the amount of staying or rather sitting power, the people would have compared favourably with any nation on earth, and against any single speaker, though capable of preaching at great length, they would have held their ground; but when they saw a relay of the brethren ready to follow and relieve one another, they held that in fairness they could not be expected to sustain their 'sederunt'; and so they went out and in."

Despite the tedium of the kirk Sabbath, Mair says, there must have been few who attended it on whom it did not make some impression for the better "as compared with the trudging on of their weekday round unbroken."

He adds:

> "The stout farmer or craftsman somewhat stiffened by toil and years, though his outward talk in the kirkyard group was of the affairs of the week, may have had a conversation within himself of a different tenor.

> "Standing above the dust of generations and the mouldering bones of some he had once known, and thinking of the time when it would be even so with himself, he may have marvelled for a space if there was not more of the everlasting in even the strains of the psalm swelling ever and anon through the abundantly broken windows of the kirk, or beyond the kirkyard walls, in the moaning of the wind far and wide over the fields, mellowing once more to the harvest.

> "But more likely than the well-to-do husbandman to be impressed by the solemn services of the day had been those to whom trouble and bereavement had come, and the quiet female strayed apart and thinking of the home with its cares and sorrows to which she must return. But as much as by any there may such a day have been remembered with affection by those who could join with them no more and might never do so again - the adventurous sons of the Presbytery who had gone forth, and strangers in a strange land fighting a friendless and perhaps a hopeless battle.

> "Often on a Sunday morning may some of the best of these, lying apart, have recalled the Sacrament Sunday of old Scotland, and phantom-like in the forest aisles have seen the serious faces of those seated at the tables, and heard in the wind the rolling of the 103rd psalm to its old familiar tune - 'O thou, my soul, bless God the Lord.'"

Some viewed the Sabbath with profound dread. For that was the day when offenders must appear in sackcloth, seated on the stool of penitence before the whole congregation, and in serious cases standing on the stool at the church door, or even chained to the external wall by an iron neck-halter as a dire warning to others also tempted to walk sinful paths. Some of the luckless are known to have undergone this brand of humiliation for as long as 20 consecutive Sundays.

"No wonder," Mair commented,"if along with this came an extraordinary reluctance and refractoriness on the part of many delinquents. Promises were given so long as they would avail; sickness and infirmity were fallen back upon; and at last many ran rampant and turned into fugitives and vagabonds and were proclaimed so in the Synod black lists, rather than enter on a penance."

Wrong-doers were generally dealt their retribution at meetings of the Session or Presbytery and I am indebted to the same writer for a picturesque cameo of a Presbytery Day in the 18th century. A considerable gathering of the laity attended, some of them elders or heritors with business to transact, and delinquents who had been summoned along with witnesses would often form a host in themselves. They would linger, in the neighbourhood of the church in which the Presbytery met.

Mair wrote:

> "Its solemn pile, rising above the humble tenements around, would probably be 'the cynosure of neighbouring eyes', though, of course, with the public house as a rival in the case of many.

> "The Presbytery's officer, on duty by the church, might sometimes venture as far as the public house, on the plea of calling 'next', and get his lips wetted behind the door, through the liberality of some delinquent."

The Presbytery minutes, in their references to dining arrangements, do not admit to venues other than 'the house' or 'the place', though there is strong evidence that the hypocritical clerics dined in the best 'oistlar ' house or hostelry available.

Mair commented:

> "In the rude and homely way of the time, the kitchen was the readiest drinking saloon. There on seats and 'deases' (long benches) many of those who had to attend on the Presbytery beguiled the time with pint or choppin jug in hand, the pots and pans around the ample fire, wherein the Presbytery dinner was preparing, diffusing an odour that must have been savoury, at least to the hungry."

Mair imagined that the dinner would have been held in the best apartment of the hostelry - "swept and garnished, the deep-set windows or winnocks boarded and with a scanty supply of wrinkled and distorting glass, the smoke-embrowned beams or rafters overhead and the genial blaze of the great peat fire on the hearth." He envisaged the "quaintly-attired brethren, with long flowing locks in the fashion of the time, save on those polls where the desolation of baldness had come" and the table with its cloth and "ample supply of viands, the wooden ladle for the broth, the finely-polished pewter or horn spoons and the antique earthenware."

"The foaming ale," he added," quaffed from the pewter or the wooden bicker, was by no means to be lightly esteemed and would atone for much now customary. Could all these things be restored for but a day, tickets of admission to dine with the Presbytery would sell at a premium! "

Religious schisms were still apparent in the parishes. The Secessionist movement (a breakaway church) was cradled at Craigdam, a mile from Tarves. Founded in 1752, it had a congregation of 130. Its first minister, William Brown, had preached earlier at Auchnagatt amid a great deal of local hostility. Dogs were set on his congregation of zealots and they were even stoned.

The site of the church was given by William, 3rd Earl of Aberdeen. For a time it was the only Secessionist church between the Dee and the Spey, and as such had a flourishing following from as far afield as Rosehearty, Peterhead and Old Deer. According to the *Thanage of Fermartyn*, the 24 members who signed Mr Brown's call to Tarves did not think of offering any stipend. When the presbytery enquired into this strange omission, they were given the reply: " The silver and gold is mine, saith the Lord of Hosts."

Born in Perthshire, Mr Brown was a man of small stature but of considerable eloquence and physical energy which earned him the sobriquet of 'the rinnin' minister'. An earnest and fervid preacher, he once ventured to publish a sermon but was told by the printer that it contained so many 'O's that his fount of them was exhausted and the printing would have to be delayed until a new supply of 'O's arrived from Edinburgh!

Mr Brown and his wife, Christian Hay from Elgin, had three sons - John, a doctor who emigrated, William, proprietor and publisher of the *Edinburgh Weekly Journal*, and Alexander, a bookseller and publisher in Aberdeen.

The next minister at Craigdam, the evangelical Rev Patrick Robertson, was an equally popular preacher - the 'Spurgeon of his day and district' according to the *Thanage*. A contemporary writer described his style thus:

> "He preached in the broadest vernacular, with a vigour in his last days almost equal to anything in the *Noctes Ambrosainae*."

In a discourse about the sisters of Lazarus, Robertson is reputed to have said from the pulpit:

> "Mary was a quait* cratur, and sat at the feet of Jesus and listened to his sweet discourse, and thocht she never heard anything like it. But Martha was a thrifty, futherin'** wife, that

quait - quiet ; **futherin'* - fussy

futherit but the hoose and ben the hoose, and had a' her pots and
a' her pans ga'en, and heard a word now and a word then, and like
ither thrifty wimen, had a gey sharp tongue of her ain, for she cudna
keep her ill tongue aff o' our Lord himsel'."

Later in the sermon, he touched on a subject about which, even today, women
tend to be rather sensitive:

"Here ye are sitten wi' yer auld withered faces that's bonnier to me
than a lass in her teens; for I ken ye hae seen sixty or seventy
summers, ilk ane o' you, and yer auld withered faces just say to me,
we hae served our Maister threescore years, and we are nae tired
serving him yet."

At a service of Communion, he was reported to have said:

"My brethren, the muckle broth pot is on today; ye sanna get
speenifas* and speenifas, but ladlefuls and ladlefuls."

Preaching on the call of Moses, he declared:

"Far d'ye think, my freens, did Moses fin' God's chosen people; far
d'ye think he fan' them, and fat were they daein'? He jist fan' them
in the land of Goschen, with their sark sleeves rowed up to their
oxters**, kirning*** amongst clay making bricks."

Asked if there was any man alive able to perfectly keep the commandments of
God, he told the questioner:

" Ye can nae mair dae it, ma freens, than a coo can clim' up a tree!"

On one occasion he preached a sermon on the woman "who, having lost a piece
of money, lighted a candle, and with a besom (brush) swept the hoose till she
found it." According to Mr Robertson, the woman represented the Church, the
candle God's Word, and the besom the discipline of the Church. Applying them
to the various churches, he claimed that in the Roman Catholic and Episcopal
churches there was neither candle nor besom - neither truth nor discipline.
As for the established kirk (like the one a mile away on its knoll at Tarves) they
had for truth but the "glimmer of a canle, and a' that they had for a besom was
but the hanle of one." In the Independent church, they had "a licht that he
would not deny but they had far ower mony besoms. Ilka member had a besom,
and he swipet, and she swipet, and a'body swipet, and atween them a' they
raised sic a stour**** that nae ane o' them cud see the canle for the clouds of
dust they had raised."

Meeting a farm servant coming home from St Margaret's Fair at Tarves, who
was needing all the road to hold him, Mr Robertson sought to pass him without
recognition. But this he was unable to accomplish. "Eh, Mr Robertson," said
the staggering parishioner,"dae ye no ken me, and me ane o' yir ain converts?"
"So yir ane o' my ain converts," said Mr Robertson. "Weel, weel man, yir like a
hantle o' my haniwark, nae muckle worth."

*_speenifas_ - spoonfuls; ** _oxters_ - armpits; *** _kirning_ - working; **** _stour_ - dust

On another occasion, Mr Robertson expressed displeasure about the number of his parishioners bringing their dogs to worship at Craigdam church. He told them he would be 'muckle obliged if the relations of these dogs would keep them at hame.'

When Mrs Robertson acquired and brought a piano to the manse at Craigdam, she and her husband were rebuked by the congregation for having allowed:

> "a serious innovation on the primitive habits of the people and a vain indulgence in the prevalent sinful pleasures and frivolities of the world."

Mr Robertson ministered at Craigdam from 1804 until 1841 when he was appointed to Charlotte Street Secessionist Chapel, Aberdeen. He died at the age of 90.

Another Craigdam minister, the Rev D.K. Auchterlonie, was an unusually picturesque figure in an age of dull uniformity in the Church. The "rough whinny knowe" on which Craigdam Church was built had come to be a recognised centre of religious life and Mr Auchterlonie dubbed Tarves a mere suburb of Craigdam!

In 1911, William Duthie of Collynie, the "Shorthorn King", was presented with an illuminated scroll by the Craigdam congregation. He had been Superintendent of the Sunday School and an elder for many years. When repairs to the Manse and other works burdened the congregation with a £ 400 debt, Duthie presented them with a cheque for the full amount. In 1915 he donated the Mrs Webster Memorial Hall at Craigdam in memory of his sister. The last service at Craigdam was held in 1958 when it was reunited with Tarves Parish Church. The building was demolished, its former site now marked by a cairn.

A Quaker meeting-house which once flourished near the farm of Auquorthies is long since gone - burned down by locals in the 18th century who did not share the views of the Friends. In fact, Quakers aroused the wrath of the kirk session and presbytery for more than a century. As far back as 1700, the local clergy complained that:

> "Quakerism doeth abound verri much in these parishes "

In 1738 the record speaks of 'swarms of Quakers' in Tarves. Sixty years later, there were one Quaker and 11 Episcopalians. Nearby Udny, however, catered for a rather more interesting religious pot-pourri - 980 members of the established church, 107 Episcopalians, 35 Seceders, four Quakers and five Roman Catholics

The district of Barthol Chapel became a Quoad Sacra Parish in 1876 and a place of worship called The Gordon Memorial Church was erected by the Dowager Countess of Aberdeen in memory of her eldest son, George, lost at sea in 1870. The first minister was the Rev Mr Forrest, who was translated to Lonmay in 1878 and was followed at Barthol Chapel by the Rev A.R. Sutter. According to the *Thanage of Fermartyn*, the Quoad Sacra Parish may be said to represent the "chapel of Futchul, the name of a district whose chapel is mentioned with the parish church in charters of 1220-29." It was in all likelihood dedicated to St Bartholomew. The Barthol Chapel Church became a linked charge with Tarves in 1958.

An unusually large proportion of the early ministers at Tarves went on to fill high theological office. The Rev William Sympill (1534) became Chancellor of the Cathedral of Aberdeen. Dr John Strachan (1659-83) was called to the Tron Church, Edinburgh, and a Professorship of Divinity at the University of Edinburgh. George Anderson (1683 - 1705) who, with his wife and seven children survived the famine and floods of King William's 'ill years' at Tarves, became Professor of Divinity at Kings College, Aberdeen, as did Dr Duncan Mearns (1801 -16) and Dr Alexander Black (1817 -32).

All the panoply of death in the kirkyard at Tarves - carved on this memorial stone are the Bible, a skull, the measurement of time, the bell used to announce death, bones, the implements of the gravedigger and a coffin.   Picture -THP

Chapter 12

Anatomy of a Kirk

by Ian Davidson, Regional Building Surveyor
National Trust for Scotland

FOR almost 1500 years, there has been a Christian place of worship in or near Tarves. We learned in an earlier chapter that St Murdebur of Leinster founded a chapel in the parish in about 600 AD. There had been a similar Christian outpost at Andet, Methlick, for 200 years longer, established by St Ninian from his base at Candida Casa in Galloway, S.W. Scotland.

The parish of Tarves was impropriated by the Abbey of Arbroath in 1189. This practice, of granting parishes to distant monasteries, drew off the major part of any endowment and worked to the great detriment of the parishes. In 1299 the Abbot exercised his power in the Court of Regality, which gave him almost Royal authority in Tarves. He was not long in exercising his judicial powers, prosecuting four local men for stealing cattle.

Although he may have had a predecessor called Maurice, the first authenticated parochial vicar, Galfried (sometimes recorded as Galfridus) de Wellys, appears in deeds dated 1322 and 1331. A chronological list of vicars and ministers from that age to modern times is given at the end of this chapter.

Of the ancient chapel of St Murdebur not a trace now remains. The church building we know today replaced the medieval kirk in 1798. It is possible that the old kirk had been there since the 13th century and may well have been constructed on the site of the 7th century Celtic chapel.

There is a description of the medieval church (as seen in 1732) in *A View of the Diocese of Aberdeen:*

> "The church has a choir and two isles (sic) : one for the Gordons of Haddo, now ruinous. Sir Thomas de Longovile (otherwise called the Red Reaver), the French pyrate, whom Wallace is said to have taken at sea, and recovered to a regular life, is reported to have died at Ythsie, and to lie at the east end of this church. It is added that the two blew stones, now on the stairhead of Tolquhon loft,whereupon now nothing can be discovered graven but a cross, were taken from his grave."

All that remains of this building is the Tolquhon Tomb, which was installed in the South Aisle in 1589 and now stands in the kirkyard to the South of today's church. Its builder, William Forbes, was a benefactor of both kirk and parish and founded a hospital in Tarves - the Bede House - which long survived him.

The Tolquhon Tomb is among those held in trust for the nation by the Secretary of State for Scotland and cared for on his behalf by Historic Scotland. It is the tomb of the 7th Lord of Tolquhon and his wife, Elizabeth Gordon of Lesmoir. It

was he who instigated a thorough and imaginative rebuilding of Tolquhon Castle in 1584, which was completed in 1589 and visited by James VI (see pages 13-14).

In 1948, W. Douglas Simpson (*A Short History of Tarves*) provided this description: " The tomb is a particularly fine one, as one might have expected from such a fine gentleman. It displays a most interesting mixture of Gothic and Renaissance elements. The general scheme remains thoroughly medieval but much of the detail is pseudo-classical in character. This is particularly seen on the arcade in front of the tomb-chest and in the balusters on either side. The grotesque animals on the external curve of the tomb arch are fashioned in the whimsical and vigorous style so often found in sculptural work of this period in North-East Scotland.

" On the dexter (the left, as one looks at the tomb) spandrel is a shield bearing the arms of Forbes, a squire's helmet and the motto SALVS PER CHRISTVM, while on the other side are the laird's initials and below it the date 1589. On the sinister spandrel a similar shield, with a man's hat for a crest, bears the arms of his spouse, Elizabeth Gordon of Lesmoir, impaled with those of Forbes, together with her initials and the description 'Dochter to Lesmor'. Portrait statuettes of the laird (above) and his lady support the tracery on either side."

The present pedimented setting probably dates from 1798. It is protected by a glass cover erected by Historic Scotland in the 1980s and is Listed Category A.

We heard (on Page 50) how famine and flood during the 'ill years' of King William ravaged the Bede House and its occupants. The *View of the Diocese* reported that in 1732 the Bede-men still received their meal and money from the William

Forbes' bequest but their slated house was neglected and in ruins. In 1735 Tarves Kirk Session was asked to produce an account of the state of the hospital. The four occupants, it was reported, had to carry in sticks and peats to Tolquhon Castle during the week and on Sunday to march to church before the laird and his lady, standing behind them during the service "counting their beads". As successors to Tolquhon, the Gordons of Haddo sustained the Bede House payments into the 19th century. There is still a fragment of a much-defaced stone slab at Bede House commemorating, in Latin, its foundation by William Forbes.

The site of the Bede-House today, with the village of Tarves to the left   Picture: THP

The Old Kirk

In 1676, the church - possibly 300 years old by then - was in serious disrepair, its roof and walls supported by props. It had dilapidated still further by 1727, with some of its lofts about to fall. A session minute of 12 June in that year reported:

> "John Pirie was appointed to speak to Sir John Paterson of Granton and the Laird of Keithfield anent repairing their respective lofts in the Church that were ready to fall."

About this time, too, the session spent £ 70. 8s on building a new loft for the poor, entered from the outside. According to the session record, James Fergusen, mason was engaged:

> "at 9d Scots per day for meat and wages to open the church wall for one entry to the loft."

To finance this, loft seats were let out from one St Margaret's Fair to the next. In July 1734 the minutes stated that:

> "Some people in ye East Loft complained of the little seat in the end of the Session Loft as obstructing their hearing the minister, wherein the Session allowed it to be taken out."

The floor of the loft must have been very open, for in April 1735 the minutes recorded that the minister, the Rev William Forbes, had received a missive from the factor at Tolquhon containing an order to all tenants who sat in the East Loft "not to trouble or molest those sitting immediately below them by throwing dust upon them."

On 13 July,1733, the session paid £46. 2s to William Armstrong and David Hodge as the balance due for casting a new bell. Sixty years later, restrictions were imposed on the use of the bell to keep it in good order. That bell did not survive, and the existing one is inscribed 'J. Warner & Sons, London, 1855,' on the waist front, with 'Tarves, September 1855' on the rear. There is also a Royal coat-of-arms and patent. The bell is rung from the ground outside the building.

The Rev Thomas Mitchell wrote in the Statistical Account of Scotland, in the closing years of the 18th century, that the church was very old and ruinous, but he did not live to see the new one built. He died in 1793.

Demolition of the ancient kirk, its lofts, tombs, pulpit and all its fabric began on 18 February, 1798. The first stone of the new building was laid on 10 March and the church received its first congregation on 7 October.

So, along with most of Scotland's pre-Reformation churches, the Tarves kirk disappeared almost completely. It has been said that this nationwide loss was due to a combination of four factors:

● Poverty of the land and people.

● Greed of the landed class and nobility.

● Neglect of the built structure - a significant factor in Tarves.

● The Reformation - this induced much wrecking during its early years and while it is true that Presbyterianism in Scotland laid a black cloth over much that was beautiful, there was some attempt at legislating for repairs to damage caused by the "rascal multitude" as John Knox described them. The First Book of Discipline in 1560 stated that churches should be:

> "repaired with dores, windowes, thack, and with such preparation within as appentaineth as well to the Magestie of God, unto the ease and commodity of the people."

It also required that idolatry be utterly suppressed. The kirk was replaced in a manner that suited the new religion which deemed that there should be no altar and that the church be centred on the pulpit.

Perhaps the deterioration of the old kirk was tied to the reversal in fortunes of the Forbes of Tolquhon family who were forced to sell their estate in 1716. By By the end of the 18th century, in any case, Scotland had witnessed sweeping changes in society. The Agricultural Revolution and the Clearances had resulted in great movements in the population and the creation of new villages. It is scarcely surprising that the winds of change in religion and wealth creation should sweep away the old kirk.

The New Kirk

The contractors for the new building were James Walker, mason, Denend; James Littlejohn, wright, Aberdeen, for the roof, galleries, doors and windows; and George Jaffray, wright, Old Aberdeen, for the remainder. It is a plain but dignified specimen of a Presbyterian preaching house. It was built on a plain rectangle, lit by four round arched windows on the south wall. There was also a flat lintelled window on the north wall and a high-level round arched window on each gable. Entrance would have been through the round arched doorway on each gable.

Identifying the original internal arrangement poses a small controversy. The Scottish Development Department listing states that the gallery dates from 1825. This appears to have been extracted from a paper by the Rev Francis Knox which described "considerable improvements" in that year. However, a gallery was included in the original specification. Knox's paper also states that after the 1825 improvements the seating was reduced by about 30 - surely unlikely if the gallery had just been built. On that basis and from examination of the flooring, the gallery almost certainly dates from 1798. Areas of flooring have clearly been replaced on the ground floor to create raked seating along the north wall, facing the pulpit. The boards are a uniform width of 150mm. Those in the gallery and to the east of the pulpit on the ground floor are of various widths up to 300mm. This suggests that the gallery and the area near the pulpit are contemporary. The SDD listing states, too, that the pulpit was formed in 1825. I have not found any evidence of this. Sadly, the session minutes of that time are missing.

The walls would have been squared granite blocks with decorative cherry cocking. This remains on the south and west walls, while the other two have been sneck-harled at a later date. The roof was completed with Scots slates. At the top of the west gable is a bird-cage bell cote.

Improvements in 1825

Knox does provide one clue to the 1825 improvements when he refers to the number of seats having been reduced by 30. There are two possible areas where this possible reduction occurred. Firstly, the pews on either side of the pulpit are asymetrical, while those to the east have been removed to make space for the choir. Secondly, there are vestibules inside each gable door which may have been added later than 1798. They certainly give an awkward plan. The astragals in a fanlight over the doors from the vestibule to the church are quite different to any on the windows.

An uncredited manuscript provides more information. It says that by 1825 the main walls had been pushed two feet off the vertical by the force of the roof and

The new kirk at Tarves (above), which received its first congregation on 7 October 1798, was built in just six months. It is a plain but dignified specimen of a Presbyterian preaching house. The Tolquhon Memorial (below), is a mixture of Gothic and Renaissance elements. It is now protected by a glass cover erected in the 1980s and is Grade A listed.

Pictures - (above) the author; (below) Historic Scotland

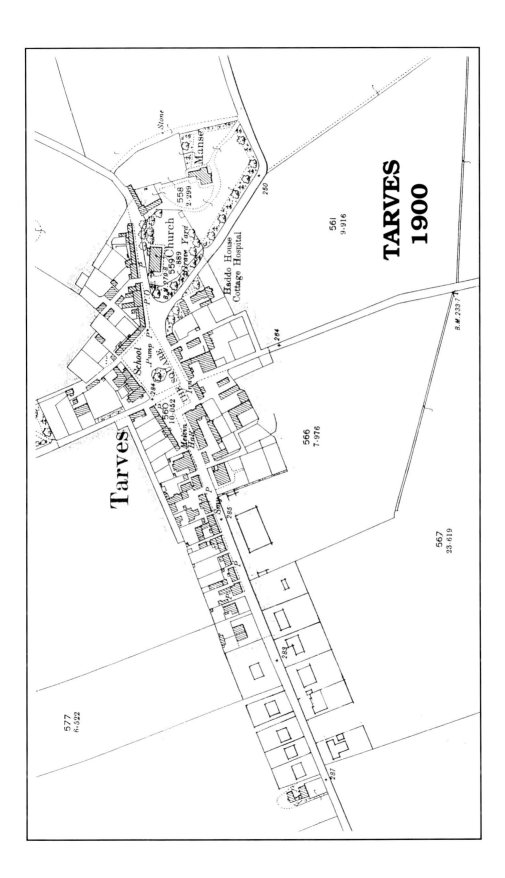

TARVES
1900

that the gables had cracked. Tie bars were then fixed to the roof timbers and the walls pulled back into place. It is unlikely that the walls were so distorted - otherwise I would have expected the roof to collapse. The tie bars are still in place, and it has to be said that they are ugly additions to the building. The only evidence of repairs to the masonry is that both the North and East walls have sneck harling over cherry cocking.

Our mysterious chronicler also stated that "alterations were made to the shape of plastering the ceiling". From inspecting the roof timbers, it can be seen that the coomb has been formed by fixing bearers to the collar of the primary truss.These look fresher than the primary truss timbers and may well be more recent insertions.

The ceiling presents a minor curiosity. The top of the rounded arch of each gable window is hidden by the flat plaster of the ceiling. The underside of the roof truss collar is below the top of the window arch and so the ceiling must have always intruded.

This does not suggest, however, that the roof void was open to view at any time. The roof timbers are undistinguished and the pointing of the upper gable masonry is poor, unlike the exterior which was finished in a most decorative manner.

The uncredited manuscript goes on to say: "Further improvements were made on the church by reseating the area and painting in 1877". The 'area' is not defined, nor the extent of the reseating. The pews are not particularly fine examples. Late Victorian joinery would have been to be of a much higher standard. The seating along the North wall has been placed on a small ramp - there is a strong possibility that this alteration forms part of these developments.

On the North wall is the boilerhouse - a stone-built mono pitch with slated roof and two lined and braced doors. The heating system has 50mm pipes running around the entire structure and radiators in the vestry.

The stone-built organ house, opened in 1892, is lit by two round arch sash windows and situated on the South wall. It is in the position once occupied by the third window. There are no written records of when it was constructed but it is a later addition to the building. Initially, Presbyterian churches did not have organs. Indeed, the Episcopal church was colloquially differentiated by being called the 'whistling kirk' - derived from 'kist o' whistles,' the Scots phrase for an organ, and the fact that Presbyterian kirks did not have one. The organ itself is in dark oak and Gothic in appearance.

The vestry and entrance porch were added to the West end in 1905. I have found a sketch proposal by the architect, James Cobban, in the Haddo House archives, dated 1903. Stylistically, it displays aspects of Scots Baronial in its crow stepped gables, Gothic in its window cills, plinth and chimney, and Art Nouveau in the stained glass, and it is respectful of the church itself with its round arched door and window openings. The entrance porch affords space for the congregation to pass into the main body of the kirk out of the wind that blows around the high walls. The pitch pine lined walls of the vestry display photographs of past ministers and elders. It sits a little uneasily with the main structure, the ridge being higher than the cill of the gable window, resulting in an uneasy break to meet the wall below the cill.

Modern Improvements

Substantial repairs and alterations were undertaken in 1953. The roof was re-slated and re-sarked. The roof timbers show considerable signs of historic water staining. At the same time, the ceiling was replaced using plasterboard, except in the gable window arches where the split lath and plaster can still be seen from the roof void. The pews were adapted to make them more comfortable, their backs being given a slight slope. The building was then re-decorated. At this time, the walls and ceiling are in pale blue and the pews in a light brown grain - in this writer's opinion, an unattractive combination.

Three decorative windows have been provided in modern times. The inaugural one was inserted into the second window on the South elevation in 1954. It is in a Gothic Revival style and is to the memory of William Still Cumming, placed there by his wife Jane. The second window is in the lintelled North window opening, dated 1969 and a memorial to the Davidson family, who farmed in the parish for many years. The third, which is a screen, is located inside the original window on the East gable. It is an unusual form, not using lead cames but glueing the coloured glass pieces together in an abstract form. It was placed there in 1979 by Mrs Pamela Cotton in memory of her husband Bruce. Sadly, it is now deteriorating and pieces of the glass have become detached. It may be necessary to remove this window to a new location where it can be safely monitored.

It seems likely that limestone used in the building of the church would have been burned in the several kilns found nearby and there is a large quarry at Auquhorthies, two miles West of the church. The granite for the church probably came from the now disused quarry at Craigdam, a mile away.

The Kirk's Ministers

Date	Name
11??	**Maurice**, was among witnesses to the foundation of St Peter's Hospital in the Spittal, Aberdeen, by Bishop Matthew de Kyninmund (1172-1199) in the reign of Malcolm IV.
1322-31	**Galfried de Wellys**, mentioned in a deed about a pension of eight merks due to the monastery of Arbroath from the vicarage tiends of 'Tarwas'. He was a contemporary of Abbot Bernard, who drew up the celebrated *Declaration of the Independence of Scotland*, signed at Arbroath by Bruce in 1320.

Date	Name
1342	**John of Munro**, mentioned in another deed about the same eight merks pension.
1493	**Sir Alexander Abercrummy**, this is the date of his death.
1493-96	**John Lumsden**, successor to the above, came from Diocese of St Andrews.
1496	**Edward Cunninghame**, Rector of Cluny, presented to the church at this date, with a deed signed at the Abbey of Arbroath before witnesses John Ogilvy of Fingask, Andrew Rossy, Patrick Uldny and Adam Patonson.
1501	**Sir Thomas Myreton**, demitted his charge after four years at Tarves.
1501-25	**Archibald Balcomy**, presented to the vicarage in 1501.
1525	**Alexander Dunbar**, was in Tarves for only one month.
1525-34	**John Reid**, Vicar of Mernys in the Diocese of Glasgow
1534	**William Sympill**, formerly Chaplain of the Diocese of Glasgow. Became Chancellor of Cathedral of Aberdeen in the same year.
1534-40	**Henry Lumsden**, nominated successor to above six months later but resigned in 1540.
1540	**Alexander Ogilvy**, last of the Roman Catholic vicars of Tarves. In that year there is a precept from Pope Paul III for inducting Alexander Ogilvy into the perpetual vicarage of Tarves on the free resignation of Henry Lumsden.
1574	**Thomas Germok**, because of a shortage of ministers, was responsible for three parishes - Tarves, Methlick and Fyvie - though he had the assistance of Donald Reoch, a Reader, at Tarves.
1593-1633	**Thomas Gardyne**, transferred from Fintray, presented to the vicarage by James VI and also to the 'modified stipend' on 1 March, 1616. He became infirm and was unable to discharge his duties, dying in 1633. One daughter married to George Merser in Aberdeen, another to John Mowat in Auquhorthies,
1633-1659	**James Moir,** MA of Marischal College, initially assistant to Gardyne, and presented by Charles I on 28 March, 1633. He remained until 1659. His son, William, an Edinburgh advocate, became Principal Clerk of Session,

Date	Name

1659-83   **John Strachane**, MA, DD, took his degree at Kings College, Aberdeen, in 1655, transferred to the Tron Church, Edinburgh, and Professorship of Divinity at the University of Edinburgh, in 1683. Died 1699, aged 64.

1683-1705   **George Anderson**, MA, DD, transferred from Methlick. Became Professor of Divinity at Kings College, Aberdeen, on 12 October 1704, preaching his farewell sermon at Tarves on 14 January, 1705. He had seven children. Died 1710, age 75.

1706-38   **William Forbes**, MA, MD, son of Sir John Forbes of Waterton, and grand-nephew of the First Earl of Aberdeen. Took degree of MD at University of Pisa and AM at Kings College. Transferred from Leslie. Died while attending the Synod in Aberdeen on 21 April, 1738, age 69. Left 300 marks to the poor of the parish. Had five sons and eight daughters, three marrying ministers at Logie-Coldstone, Towie and Crimond. Wife was Janet, daughter of James Gregory, Mathematics Professor at Edinburgh University.

1738-65   **Alexander Howe**, son of the minister of Birse, transferred from Methlick and was presented by William, Earl of Aberdeen. Died at Newhills where he had gone to assist his brother at a communion service on 3 September,1765. Married to Margaret Nichol and had two daughters. Published 17 sermons.

1766-93   **Thomas Mitchell**, was initially a missionary at Portsoy, transferred from Tarland and presented by George, Earl of Aberdeen. Reported on the community in the *First Statistical Account of Scotland*. In the year he came to Tarves he married Mary, daughter of Donald Mackenzie of Dalmore. Had one son, George.

1794-1801   **Alexander Knolls**, transferred from Methlick, age 79. During his time the old kirk was demolished and the new one built. Wrote in the *First Statistical Account of Scotland* about Methlick, to which he had been ordained in 1746.

1801-16   **Duncan Mearns**, MA, DD, son of minister of Cluny. Born 23 August, 1779. Degree from Kings College, and licensed 27 June 1799. Presented by George, Earl of Aberdeen, and admitted assistant and successor 13 November, 1799, age 20. Demitted office 10 October 1816 to become Professor of Divinity at Kings College. Died 1852, age 72.

Date	Name
1817-32	**Alexander Black**, MA, DD. Graduated at Marischal College, Aberdeen 1 April, 1807. Presented by George, Earl of Aberdeen, November 1817. Took doctorate at Marischal College in 1824 and became professor of Divinity there in June 1832. Died 1864, age 72.
1833-70	**Francis Knox**, MA, son of Little Ythsie farmer, graduated Kings College, 1822. Became Assistant Schoolmaster at Tarves. Licensed December 1830, and presented by George, Earl of Aberdeen. Died 1870, age 67. Wrote account of Tarves in *New Statistical Account of Scotland.* The *Thanage of Fermartyn* says of him: "He was a very amiable man, respected and beloved by the whole of his parishioners, amongst whom he was born, lived and died."
1871-1916	**John Pringle**, MA, from Greenlaw, Berwickshire, son of a land steward. Graduated University of Edinburgh 1862, where he was a member of the Missionary Association. He was a schoolmaster for a time. Presented 1871, demitted office 1916.
1917-29	**Alexander Wood McNair**, born in Greenock, November 1879. Went from Glasgow University to Logie-Buchan in 1913, and was a forces chaplain at Dieppe during the First World War. Presented at Tarves, February 1917.
1929-47	**James Murray**, MA, had a First in Philosophy at the University of Aberdeen. Ministered later at Greenock St Marks and Newtonmore. Died 18 July, 1993.
1947-51	**Alistair Sutherland**, MA, reached Tarves from Kilmuir Easter in 1947. Moved to Stichill in 1950. Died 1 March 1993.
1951-63	**Charles Henry Stuart,** MA, ordained at Lanark 1942, was Royal Artillery chaplain 1942-46, ministered at North Berwick Blackadder before reaching Tarves in 1951. Later ministered at Duddingston,Edinburgh, Echt and Midmar. Died 1995.
1963-79	**Alasdair W. Macdonnell**, BD, came to Tarves 25 July 1963. Moved to Haddington St Mary's in 1979. Retired to Gifford.
1980-91	**Dr William M. Murdoch**,B Sc, BD, Ph D, STM, came to Tarves in 1980. Became Chaplain of Aberdeen University in 1991.
1991	**Leslie McEwen Barrett,** BD, FRICS, trained for the ministry at St Andrews and the parish of Anstruther. Formerly a Chartered Surveyor in Edinburgh. Inducted to Tarves in June 1991.

Chapter 13

Castle In The Air

HIDDEN in a charming setting among fine old trees on a hill from which it once dominated the Tarves countryside, is Tolquhon Castle. This once glorious 16th century pile, now in the care of Historic Scotland, exercised a profound influence on those who occupied the farms and crofts that lay scattered below its battlements.

The Thanage of Formartine was divided in the 15th century between the two heiress daughters of Sir Henry Preston of Fyvie. One married Alexander Meldrum, who inherited the Fyvie half of the thanage, the other - Marjorie - was given title to the Tolquhon portion and married Sir John Forbes.

Sir John was the fifth in line of descent from John de Forbes, who flourished in the reign of William the Lion. Marjorie made over Tolquhon to her husband in a charter dated 16 July, 1420. The oldest surviving part of the castle, the rump of a tower house known as Preston's Tower, was either built by Sir Henry or by his son-in-law early in the 15th century. It was the main residence until 1584 when William Forbes, the 7th laird, embarked on a five-year reconstruction project.

According to the *Thanage of Fermartyn*, John Forbes - son of Sir John and Lady Marjorie - was accused, along with a relative, James Forbes, in 1448 of abetting Sir Andrew Morison, Chaplain, in a suit at the Market Cross, Aberdeen, against Nicholas Blair, Chaplain to William, Lord Errol, Constable of Scotland. Sadly, the ancient record does not reveal the nature or outcome of the proceedings.

There is a similarly oblique reference to Sir John's grandson, Malcolm, being involved in a contract in 1501 between William Hay, Earl of Errol, and Thomas Kinnaird, for the "redemption of a reversion from Malcolm Forbes of Tolquhon for the lands of Sithan (Shethin), Rawak and Craigie for the sum of four hundred merks." There is a frustrating absence of further detail in the record.

Tolquhon - An Ancient Pile

From its bluff above the Tarves countryside, Tolquhon Castle exercised a profound influence upon the folk who occupied the farms and crofts at its feet. Today, its sylvan setting is the haunt of lovers, and tourists who stray from the main road in the valley. Pictures - the author

The 7th laird, William Forbes, succeeded to Tolquhon early in life after his father's untimely demise at the Battle of Pinkie in East Lothian in 1547. William emerges from history as a colourful, respected and cultured personality. In 1550 he was "bound over in two thousand pounds for his soune (son) and his friends not to trouble the Provost and Bailies of Aberdeen." Though the record is again agonisingly deficient in detail, the action was almost certainly connected with the constant municipal turmoil in Aberdeen at that time as the crafts and guilds sought fairer representation in running the town's affairs. Forbes was admitted a burgess of Aberdeen in 1578.

In 1581, Forbes received permission under the Privy Seal, because of an eye ailment, to eat flesh during the prohibited period in Lent and to "remain at home from all King's raids, sending a friend with his men." The affliction was described thus:

> "ane dolour and diseaiss in his ene, proceiding be ane distillatioun out of the heid."

He was a generous man, building a memorial aisle in the parish church and establishing a hospital for the poor in Tarves (described in the previous chapter). A climax to the full life led by this unusually benign and respected laird was reached towards the end of his days when, in failing health, he started the reconstruction and extension of his castle. An inventory, compiled in 1589, shortly after the five-year project was completed, refers to:

> "my hallis (halls), galleries, chalmeris (rooms), vardrope, kitchingis, stabillis, sellaris (cellars), lednaris (larders), pantreis, librellis (libraries) or wyther (other) office houssis."

There are also references to:

> "buikis (books), bedding, tapestrie, neprie (table linen), timmer (wood) wark, artalryie (canon), wther furniture insycht and plenishing."

A number of volumes from his library, bearing his distinctive flowing signature, have survived, as well as four bronze canon bearing his monogram and motto, SALUS PER CHRISTVM - 'Salvation Through Christ.' A surviving inscribed panel beside the gatehouse declares:

> "AL THIS WARKE EXCEP THE AVLD TOVR
> WAS BEGVN BE WILLIAM FORBES
> 15 APRILE 1584 AND ENDIT BE HIM
> 20 OCTOBER 1589"

It was surely a noble and spacious residence, among the grandest of its time. A rectangular block enclosed a neatly cobbled open courtyard. The main house, situated opposite the gatehouse, was flanked by service buildings and other structures, including a dovecot. Over the entrance to the castle was the Forbes coat-of-arms and that of James VI, who visited Tolquhon at the completion of the works.

An artist's impression of how the West gallery of Tolquhon might have looked just after completion of the building project.   Picture by kind permission of Historic Scotland

As a 'shop window', the gatehouse presented an impressive facade, richly adorned with armorial panels, sculpted figures and decorative gunloops. The oldest part of the castle - the Preston Tower with its 10-foot-thick walls - is now largely a shell. A feature of great interest is the castle's main bakehouse with two brick domed ovens, behind which was a pit-prison, reached through a hatch from the floor above. At least it would have been warm in there! There was also a brewhouse and a gallery where the family could take their exercise during inclement weather which prevented them from using the pleasance and formal gardens outside.Twelve square recesses in an outer retaining wall facing the pleasance originally housed bee-hives.The initials of the master mason responsible for the new buildings, Thomas Leiper, are carved on a skew-stone on top of the drum tower of the main house. Leiper also undertook building work at Schivas and Udny Kirk, and his son John was engaged in a similar capacity at Castle Fraser.

After the Royal visit to his new castle, William Forbes had but a few years remaining in which to enjoy the pleasures of his impressive home. He died in 1595 and was laid to rest in the memorial aisle he had created at Tarves Kirk.

William and Elizabeth had enjoyed a long and happy marriage. Not so one of their grandsons, Alexander, who died early in life, a bachelor jilted by his lover, Sophia Hay. The story was picked up by a balladeer:

" Word has come to young Tolquhon,
  In his chamber where he lay,
  That Sophia Hay, his first fause
      fair love,
  Was wedded and away.
  Sophia Hay! Sophia Hay!
  My love, Sophia Hay!
  I wish her ance as sair a heart,
  As she's gi'en me today,
  She thinks she has done me
      great wrang,
  I do not think it so;
  I hope to be in quietness,
  When she shall live in woe.

She'll live a discontented life,
  Since she has ga'en frae me;
  O'er soon, o'er soon, a weed of green,
  Will shortly cover me!"

Sophia Hay married Lord Melgum who was burned to death in the tower of Frendraught in October 1630. Her former lover's prophecy was truly fulfilled..

" And oft she cried, alas! alas!,
  A sair heart is ill to win,
  I wan a sair heart when I married him,
  And the day is well returned again."

A banquet in progress in the first floor hall, as it might have looked at the conclusion of the project in 1589.

Another of the Tolquhon family, William, who was described by a contemporary as considerably skilled in conducting courts and trials, was one of two commissioners appointed by James VI in 1608 to investigate the "dearth of buits and shoone" (scarcity of boots and shoes) in Aberdeenshire.

In a letter to Walter Forbes at Tolquhon, said to be in the handwriting of Charles II, the king forbade Huntly to make any levy on Tolquhon or to make the laird turn out to arms because he was past 60 and his son, Alexander, was already in command of a regiment of foot. As one of three Aberdeenshire colonels serving in the Scottish army of Charles II, Alexander, the 10th laird, had the honour of saving his sovereign's life at the Battle of Worcester in 1651.

This has been gleaned from family papers:

> "Sir Alexander, at Worcester, commanded a troop of horse raised by himself, and when the King's horse was shot under him, he defended him by his troop; and while General Lesley seem'd unconcerned, with his cloak muffl'd up to his chin, and beheld the rout of the King's troops, he kept the enemy at bay, mounted the King on his own horse, put a soldier's coat and a bloody handkerchief about him, and, sending him safe off the field, he kept the enemy still engaged till he was shot through both the calves of the legs.

> "He lay among the dead until next day (some say longer), when, being observ'd to have life, he was taken care of by a lady in the neighbourhood, who ventured to show him that kindness. The story of that lady's falling in love with him, and his concealing his being a marry'd man till he was recovered, perhaps, is fanciful."

The laird was knighted for this service. He had married in 1649, to Dame Bathia Murray, daughter of the Laird of Blackbarony and widow of William Forbes of Craigievar. They had no children. A strange story about Sir Alexander, which appeared in *Chambers' Domestic Annals*, confirms the tales of dotage in his later years. It was provoked, it appears, by the supposed disappearance of two valuable drinking cups after a convivial evening at Tolquhon when the laird's guests were Ogilvie of Forglen, Sir John Falconer and Lord Pitmedden. Tolquhon wrote to Ogilvie about the cups, asking if he could cast any light upon their disappearance. Though feeling slighted by the inference, Ogilvie replied that he had never seen the cups. The laird responded with an apology and the camaraderie of the past appeared to have returned.

The story was recounted in the *Thanage of Fermartyn*:

> "Afterwards, on Ogilvie refusing to take part with him in quarrels with a third party, Sir Alexander Forbes appeared to have conceived a malicious feeling towards him. To wreak this out, he raised an action against him in the Court of Session, on the allegation that he fraudulently abstracted the cups.

"When the case was called, Tolquhon had the confidence to appear personally at the bar, and own and countenance the same, and crave Ogvilvie's oath of calumny anent the defamatory libel. After Ogilvie had thus acquitted himself, Tolquhon craved permission to enter on a proof of the libel by witnesses, which the Lords granted.

"While the matter was pending, Tolquhon frequently upbraided Ogilvie with the terms 'cup stealer' and 'cup cheater'; nor did he hesitate to resort to legal quirks for keeping the charge as long as possible on the head of the accused. At length the case came on, and being found solely without evidence, was pronounced to be altogether founded in malice.

"A subsequent process by Forglen against Tolquhon was undefended by the latter who was amerced (fined) in twenty thousand merks, whereof one half was adjudged to the aggrieved party."

The cups were later found in the hands of a goldsmith in Aberdeen, left there for repair by their careless owner who had forgotten all about them!

The old laird's mounting imprudence was reflected in unwise financial adventures, including investment in the doomed Darien Scheme. His death, without issue, left the heavily burdened estate to his brother, Thomas Forbes of Auchry, whose son, William, succeeded to it in 1704. He did not enjoy the estate for long. Sir Alexander's creditors closed in, procuring the estate's sale by order of the Court of Session. William, aggrieved by the manner in which the ruling had been obtained, refused to quit the castle until, on 25 September, 1718, it was attacked by a military unit and himself wounded and taken prisoner.

The lands of Tolquhon were sold in November 1716 to Lieutenant-Colonel Francis Farquhar, who passed them on to Sir John Paterson, son of Sir William Paterson, Clerk to the Council under Charles II, and grandson of Bishop Paterson of Ross. From Sir John they passed to William, Earl of Aberdeen.

The ancient family seat of the Forbes ceased to be a residence of gentry and ended its days as little more than a farmhouse, remaining inhabited until the middle of last century. The historian John Hill Burton wrote at that time:

"A more melancholy place, nor one better fitted for the residence of an un-earthly guest, cannot well be conceived. Neglected, stagnant waters accumulate about decaying wood, and through some scattered trees appear the long-neglected fragments of pleasure-grounds. The ruins themselves are made fruitful by the soil deposited on them by rotting timber. They are in that most melancholy state of transition from a habitable condition to a mere mass of bare walls. Doors with their huge iron-knobbed locks still swing on their fantastic curling hinges; and not so many years ago, in one of the upper rooms, stood the almost architectural fragments of a gigantic carved bed."

Sometime last century much of the inner side of Preston's Tower, above its vaulted basement, fell into the courtyard, blocking it with debris. Decay was continuous until 1929 when the ruins were transferred by the Earl of Aberdeen into state care, and latterly into the stewardship of Historic Scotland. The transformation achieved since then is a tribute to those who undertook the daunting task of restoring glory to the remains of an ancient pile so important in the history of our parish.

An effigy of the laird, William Forbes, commemorating completion of the castle extensions in 1589.

Picture - Historic Scotland.

Gateway to history - the first view which the visitor has of the once-grand house that was Tolquhon.

Picture - the author

Chapter 14

In Great Hooses

W HEN Haddo House rose near the ruins of the old Place of Kelly in the early 18th century, it was both a revolution and a revelation. It was revolutionary in house design trends of the period and a revelation in style that would advertise the patrician superiority of its occupants. The Palladian mansion planned by William Adam for William Gordon, 2nd Earl of Aberdeen, brought stone and mortar at its finest to a bleak, almost treeless landscape.

In 1732 John Baxter, who was overseer of the construction work, was paid £ 25. 16s 3d to remove the ruins of the Place of Kelly, despoiled by marauding Covenanters nearly a century earlier. Today, with its lakes, country park and immaculate tree-lined avenues, Haddo House is a welcoming place in the care of the National Trust for Scotland. The lofty facade, with curving staircases to the first floor, and great wings reaching round on either side, appear to envelop the visitor, beckon the stranger towards a tour of its gracious rooms and halls, redolent of the history of a famous family. Out-of-doors, there is splendid relief for the jaded city dweller in the form of sylvan walking routes, a deer park, hides for the bird-watcher, a 'nature room' widely used by school visitors, equestrian pursuits, tennis courts, pheasant and partridge shooting and picnic areas.

The Aberdeens and their kinfolk have lived in or around Haddo for 500 years - an illustrious family which has produced admirals and generals, diplomats and Members of Parliament, a bishop, a Chancellor of Scotland, a Viceroy of Ireland, a Governor of Canada, and a Prime Minister of Great Britain. The latter, George, 4th Earl of Aberdeen - the 'Premier Earl' - was a model landlord who did much to enhance his estates by drainage, planting, restoration, building and effecting improvements in the conditions of his tenancy. When he died in 1860, they commemorated him by erecting the angular granite tower, the Prop of Ythsie, which dominates the Formartine countryside.

Haddo House - " it belongs to the time when men recognised that they could forget tall fortress-like towers."

In *A Souvenir of Haddo House*, written in 1958 by Cosmo Gordon of Ellon, and updated by David, 4th Marquess of Aberdeen, in 1974, it is said of the House:

> "Haddo belongs to the time when men recognised with relief that even in Scotland they could live safely in houses with large windows and airy rooms and could forget the tall fortress-like towers, many of which had been built in Aberdeenshire less than a century before. It is a house, not a castle, but when first built the new Haddo must have looked as modern to some of its neighbours as constructions of glass and steel look to us today."

Fifty years after the opening of Haddo, the neighbouring branch of the family at Castle of Gight fell on hard times and their stronghold was put up for sale by Catherine Gordon, wife of the profligate Captain 'Mad Jack' Byron and mother of only child George, who became Lord Byron of Newstead Abbey. A prophecy, presumed to date from the time of the itinerant poet Thomas the Rhymer, had forecast:

> " When the heron leaves the tree
> The laird of Gight shall landless be."

The lands of Gight passed to Haddo, as did the herons which had once nested below the castle beside a fish-rich pool on the River Ythan. The herons flew off to Haddo where their untidy tree-top nests can be seen to this day. The castle was abandoned and became ruinous. The prophecy had been fulfilled.

Close to Haddo, too, at the spot where the Kelly Burn runs into the Ythan, Sir Thomas Menzies of Cults procured the famous pearl which found its way into the Scottish crown. Sir Thomas travelled to London to present it to the king in 1620 and was rewarded with "twelve or fourteen chalders of victuall about Dumfermling (sic) and the custom of merchant goods in Aberdeen during his life."

In the lush greenery of Haddo on a summer afternoon, it is difficult to conceive that here, tragedy walked hand-in-hand with fame, sorrow with joy, and that the lives of the owners rather than the fabric of their gracious house was what so profoundly affected those who shared their landscape.

Space limitations necessarily restrict this account of the illustrious, but often damned, family which occupied the former Place of Kelly and its grander 18th century successor. Some of the pinnacles and troughs in the family record must suffice in this wider history of the parish which was part of its fiefdom.

● According to *Crawford's Peerage*, the Gordon family was descended from Sir William Gordon who swore fealty to Edward 1, 'Hammer of the Scots', though there does not appear to be any corroborative evidence.

● 1402 - Sir Adam Gordon, slain at the Battle of Homildon, had minor land holdings on the Banks of the Ythan.

● 1467 - a charter by William Foulerton of Aberawne conveyed to James Gordon the lands of 'Haldauch' on the Ythan at an annual rent of ten mcrks. This is the first identified connection of the Gordons with Haddo. James Gordon married Canea Harper, heiress of the "sunny half of Methlick". Two years later, another charter conveyed the remainder of the lands of Haddo to James Gordon, together with the "shadow half of Meikle Methlyk except for one habitation described as 'Le Chrystis croft".

● 1482 - a charter by David Annand of Ouchterellon conveyed to Patrick Gordon of Methlick the lands of Park of Kelly and Owerhill (Ordhill). This was the first Gordon acquisition of a portion of the estate of Kelly, which had belonged in the 13th century to Alexander Comyn, Earl of Buchan, bitter adversary of Robert the Bruce. Further Gordon acquisitions followed at this time, including 'Knockinblewis, Breckoh, Glassach and Auchadlie'. James Gordon acquired Mains of Kelly upon paying £6. 0s 4d to the Abbot and Convent of Lindores. The whole barony of Kelly, as well as Haddo and Methlick, gradually became the property of this branch of the Gordon family.

● 1515 - though recorded as having had many bastard children - 'filio carnali' and 'bastardis filiis' - Alexander Gordon was appointed Bishop of Aberdeen.

● 1575 - what was to become a notorious branch of the family obtained a grant of the lands of Tillyhilt. This was the graceless enclave that produced John Gordon, the bully and profligate who terrorised Formartine and Buchan, and Agnes Gordon who 'cast her glamourie' over her cousin, Haddo, winning him from Helen of Udny, to whom he was betrothed. Their grotesque antics were outlined earlier earlier in this book.

● 1580 - steps were taken by the Government to end deadly feuds between the Forbes and Gordon families, in which James Gordon of Haddo was much involved.

● 1582 - James Gordon of Haddo and Methlick obtained charters from James VI bestowing ownership of the lands of 'Kirktown, Tarvis, Brakla and Tullielt' as well as confirmed patrimony of Methlick and Haddo.

● 1644 - Covenanters sacked the Place of Kelly and captured Sir John Gordon of Haddo, who was later executed at Edinburgh for his loyalty to King Charles I.

● Sir George Gordon (1637-1720) was a Member of the Privy Council and a Lord of Session under the title of Lord Haddo. In 1681 he was appointed President of the Court of Session and then Chancellor of Scotland. He became 1st Earl of Aberdeen in 1682 and played an influential role in the Treaty of Union between Scotland and England.

● William, 2nd Earl of Aberdeen (1679-1746), though one of the representative peers of Scotland, did not take an active part in public life, preferring to increase and improve the family property, acquiring Tolquhon, Fyvie and other estates. He commissioned William Adam to design Haddo House.

● George, 3rd Earl (1722-1801), sometimes known as the 'Wicked Earl' on account of his womanising and self-indulgence, always referred to himself as 'Us'. He purchased three great houses at Cairnbulg in Buchan, Ellon Castle, and Wiscombe Park in Devon, in each of which he had mistresses and children.

● 1815 -The 4th Earl's brother, Sir Alexander Gordon, Lieutenant-Colonel and Aide-de-Camp to the Duke of Wellington, was killed at the Battle of Waterloo. Sir Walter Scott declared:

> " And generous Gordon, 'mid the strife,
> Fell while he watched his leader's life."

An obelisk erected to his memory in the grounds of Haddo is said to be of the same form as one which marks the spot at Waterloo where Sir Alexander fell. The latter bears an inscription, in both French and English:

> "Sur le champ de Bataille"

> "Sacred to the memory of Lieut-Colonel Sir Alexander Gordon, Knight Commander of the most honourable Order of the Bath, Aide-de-Camp to Field Marshal the Duke of Wellington, and also brother to George, Earl of Aberdeen, who in the 29th year of his age terminated a short but glorious career on the 18th June, 1815, while executing the orders of his great Commander in the battle of Waterloo. Distinguished for gallantry and good conduct in the field,

he was honoured with repeated marks of approbation by the
illustrious Hero, with whom he shared the dangers of every battle
in Spain, Portugal and France, and received the most flattering
proofs of his confidence on many trying occasions. His zeal and
activity in the service obtained the reward of ten medals, and the
honourable distinction of the Order of the Bath.

"He was justly lamented by the Duke of Wellington in his public
despatch as an officer of high promise and a serious loss to the
country; nor less worthy of record for his virtues in private life,
his unaffected respect for religion, his high sense of honour, his
scrupulous integrity, and the most amiable qualities, which
secured the attachment of his friends, and the love of his own
family. In testimony of feelings which no language can express,
a disconsolate sister and five surviving brothers have erected this
simple memorial to the object of their tenderest affection."

● 1820 - William Gordon, a Vice-Admiral, became a Member of Parliament for
Aberdeenshire.

● The ' Premier Earl' - George, 4th Earl of Aberdeen (1784-1860) - accompanied
Lord Cornwallis to negotiate with Napoleon the Peace of Amiens. He was present
at the battles of Dresden and Leipsig where he developed an aversion to war.
Nevertheless, when Prime Minister (1852-55), he shouldered much of the blame
for projecting Britain into the Crimean War, a largely inevitable but very costly
confrontation. His interest in Grecian culture earned him the name of 'Athenian
Aberdeen'. When retired from public life, he devoted himself to major works of
improvement on his estates and to bettering the lot of his tenantry.
The 100-foot-high Prop of Ythsie is a permanent reminder of that tenantry's
gratitude.

● mid-19th century - Alexander Gordon, KCB, was an Army General; Douglas
Gordon was Chaplain to the Queen; and Arthur Gordon was, successively,
Governor of Trinidad, Mauritius, Fiji, and Ceylon.

● George, 5th Earl (1816-64), was an Aberdeenshire MP but died young
following a long illness. He devoted his final years to philanthropic and pious
causes.

● George, 6th Earl (1841-70), sometimes known as the 'Sailor Earl', went to sea
as an ordinary seaman, sailing under the name of George Osborne. Became a
captain but was drowned at sea when, as first mate on a three-masted schooner,
the *Hera*, sailing between Boston and Melbourne, he was swept overboard
during a storm. When Barthol Chapel was erected into a Quoad Sacra Parish in
1876, a church called The Gordon Memorial Church was erected by the
Dowager-Countess of Aberdeen in memory of the son lost at sea.

● John, 7th Earl (1847-1934), was Lord Lieutenant of Aberdeenshire, Lord High
Commissioner of the General Assembly, Viceroy of Ireland, and Governor-

General of Canada (1893-98). The Earl and his wife, Countess Ishbel, lived a very full and somewhat extravagant life at Haddo and in Ireland and Canada, about which she wrote in her book, *We Twa*, a title which came to refer to a couple who were clearly engaged on a life-long love affair. Ishbel Maria was the youngest daughter of Sir Dudley Coutts Marjoribanks, who became Lord Tweedmouth. John became the Marquess of Aberdeen and Temair in 1916.

● Their eldest son George, 2nd Marquess (1879-1965), succeeded to an impoverished estate and provided funding to rescue 'We Twa' from their overspending. Agriculture went through difficult times between the wars and much careful 'housekeeping' was required to keep the estate solvent. In 1920 some 45,000 acres of the Haddo House Estate were sold, with most of it acquired, fortunately, by those involved in agriculture locally. George was Chairman of both Housing and Parks on London County Council. He became Lord Lieutenant of Aberdeenshire in 1934. In 1930 the family wing at Haddo was gutted by fire. George had no children.

● His brother, Dudley, who became 3rd Marquess (1883-1972), was an engineer and industrialist who, in the First World War, had commanded the 2nd Battalion of Gordon Highlanders and was awarded the DSO.

● David (1908-74), Dudley's son, became the 4th Marquess. He was mentioned in despatches while serving with the Gordons during the Second World War, was Prior of the Order of St John in Scotland, Chairman of the Scottish Landowners Federation, Convener of Aberdeenshire Education Committee, and Lord Lieutenant of the County. With his wife, June, he made Haddo a centre of the arts which has few equals, bringing together parishioners, townsfolk, artists and professional musicians in a community of music-making and thespian pursuits which enrich everyone. The Haddo House Choral Society has a national reputation. Before his death, David started negotiations to transfer Haddo House to the care of the National Trust for Scotland and 180 acres of its park to Grampian Regional Council as a County Park. Five years later the House and its policies were opened to the public. David's widow continues to live at Haddo.

● David was succeeded by his brother Archie, 5th Marquess (1913-84), who spent 32 years on the staff of the BBC, was head of Radio Talks and Documentaries, and producer of the *Week in Westminster* series.

● The 6th Marquess is Archie's youngest brother Alastair, born in 1920, and residing in Berkshire. His son, Alexander, born in 1955, is Earl of Haddo. He has recently built a house within the walled garden for the family's continuing use when the final family-occupied wing passes to the National Trust.

A Scottish Garden

PITMEDDEN, more renowned today for its grand formal garden than its house, lies close to the village of that name and is just three miles south of Tarves. The house was anciently owned by a family called Panton, first mentioned about the

Pitmedden Garden - magnificently restored to reflect its 17th century origins.
Picture - Doug Westland

end of the 14th century. The property was purchased in 1619 by James Seaton of Bourtie, who married a daughter of William Rolland, Master of the Mint in Aberdeen. His brother, John Seaton, accompanied the Earl of Errol as High Constable of Scotland at the coronation of King Charles I and, as a Royalist, did much to promote the king's interests.

Commanding a detachment of Loyalists at the Battle of the Brig o' Dee in 1639, he was shot through the heart, aged just 28. A handsome man, his early death was recorded in the ballad, *Bonnie John Seton of Pitmedden.* On account of his loyalty, his infant sons were subjected to severe hardship and Pitmedden was plundered by the Covenanters. One son, James Seaton, died of wounds received in a naval engagement with the Dutch when they attacked the English fleet at Chatham in 1667. His brother, Alexander, sat in the Court of Session as Lord Pitmedden. Because of his opposition to King James VII, however, he later lost office as a Senator of the College of Justice and was forced into private life to rebuild his mansion house and, in 1675, to lay out the beautiful formal gardens which have been restored by the National Trust for Scotland and are enjoyed by so many today. His son, William, was one of the Commissioners appointed to engineer the Parliamentary union between Scotland and England in 1707.

No records have survived to show what the early gardens looked like. A fire in 1818 destroyed the Seaton family home as well as any plans there might have been of the original garden. When the National Trust took over the garden in 1952, it inherited a superlative working market garden developed over several decades of this century by Alexander Keith and his son, Major James Keith, and set within the lower part of a much older walled garden. Since then the Trust has magnificently restored the Great Garden to reflect its 17th century origins. Major James Keith was a leader in improving agricultural techniques, outputs and income, and farmed extensively in the local area as well as in East Anglia. He was Chairman of the North of Scotland College of Agriculture.

A woodland walk, wildlife garden and picnic area were created but a new dimension was given to the Pitmedden complex in 1977 when the trustees of William Cook of Little Meldrum, Tarves, donated his lifetime's collection of agricultural and domestic artefacts. The items, known as the Cook Collection, were augmented by donations from all over Scotland, enabling a Museum of Farming Life to be established at Pitmedden. Mr Cook's son, Lindsay, who farms near Tarves, helped identify many of the items and advised on their former use.

Out Shethin Way

FOR long an independent property, Shethin, in the east of the parish, emerged in written history among the charters of Robert III. It was purchased from John Maxwell of Pollok early in the 15th century by John de Ogiston, an influential family with much land in Morayshire and Aberdeenshire. The Ogstons (as the name became) later added Crag (probably Craigies, Tarves), and Rawyston (Raxton) to their holdings.

By the 17th century, however, Shethin belonged to a branch of the Seaton family, distantly related to the Seatons of Pitmedden. An earlier chapter in this book recorded the tribulations of William Seaton of Shethin who fell foul of the Covenanters in 1644. His home was "pitifullie plunderit and spolzeit" but at least he escaped with his neck, unlike his gallant but luckless neighbour Haddo.

Shethin was ultimately merged with the estates of the Earl of Aberdeen but was farmed for over two centuries by the Hay and Shepherd families.The Hays produced some notable sons:

● Sir John Hay, KCMG, President of the Legislative Council of New South Wales.

● Captain Patrick Hay, wounded at Waterloo, was later Aide-de-Camp to the Governor of Madras.

● Alexander Hay, who was the first farmer to introduce Shorthorns to Aberdeenshire.

●William Hay, his brother, also a famous breeder of Shorthorns, was the first in Aberdeenshire to win a prize at the Smithfield Club Show. He was also the first to send cattle by rail to London.

For a full story on the famous Shorthorn and Aberdeen-Angus breeders at Tarves, see Chapter 17.

In *A View of the Diocese*, a chapel at Shethin is mentioned, located near the site of the mansion house. Some remains were found and the font was removed to Ellon Castle. There was also at one time distinct traces of a hilltop camp, though its origins were unclear. There are 10 well-preserved standing stones in a field west of the farmhouse.

Along at Cairnbrogie

ANOTHER property well known for its associations with the Shorthorn, Cairnbrogie originally formed part of the numerous estates assigned to the Abbey of Arbroath. In the mid-17th century it was owned by an Aberdeen lawyer, Alexander Davidson. In the following century it became part of the Aberdeen estates, though rented for many years by the Marr family. When Captain John Marr (of the Udny Volunteers) came into possession in the 1790s, there was much wasteland about the farm which he recovered, drained and enclosed, bringing it into a high state of cultivation.

His son, George, an MA graduate from the University of Aberdeen, was the author of a widely-read essay on the agricultural labourer and the best means of improving his conditions. He further improved the farm and bred a fine herd of Shorthorns. Of his own very large family of 14, no fewer than eight were wiped out by diptheria in one month in 1862. His heir, John Marr, an Aberdeen graduate, too, was Commanding Officer of the Tarves Volunteer Corps, which included Lieutenants George Shepherd of Shethin and Sam Davidson of Northseat of Auchedly. He was a renowned breeder of Clydesdale horses.

Up at Schivas

AT THE northern extremity of the old Tarves parish and approaching its highest point at the 578-foot Hill of Skilmafilly, is the castellated house of Schivas, once the centre of the barony of that name. It was once annexed to Methlick but was returned to Tarves in 1610. The original owners rejoiced in the property's name - Schivas, Schevez, Shives, or de Syves, according to the spelling in vogue at the time or the idiosyncracies of the chroniclers.

One member of the family, Andrew de Syves, was Rector of Aberdeen Grammar School in the early 15th century. Another, William Schevez, was Archbishop of St Andrews (1478-1497). By all accounts, he was a turbulent cleric who made enemies easily, dabbled in medicine and astrology and was even rumoured to indulge in the black arts. He was, nevertheless, a scholar of some note and prized his personal library, some of the volumes from which are preserved at the University of Aberdeen. He started his career as physician to King Henry III, becoming his personal friend and crony.

The Schivas estate passed to the Gray family, an early member of which was William Gray, a burgess of Aberdeen, who had amassed a considerable fortune as a trader. In 1512, his son Alexander acquired the Schivas lands and his grandson, Gilbert Hay, built the House of Schivas some years later, to the designs of Thomas Leiper, the master mason of Tolquhon fame.

The Grays of Schivas - staunch Roman Catholics - fell foul of the Reformed Church of Scotland which was in the throes of persecuting all other forms of Christian belief. In 1608, Thomas, the kirk officer at Tarves, delivered a summons to James Gray, son of the laird, to appear before the Presbytery of Ellon. On arrival at Schivas, Thomas "wes informit be ye servands of ye place of Scheves that he was thair, and he saw ye said James' cloak and sword and ryding geir in ye hall." On being told that James did not recognise the summons or the Presbytery, Thomas fixed the missive to the front door of the mansion and returned to Tarves. On a second occasion, James rejected another summons owing to "ye rochness of ye wedder."*

In 1624, Gilbert and Patrick Gray were accused of apostacy, though the Presbytery heard from the Tarves minister, the Rev Thomas Gardyne, that they "war baith past south as he hopit not to return shortlie." In 1639, the laird was summoned for "having laitlie ane bairn baptized be ane priest". In 1663, Andrew Gray's wife, Marie Gordon, was also chastised by the Presbytery but ignored their summons, resulting in her excommunication, with her daughter, in 1668. The family built an altar recess to enable them to worship in their own home.

The Schivas property passed, through a Gray heiress, to Alexander Forbes of Craigievar in 1703. North-East and South-West wings were added to the house in 1750. In the next century it went to Alexander Irvine, Laird of Drum, after his marriage to a daughter of Hugh Forbes of Schivas. The Schivas estate was sold to the 'Premier Earl' in 1844. It was burned out by an accidental fire in 1900. In the Spring, a blackbird had built its nest in one of the 'lums' of Schivas. Later in the year, a large peat fire was lit and the nest caught fire, spreading to the joints in one of the upper floors, and soon the entire building was engulfed in flames. It was subsequently rebuilt and extended by Lord Aberdeen.

In the large disposal of Aberdeen family-owned lands between the First and Second World Wars, Schivas was purchased by James Burr of Tulloford, Barthol Chapel. A succession of owners since then has included Colonel Arthur Brooke of Fairley and Lord Catto. It was purchased in 1931 by the then Sir Thomas Catto of Peterhead, who carried out extensive alterations and improvements, to designs by J. Fenton Wyness. Sir Thomas was elevated to the Peerage in 1936 and was Financial Adviser to the Chancellor of the Exchequer during the Second World War. Today, Schivas is the home of his grandson, the Hon Innes Catto.

Near Schivas stands the 'Howff' - the burial enclosure of the Forbes family. It bears the initials of Hugh Forbes of Shivas and his wife, Christian Garden, who, during the snow-wrecked harvests of 1782-83 which brought the tenantry to their knees once more, provided work for them by employing them to clear the fields of boulders. They were still trying to bring in the harvest in December 1782. A relief fund, led by Aberdeen Town Council, was launched when only two weeks supply of cereals remained in the town and district. Grain was purchased

* *"ye rochness of ye wedder"* - *"the roughness of the weather"*

from England and the Continent. On Christmas Eve, 1782, a meeting of the county's landed gentry met in Aberdeen to discuss the crisis and it was calculated that 220,000 bolls of corn were needed, over and above the harvest, to feed the townspeople and country folk. Economies were made by ceasing the malting of barley, the group's concerted actions saving the town from famine.

If any single event could be said to have provoked the widespread improvement of Tarves farming practices dating from about that time, it was those two years during which the corn was destroyed and famine loomed. Many of the unprogressive farmers and crofters whose methods of husbandry had been inherited from time immemorial, at last opened their fields to turnips, potatoes and sown grass. The era of 'The Improvers' had arrived.

The house of Schivas is said to be haunted by the benign ghost of the beautiful Mary Gray who had spent a happy 17th century childhood there, with her brother as the only companion of her age. At 18 she fell in love with her kinsman, John Leslie, but Mary's father frowned on the romance and chose an older and wealthier husband for her. Mary was virtually imprisoned in her new home, closely guarded to prevent her escaping. However, escape she did, with the help of her lover who was waiting with a horse. They rode off into the night and were married by a priest at a wayside chapel.

When Mary returned to Schivas, she found that her father had died and her brother was the new laird. It is said that on the anniversary of Mary's return to Schivas, the ghost of the happy girl flits over the paved courtyard before passing through the great studded door and up the spiral staircase to the little room of her childhood.

Schivas House, home to a happy ghost.　　Picture - the author

Chapter 15

A Class Of Their Own

IN the Spring of 1996, the youngsters of Tarves Primary School were using personal computers, telephone modems and electronic mail to exchange classroom projects with children in Australia, Norway, the United States, Chile and Canada. In modern parlance, they were 'surfing the Internet' as part of a drive to broaden their knowledge of the world at large and to let others into their own world in Formartine.

"We are trying to open up the world for them and taking maximum advantage of modern information technology in so doing," said their visionary Head Teacher, Marek Gorski. "We are leading the way in this part of the country."

The children were participating in a European Union programme which aims to promote co-operation between schools, encourage pupil contact, foster the European dimension in education and improve knowledge of cultures and languages.

How very different, one might think, from the dark days when Tarves was an obscure backwater in which any brand of formal education was unknown. And yet, 150 years ago, Latin and Greek were being taught in the building in the Square which is now occupied by the doctors' surgery.

From the early 19th century, at least, great emphasis was placed upon the teaching of the Three R's - reading, 'riting and 'rithmetic - which have stood the test of time so well in Scottish Education.

Little has been recorded of the earliest forms of education, especially in rural districts like Tarves, though we know of the existence during early Christian times of monasteries and seminaries where emphasis was laid on religious teaching, together with some instruction in ancient languages and astronomy. It is likely that monasteries situated in the countryside also gave some attention, for practical reasons, to instruction in agriculture and affiliated crafts.

Cathedral and abbey schools appeared in medieval times, though these were situated largely in centres of population and would not have drawn their scholars from remote parishes. The first Scottish universities appeared on the scene in the 15th century (Aberdeen in 1494), though these were initially the exclusive domain of the rich. In 1496 an Act of the Scottish Parliament aimed to introduce a form of compulsory education, but this was confined to the eldest sons of ruling barons.

The Reformation in the mid-16th century provided the first blueprint for universal compulsory education in Scotland. The Reformation's *Book of Discipline* in 1559 described an elaborate scheme of national compulsory education targeted at instilling "wisdom, learning and virtue" into the youth of the land so that the Church should have an adequate supply of ministers and the nation its necessary administrators. Every kirk was to have its school, though in rural parishes the minister or reader could undertake the task of instructing the children in "the rudiments" as well as in "the Catechism of Geneva" - Calvin's. Every "sizeable" town should have a schoolmaster able to teach Latin and Grammar and every "notable" town should have a college in which should be taught Latin, Greek, Logic and Rhetoric. Those at college who showed an aptitude for learning should proceed to a university.

Also laid down was the time to be spent in every educational stage, as were the qualifications needed for progressing from one stage to the next. Those who qualified would be obliged to proceed, even if their parents objected, and bursaries would be made available to remove parental obstacles. University students would be drawn from all classes and at the age of 24 should be ready to enter the profession of their choice.

Theory was one matter, practice another. It would be many years before John Knox's blueprint became reality, since it was much too ambitious for that turbulent era. However, it was the seed from which grew educational progress over the following three centuries, turning the ideas of the Reformers into the foundation stones of modern education.

The parish school at Tarves first appears on record in 1611 when William Mill was schoolmaster. Nine years later, his successor, John Lowrie, had an unsavoury association with the vagabond John Gordon of Tillyhilt (documented in Chapter 2). About that time, the fee for attending the parish school was 10s per annum for "inland bairns" and 16s for "boarders." By 1624 a schoolmaster was in residence but he did not have a schoolhouse. For a time, the kirk loft was used, but the school was discontinued during Covenanting times. We do not hear about it again until 1687 when William Greig, the schoolmaster, was in trouble with the Presbytery of Ellon, having neglected his duties for revelry in the alehouse he kept in the village. His subsequent fall from grace was recounted in Chapter 7.

The countryside was rocked in 1690 by a tragedy in the parish school at nearby Methlick. Three boys there were killed during a thunder-storm and the schoolmaster was severely injured. According to the Rev Alexander Knolls, the

Methlick minister, writing for the *Statistical Account*, the then minister's pregnant wife had also been there and was so distressed by the tragedy that " the child she brought forth some time after was born paralytic and continued so until her death."

In 1729, the Tarves school was so dilapidated that the master was obliged to teach in a barn. It was therefore decided to build a new schoolhouse. It was to be 30 feet by 12 feet within the walls, and 6 feet high to the wall heads, built of stone and lime and with a turf-covered roof.

As W. Douglas Simpson says in his captivating *Short History of Tarves*:

> "Nothing does the old-time Church of Scotland greater credit than the persistence with which its kirk sessions and presbyteries struggled, in the teeth of penurious heritors and against every other conceivable obstacle, to promote a competent school in every parish. Not that the relations between minister and dominie were always happy. At Tarves in 1759, the minister (the Rev Alexander Howe) confessed to having given the schoolmaster - to be sure, a mere lad of eighteen - a 'lunder' on the shoulders with his staff, which he represented had a good effect on him, and that to the conviction of his own parents and of all concerned in him: and that all the parish of Tarves were satisfied that he was become a new man since he received that chastisement."

In 1793 the average number of scholars in Tarves was 30. The schoolmaster's salary was £ 4 sterling from the parish, plus school fees. In 1799, the Church's General Assembly enjoined presbyteries to be diligent in the exercise of their legal power to supervise all schools within their bounds. A new impetus in education ensued during the early years of the 19th century.

In 1837, a new school and schoolhouse were built on the North side of the Square, with the schoolmaster enjoying, like his successors, the fruits of the educational endowment known as the Dick Bequest. According to the Rev Francis Knox, the new school was built on a very liberal scale and was extremely neat and substantial. There was also a school at Craigdam, endowed by an individual by the name of Barron, whose bequest of £ 600 underwrote the schoolmaster's salary. The trustees overseeing the fund were the Craigdam minister and two of his elders. At a third school, in Barthol Chapel, the teacher had a house and croft provided for him by the Earl of Aberdeen, and there was another school at Auchedly.

Knox also reported:

> "There are three other schools whose teachers have no endowment but depend for a poor and precarious livelihood solely upon the fees paid by their pupils. The total number of scholars attending all these seminaries is, on average, from 300 to 350. There are also several Sabbath schools in the parish and the minister gives instruction in the principles of Christian knowledge."

Schooldays

The girls' school in Manse Brae, which became Tarves Cottage Hospital, joined with the boys' school in 1883 (above). It was a fine granite building endowed by the Earl of Aberdeen in 1837. The school photo (below) - a serious occasion! Beneath walls hung with maps of far-away places, sit the scholars of Auchedly at the turn of the century.

Pictures courtesy THP

Writing at the same time - 1842 - Methlick's minister, the Rev James Whyte, reported that in the parochial school, Latin, Greek and Mathematics were taught "when required", in addition to reading, writing and arithmetic. There were also three 'adventure' or endowed schools. Neighbouring Udny had an 'Academy' attended by some 30 'gentlemen's sons'. It was described in the *Statistical Account* as " the means of giving better education to the parishioners than any of their neighbours had an opportunity of obtaining."

The reporter, the Rev John Leslie, added:

> "Many of the younger farmers belonging to the parish who received their education at the Udny Academy, attended several sessions at the Aberdeen universities. Some of the parishioners' sons became professional men, who, had it not been for the academy, would have been in humble life. There is not a person in the parish above fifteen years of age who cannot read or write."

At the great religious cleavage in 1843 known as the Disruption, the Free Church was faced with an educational dilemma. Hitherto, responsibility for education had rested with the Church of Scotland. By law, parochial schools had to be provided and maintained by the heritors but supervised by the Church. In addition, there were schools supported by the *Society for the Propagation of Christian Knowledge (SPCK)*, a church society, and others were built and maintained by private benefactors. Since teachers who were aligned with the Free Church were to be dismissed, a means of employing them had to be found. Within a year more than £ 50,000 had been raised and the Church undertook their maintenance. Two teacher-training schools were founded and public grants were made to schools certified as efficient by Government inspectors.

In 1869, shortly before the Education (Scotland) Act was passed, taking all denominational schools into a national system, it was reported that the Free Church had almost 600 schools and had raised £ 600,000 for educational purposes since the Disruption. Management of the nation's schools was transferred to elected school boards in 1872. Full-time primary education became compulsory for all children, effectively taking child farm labour out of the market. From time immemorial, children had worked as herds in the summer and had laboured during the harvest weeks, when school attendances were greatly depleted.

For a number of fascinating cameos of the 19th century schools in Tarves and Methlick I am indebted to Grampian Regional Council whose Education archives in Old Aberdeen I was permitted to examine in some depth.

On a school inspector's visit in the 1830s, for instance, the schoolmaster at Tarves was reported to be 82 years old and ailing. The turf-roofed school had been flooded that morning, torrential rain filling gaping holes in the clay floor. The master, George McNaughton, was described as being in such an infirm state that "it is not probable he will survive many months." The schoolhouse was said to be large but in a "very shabby state" and only a part of it floored.

Incredibly, there existed a parallel situation at Methlick where schoolmaster George Pirie, in his late 70s, had lost the use of both legs and was obliged to use 'stilts' and crutches. Nevertheless, the inspector was able to report that Pirie maintained discipline and was an effective teacher. He was assisted by his son, John Pirie, who was also apparently in ill health. The inspector was particularly impressed by the manner in which the Piries handled religious instruction:

> "The seriousness and propriety of spirit which characterise the scriptural lesson may be attributable in some measure to the influence of Sabbath Schools which are largely attended in this parish and the recognised importance thus attached to religious instruction."

At Tarves the inspector heard three Latin scholars read a passage from Nepos rather better than had been achieved at Methlick:

> "One lad, a shoemaker, reads Latin half the day and works the other half. He only began at Martinmas and is already translating Nepos and making good versions."

The Tarves master in 1848, George Melvin, known as "Dickie" on account of the shortened leg with which he was afflicted, was regarded as something of an eccentric genius. He evidently taught Arithmetic in a rather singular way. The number 10,875 was quoted as being "one decade of thousands, no single thousand, eight hundreds, seven decades, five units." Reading performance by two pupils studying Latin from Livy was observed to be "excellent, being deliberate with comparatively little of coarse pronunciation, and sound intelligence." Knowledge of English Grammar was acclaimed and the overall impression created was of "a state of high efficiency with information communicated in a manner which is not only original but strikingly impressive."

Unfortunately, Melvin's nonconformity appears to have worn thin during a later visitation when the inspector commented rather icily on Melvin's refusal to use the lesson books generally employed in parish schools:

"The oldest class was using the Illustrated London Reading Book - compiled apparently from the Illustrated London News. Beginners use a primer full of engravings from the same press. They also use a tract of Messrs Chambers on the History of Scotland. People are becoming dissatisfied with the condition of the school - a feeling attested by the decreasing number of pupils. The question is whether it is practicable to check Mr Melvin's evident tendency to what is novel and eccentric and to reconcile him to patient assiduity and labour in the beaten track of duty." Ouch!

Melvin was clearly having a bad day, for the inspector was also highly critical of the scholars' reading and spelling. And there was another bad day in store. A repeat visit by the same inspector heaped opprobrium on Melvin for "inferior" reading, "lamentable" Bible knowledge, and "slovenly" writing!

Schoolmaster George Melvin - eccentric genius?   Picture - THP

The inspector concluded:

> "They do not know the meaning of words such as Papist and
> Protestant. On the whole, the school shows no indication of having
> made any progress since the last visitation. Mr Melvin was
> requested to procure a more efficient assistant."

George Melvin's brother James was Rector of Aberdeen Grammar School where
a severe exterior earned him the nickname of "Grim". George was in many ways
a man ahead of his time, yet truly of the 'old school' in his belief that liberal
application of the strap was an incentive to learning. On one occasion, when the
boys failed to come in at his call, he started to thrash some 20 of them but
half-way down the line was so exhausted that he threw the strap from him,
declaring: "God knows I have done my duty! "

He did not encourage complaints about his scholars. There was the time when
an old woman ran into the school with the fragments of a 'trackie' (teapot) in her
lap, declaring: "See what yer loons hiv deen this foreneen - threw steens doon
my lum and broke my teapot." Old Melvin told her:"Go hame, wifie, what
business had you with your trackie at your fireside at this hour of the day?"

Chuckled about for many a day in the Tarves countryside was an incident which
followed the official opening of the Inverurie to Oldmeldrum railway branch line,
at which Melvin, his servant James Mitchell, and farmer John Duncan of Newseat
had refreshed themselves overwell. Driving home in Melvin's carriage and pair,
with Duncan on the reins, Melvin beside him, and in the small back seat hung

on at the rear, Mitchell, carrying Melvin's crutch, and Francis Morrison with his fiddle, they came rattling home by Auquhorthies. The speed and the condition of the road proved too much for the back seat, which fell off, pitching the two men, crutch and fiddle into the dirt. As the trap retreated in clouds of dust, they shouted in vain. "Some midnight revellers!" said Melvin as they sped on into Tarves village. On arrival there and discovering the absence of the back seat, Melvin shouted in vain for "James! James!" He was unable to move without his crutch, and John Duncan was too tipsy either to support him or get out of the cart. Much to the amusement of early-rising Tarvesians, the befuddled pair drove noisily around the village until James, carrying the crutch, and Francis with his fiddle, staggered in from Auquhorthies.

Wayward master or not, Melvin's lasting memorial to Tarves is the Melvin Public Hall, centre of so much of the village's activities over the past century. He left the residue of his estate - about £ 400 - to be used " for some public purpose." One of his former pupils, William Duthie, of Shorthorn fame, secured its use to build a public hall, himself subsequently leaving £1000 for its improvement and extension. It replaced a ramshackle building called the 'Temple' which had served the social needs of earlier generations. When, on a visit to Haddo House, millionaire Andrew Carnegie heard from William Duthie that Tarves was the first country parish in the North of Scotland to adopt the Free Library Act, he offered £ 100 to build a library room, known today as the Carnegie Room.

The former Cottage Hospital on Manse Brae, Tarves, endowed by the Earl of Aberdeen, was a girl's school from 1875 to 1883 when the building was converted to hospital use. The east wall of the hospital, now in use as private dwellings after a spell as a garage, retains a bronze commemorative plaque with a decorative bas-relief to Mary Jane Greenhalgh, the nurse until 1890.

The carefree days of childhood in these far-off times were entrancingly recaptured many years later by Charles Davidson in an eulogy in Aberdeen's *Bon-Accord and Northern Pictorial* which he entitled 'When Simmer Days Were Fine.' Son of a long-established Tarves family which had produced an Archbishop of Canterbury, Davidson was a lecturer in Spanish at Aberdeen University in 1938 when he engagingly wrote of "a little kingdom, compact and trig and self-contained."

Among his earliest recollections was the "dame's school " in the woods of Schivas kept by Miss Mary Garden - "one of the most remarkable teachers I ever knew." He recalled:

> "We walked three miles every day to the little thatched, one-roomed house in the wood. It was a most cosy hoosie, with a roaring fire in winter. There were about thirty pupils on the roll. We did not creep unwillingly to school: we were all eager to submit ourselves to the kindly influence of this gentle lady who taught us our rudiments. Her rule was the rule of love. I cannot remember any punishment ever being inflicted, for none was required. Every boy or girl who had the privilege of being taught by her felt the benign influence that she radiated on all.

"School began with a hymn, a favourite being 'There Is A Happy Land', followed by a prayer, and the school day ended with a hymn, followed by a sort of 'Search The Scriptures'. She would say 'St John, 5th chapter, 3rd verse'. There would be a rustle among New Testaments and the one who was first to read the verse would get out of school first. And so on to the last scholar. None escaped. It was a 'Search The Scriptures' without tears."

" Faithful Unto Death"

The plaque erected by Lord and Lady Aberdeen at the former Cottage Hospital is to its first nurse, Mary Jane Greenalgh, who was only 42 when she died.   Picture - THP

He added:

> "The fees were only a few shillings a quarter. Miss Garden lived at her brother's croft, a half-mile away, and after the lunch or 'piece' interval almost the whole school would go to the Quarryhole, half-way, to meet her, to see who would have the honour of being led by the hand - one on the right and the other on the left - back to school. If ever there was a saint among women, Mary Garden was one."

Davidson revelled in the joys of the barefoot trip to school :

> "The soft plop, plop, of barefeet in the dust. Half-way down the brae, below a broom bush, a partridge's nest where once 16 eggs were laid, and farther down a thicket of yellow rasps - a sore temptation. Beyond, a well of purest water, where dwelt a wily trout. We approached his lair on tiptoe but what we generally saw was his tail disappearing up the drain. At many of the farms there was a well-trout, one of which I almost managed to tame with mealocks (crumbs). And then in the burnie which flowed from the well we laid horse hairs in a sort of dam to see if they would turn into eels!

> "Then there were the esks that, when you bent to drink from the burn, were liable to jump down your throat and take up their abode inside you! And the moment when the tadpoles dropped their tails was always a mystery. Next came a wooden bridge over the Ythan at Mill of Auchedly, and, lo, we were in Buchan! An international boundary! Soon we crossed the little uncultivated corner of Michael Muir and here on its heathery stretch skylarks and meadow pipits abounded and whinchats and blackcaps were also to be found. A little off the road was a forbidding and stagnant pool, full of all sorts of mysterious beasties - at the bottom, slow movers and on the surface swift darters, those burnished water beetles that skipped so nimbly and hid under projecting docken leaves. Wild rasps and blaeberries flourished nearby."

And so the barefoot scholars of that time 'plopped' on up the brae to the friendly wood, past the camps of tinkers:

> "Sitting, bronzed with the sun, mending iron pots, pans and pails round blazing fires.We gave them a wide berth. Their dogs showed their teeth in warning snarls ".

The senses are quickened by Davidson's account of the simple joys of that vanished era:

> "The cushie doos, the speelin' o' the trees to get their eggs! And the simple improvised games at school - bools, tackie and 'Rise, Sally Walker'. And one where we all joined into a long queue, each holding on to the waist of the one in front, with a bold lad outside who tried to burst through the line or seize the last one in the row. The leader of the queue said 'Who goes round the house at night?' 'None but bloody Tom' was the answer. 'Don't steal none of my chickens away,' warned the leader. 'None but this poor one' snapped the attacker, trying to pounce on one of the flock. The captured ones attached themselves to the robber's queue."

Returning homewards, youngsters checked lines set earlier in the river for eels:

> "We got twopence a head for a really good whopping eel from a woman who lived nearby. For a fair-sized eel we got a slice of bread and butter with a thick coating of blackcurrant jam.Then there was the guddling for trout along the burnside, where you knelt, and gently feeling with your fingers below the bank, you might have the luck to tickle a trout. Gently tickle his stomach and then grip hard and fling him on to the bank. Great fun! But sometimes there was a sharp-toothed black water rat in hiding, and his bite was not pleasant."

A seductive lure was the sight of herons fishing in Northie's Burn:

> "We crawled up by the haugh where two Bronze Age swords had been found, and where my great-grandmother used to steep her flax, to the shelter of the broom, and then, peering through, we could observe at our leisure his lordship the heron standing meditatively on one leg, motionless, with head on one side, watching for his prey. Suddenly, like a flash, down darted his beak to grip a wretched, squirming eel. Solemnly, he strode to the bank and tried to gulp down his prey, but it came writhing out again from his gullet. So, smiting it vigorously against a stone, he would at last succeed in swallowing it, birsin' it doon with contracted neck till the gastric juices came to his aid. Not far away we caught a fine sea trout with a neat bite out of his neck. An otter had been at work. We once caught a lamprey, with all his long row of suckers.

> "On the land beyond the burn was what had been in olden days a moss moor which stretched, within memory, all the way to Ellon. This was the breeding place for innumerable tenchats and even curlews and oyster-catchers. Such is the atavistic memory of birds that visit their ancestral haunts."

And what of the pearl-fishers in that far-off time? Since it was on record that the biggest pearl in the Scottish crown had come from the Kelly Burn where it joined the Ythan, it was scarcely surprising that some believed there was a still bigger treasure lying in wait for the diligent searcher.

Davidson:

> "We fished for pearl mussels in the river, using an old triangular harmonium box with seams caulked as our treasure ship. We propelled our Argo upstream while one of us sat in the prow with a cleft stick with which the mussel was held. We did not have great luck.

> "And then in the woods of Haddo was the heronry, near the lower lake, where, wearing our oldest clothes, we speeled the trees, slimy with discharges from above. At the top were huge, untidy, cart-wheel nests where the occupants sat clappering their bills and flying off with loud discordant squawks. Their dirty bluish-green eggs were a great prize, but sometimes, when young ones were in the nest, a shot of slimy liquid met us from the nest, malodorous as the discharge from the skunk."

Schoolboys in the late 19th century wore breeches and long stockings with a jacket whose Eton-style collar was easily wiped clean with a wet cloth. They wore strong boots in winter and went barefoot in summer. Girls wore long frocks and pinafores with black knitted stockings and button boots. Truancy gave as much concern then as it does now but the expedient of posting the name of truants on the church doors at that time appears to have worked wonders! A brief entry in one school register noted:

> "Deterred by the posting of names at the church doors, there were
> fewer truants this week."

The school which Tarves children attend today, situated on the South side of Duthie Road, was opened in 1911, succeeding the earlier one built by the Earl of Aberdeen in 1837. At the beginning of the 20th century, four schools in the parish dealt with the education of 388 children. Today, there are only two schools - Tarves and Barthol Chapel - catering for just over 220 children. Tarves, the larger, has 170 children on its roll. The eight-classroom establishment,formerly a junior secondary, was reduced to primary status in 1978. From the age of 12, pupils are now bussed to Ellon Academy, one of the largest senior secondary schools in Scotland, with a roll of 1700.

Tarves is one of 20 local schools feeding more than 300 pupils into Ellon Academy each year. Its head teacher is a member of the school board at Ellon and also advises his own school board at Tarves.

Marek Gorski leads a team of seven teachers at Tarves, which is supplemented by visiting specialists in art, physical education, drama, home economics, music and instrumental tuition. There is also a learning support teacher to assist less able children.

As an adviser to the school board, Marek heads a regime which sets great store on consultation with and involvement of the community. A notable recent example of this was a letter and questionnaire to parents and a pupil questionnaire seeking views on the school's future homework policy. Full feedback was given when the opinions of parents and pupils, and those of the staff, had been collated and analysed.

"We had a huge and very positive response from parents," Marek said. " It served to reflect generally the view of teachers that we were well in touch with the community's wishes - which was gratifying in itself - but, more importantly, it enabled us to write a policy document which was precisely aligned with what parents and pupils said they wanted. It helped us, too, to explain to parents for the first time the place that homework has in the curriculum."

The Scottish trinity of reading, 'riting and 'rithmetic are still to the fore, with the five areas in the school curriculum being Language, Mathematics, Expressive Arts, Environmental Studies and Religious and Moral Education. The programme is more than a set of subjects, however, contributing, as it does, to the personal and social development of the child.

The Environmental Studies aspect of the school year, for instance, is designed to teach pupils about the world in which they live, investigating and understanding their environment and developing informed attitudes to environmental issues and their own health and welfare. History and Geography have moved on, a very long way, from that which the previous generation learned at Tarves. The children now investigate transport and communications networks at home and further afield, and study the ways in which our communities are run. The educational tools available to them are a quantum leap from those used by their grandparents in the immediate post-war years. The video recorder, personal computer and modem have replaced the slates and pencils of that under-privileged era. Horizons have broadened beyond belief - the author might have been excused his surprise on learning that the rural school had recently been the scene of a truly authentic Japanese tea ceremony, organised by a kimono-clad Japanese student teacher who also gave demonstrations of oragami and Japanese writing and drawing. Or his wonderment at a 10-year-old confidently employing the Internet and associated communications technology to send text and photographs of a classroom project to another school many thousands of miles away.

This pioneering country school erected its own emblem above its front door early in 1996 - a logo comprising the landmark Prop of Ythsie encased in barley sheaves. It was designed by Danny Ross, owner of the nearby Tolquhon Art and Sculpture Gallery, and cast in metal by Stanley Klimkowski, a Polish friend of Marek Gorski and blacksmith at Lumsden on Donside.

What would those old dominies, Melvin, McNaughton and Pirie have thought of it all? We rather think they would have approved.

Head teacher Marek Gorski and some of the Tarves schoolchildren with their own school logo.   Picture courtesy of Marek Gorski

Chapter 16

A Time For Renewal

C HANGE was in the air, everywhere. It had come slowly to the North-East but the first shoots of renewal were appearing in Formartine. The vision of the 'Improvers' and the Agrarian Revolution, already well established in the South, were at last reaching Tarves.

Culloden and the cause of the Jacobites had passed into history. Indeed, Tarvesians had little of moment to recall from that inglorious episode in the annals of Scotland. Just one of their number, a crofter named James Auld, had answered the Pretender's call and failed to return to the parish after the cause perished in the bloody soil of Culloden. In the fading recollections of older folk, too, was a skirmish at Inverurie in December 1745, the last pitched battle to be fought in the North-East.

Government forces commanded by MacLeod of MacLeod and Munro of Culcairn had been quartered along Inverurie's main street and in scattered encampments in nearby fields. They were taken by surprise in a dusk raid mounted by Jacobite contingents under the leadership of Lord Lewis Gordon and Gordon of Avochie, and within 20 minutes Inverurie was in rebel hands. A handful of men died on both sides, the rebels also taking a number of prisoners who had been unable to escape.The encounter had no effect, however, on the outcome of Prince Charles Edward Stewart's forlorn bid for the throne.

That had been all of 50 years ago. In more recent days, the horrors of the French Revolution had been finally brought to an end but the threat of an invasion by Bonaparte had been underlined by a Paris edict authorising the seizure of any neutral vessels transporting British goods.

Fear gripped those who lived near the Scottish coast, not least the folk who relied upon the little port of Newburgh as an outlet for their grain and woven goods and, for those who had made a start to improving their farms, incoming supplies of timber, lime and bones for use on the land. The wide dune-fringed river mouth at Newburgh would make an ideal landfall for invading French forces.

The invasion did not come, yet life would never be the same again for the folk of Tarves and other backward parishes who had resisted change during most of the 18th century. A *Society of Improvers in the Knowledge of Agriculture* had been founded in Edinburgh as early as 1723, with 29 Aberdeenshire men among its members. In 1730 a *Small Society of Farmers in Buchan* was established and in 1784 was born the *Highland Society*, which in time became the *Royal Highland and Agricultural Society of Scotland.*

Nevertheless, according to William Alexander, that prodigious commentator on North-East farming affairs, little progress was made until the closing years of the 18th century. He wrote:

> "The body of tenants and sub-tenants continued to live on in their old meagre way; a good deal of the land was in run-rig, with a common fold for the cattle; there was no rotation of crops, cereals, oats and bere or barley being grown continuously till the land was exhausted and full of weeds, and would yield no more, when it was allowed to run out and lie fallow for some years. In winter, when cattle could not be herded out, they were fed almost wholly on oat straw; and when the winter happened to be long and severe, the poor starveling animals were reduced to skin and bone. The ordinary dietary of the people, moreover, was what the poorest labourer in town or country would not submit to now."

The sweeping changes which transformed the countryside were, from their inception, driven by the landed proprietors. The tenants, as described by Alexander, were universally poor in means and inefficient as cultivators. They were generally averse to change in their old and outworn modes of husbandry and, in many cases, not only slow to adopt improvements but stoutly opposed to those forced upon them.

Once change became inevitable, however, these dour men set to with a gusto unmatched in living memory. During much of the 19th century, in fact, the drive behind improvement became so far devolved that the tenants either directly carried out, or met the charges of carrying out the greater part of the improvements effected.

No-one was closer to the revolution in the Tarves countryside than its much-revered minister, the Rev Francis Knox, himself the son of a farming dynasty at Little Ythsie. Reporting in the *Statistical Account of Scotland* in 1842, he wrote:

> "The improvements introduced by the landowners towards the conclusion of the last century were at first but slowly adopted by the tenantry. Depressed by bad seasons, and deficient in capital, they had neither the courage nor the means to attempt expensive innovations. The rise, however, in the price of agricultural produce which succeeded the breaking out of war between this country and France, by increasing the capital of the farmers, enabled them to take

advantage of the more decided and valuable improvements. Draining, enclosing, a better system of cropping, superior agricultural implements, and application of the great stimulant, lime, became general, and from this period the progress of improvement was extremely rapid. "

Knox reported that besides the profits realised by the new system of husbandry, an additional stimulus was given to the exertions of the tenantry by the abolition of thirlage to particular mills, and of the pernicious practice of taking 'grassums' (bribes) on the renewal of leases, as well as the letting of farms over 19-year periods on favourable terms for the occupiers. Through the industry of the tenantry and encouragement given by the landlords, the parish became highly cultivated and productive, he said.

The potato, discovered in the 16th century, began to be cultivated on a grand scale. Farmers sought means of cutting costs and boosting efficiency to wrest the maximum from their land. To new entrepreneurs, the land became a vehicle for wealth generation, and profit-making methods were devised to secure that end. A flood of new ideas was applied to farming, among them the use of root crops like turnips and swedes, which could be grown to feed livestock during winter months. The turnip also helped to break up the land during the savage Scottish winter. New concepts about scientific stock-breeding were also appearing and farmers embarked on experiments with different strains of animals.

The enclosure movement and scientifically-based rotation of land use in different years also encouraged extensive improvements in the form of hedging, drystone dykes and drainage. This made for better use of the soil, boosting its fertility and restoring it more rapidly. New machinery like Tull's seed drill, together with improved hoeing, ploughing, reaping and threshing devices also enhanced land use. It was the more prosperous farmers, of course, who benefited most from the new technology.

The land, according to Knox, was worked on five, six or seven year courses, depending on its quality. In the five years course, turnips were followed by barley or oats the second year, pasture or hay the third, pasture the fourth and oats the fifth. In the six years course, the land was pastured three years, and in the seven years course two crops of oats were taken after three of pasture. Crofts and small possessions were generally worked on the five years system, the more extensive farms on six or seven years.

Turnip sowing, mostly of the yellow kind, started at the end of May, with about one-fifth of all the arable land under turnips at any one time. Potatoes were at first cultivated solely for consumption by the inhabitants until it was realised how lucrative were the town markets. Drill husbandry was universally employed and manure consisted of farmyard dung and crushed bones. Some farms used sheep to eat part of the turnip crop off the ground but most was consumed in the stalls of the farmsteads because of the profits to be made from raising cattle.

Grain crops were cut with what was known as the Aberdeenshire scythe. The scythe, fitted with a cradle, was widely used, performing more work than the common sickle with greater ease to the labourer, it was said. It also lifted more straw off the ground, getting it ready sooner for the stackyard. Threshing machines started to appear on the principal farms, some powered by water, others by horses. A steam one was in operation at Shethin.

Long-horned Aberdeenshire cattle were being succeeded by the polled breed of Buchan, latterly crossed by imports from Galloway. In the 1840s, these fetched upwards of £25 a head when three years old, sold either to fleshers in Aberdeen or consigned to London's Smithfield Market by steamers sailing from Aberdeen.

The land was largely worked by horses. In plough and harrow they were yoked in pairs, though singly in carts. Domestic poultry were reared on every croft, mainly for market. Though scarcely an El Dorado, it was altogether a more benign living than that endured by the early Tarvesians.

Knox's intimate review of the farming scene, of which his family had been a part for many generations, is an invaluable source for those who wish to understand how everlasting change came to the landscape and to the lives of those living within it. Recalling the season's round, he wrote:

"As the turnips are cleared off, the land is ploughed, if possible in dry weather, and in the following Spring is sown chiefly with oats, though a portion of the best of it is commonly reserved for barley or bear, the latter being in most cases preferred on account of its superior earliness. Little more hay is cut than is necessary for the horses kept on the farms. The grain produced is of excellent quality, bear and barley weighing in good seasons from 52 pounds to 56 pounds, and oats from 40 pounds to 45 pounds per imperial bushel. Most of the pasture is rich, white or Dutch clover being indigenous on the drier soils. Thrashing machines have long been in general use on the principal farms, some of them being moved by water, and some by horses. Indeed, where water can conveniently be obtained, they are now to be seen here on possessions of as small extent as thirty acres. Some years ago, Mr Hay erected one on his farm at Shethin, of which steam is the moving power, and it continues to answer his utmost expectation.

"Bones were first used as a manure in this parish in 1827. They have added much to the fertility of the soil. From 8000 to 10,000 bushels are now laid on annually. The latest improvement introduced is furrow-draining, which promises to effect as great an amelioration on the heavy land as bones have done on the lighter soils. Very few sheep are kept, except on the Earl of Aberdeen's home-farm, part of which is situated in Tarves. Some swine are reared, regarded as advantageous merely for eating up garbage which would otherwise be lost. The usual sorts of domestic poultry are to be found in our barnyards, but they are reared for the supply of the home larder, and never for sale."

"Most of the farmhouses and steadings on the Earl of Aberdeen's estates have lately been substantially rebuilt with stone and lime, and covered with slate. The slates, and some assistance in wood, are afforded by the proprietor; the rest is done at the expense of the tenants - stones, however, being everywhere so plentiful, that they are to be had for the quarrying and carriage. The principal farms are enclosed with stone dikes, the material in most places being found in abundance upon the land. There are some thriving thorn hedges, and had it not been for the superfluity of stones, such enclosures would have been far more common than they are, and would have added much to the shelter and beauty of the district. Indeed, we can suggest no greater improvement for the appearance of the parish than their extension. On the whole, Tarves is slenderly wooded, which is to be regretted, as respects both utility and beauty."

Farm and domestic servants were engaged by the half-year at feeing markets held throughout the countryside. Ploughmen were paid between £ 6 and £ 8 the half year, boys and labourers from £ 3 to £ 6. Some of the married men had houses from the farmers and a 'cow's keep' (or one and a half pints of milk per day), with a patch of ground on which to grow vegetables, the remainder of the wages being paid in money, meal and potatoes. In gardens, the raspberry, gooseberry, blackcurrant and strawberry were produced in abundance.

Many of the jobbers, ditchers and day-labourers rented small crofts and when the weather permitted were in full employment at between 10s and 12s a week. Masons, carpenters and other artisans earned between 2s 6d and 3s a day. Women engaged by the half-year received, besides board, between £ 1. 10s and £ 2 in winter and £ 3 to £ 3. 10s during summer. At hoeing time they earned 8d a day, plus their food, and about £ 2 for a whole harvest when women's work was to secure the corn into sheaves.

The food of the labouring classes comprised oatcakes, oatmeal, cabbages, kail, turnips, potatoes, cheese and other dairy products. Home-brewed beer was allowed them during harvest and at other times when the work was severe. At the time of Knox's commentary - 1842 - the parish was served by good turnpike roads linking it with the ports of Aberdeen and Newburgh and markets at Oldmeldrum and Inverurie.Within its own boundaries, Tarves had several ancient markets or fairs for horses, cattle and grain, all of them well patronised. Fewer hands were employed in agriculture as improved methods of working and the drive for efficiency - now in full bloom - pushed labourers into the towns to seek an alternative living. The parish population had fallen from 2346 in 1755 to under 1800 by the turn of the century and it was well into the 19th century before it regained its former level. In the wider world, Faraday had created an electric motor, Trafalgar and Waterloo had been fought and won, Macintosh had fashioned a new type of raincoat and Lord Byron was a Greek hero. Sir Walter Scott was scaling the literary heights, the first wagon train had crossed the Rockies and George Stephenson had opened the world's first passenger railway between Stockton and Darlington.

In his *Journals* in 1838, Lord Cockburn wrote:

> "I know of no part of Scotland so much and so visibly improved within thirty years as Aberdeenshire. At the beginning of that time the country between Keith and Stonehaven was little else than a hopeless region of stones; there was nothing but large white stones, of from half a ton to ten tons weight, to be seen. A stranger to the character of the people would have supposed that despair would have held back their hands from ever attempting to remove them. However, they began, and year after year have been going on, making dykes and drains and filling up holes with these materials till at last they have created a country which, when the rain happens to cease and the sun shines, is really very endurable."

Knox, too, commented on the boulder-strewn landscape:

> "The rocks are all of the primitive order, and, with the exception of some limestone, consist entirely of gneiss and granite alternating with each other. These rocks are, in some places, buried to a great depth beneath diluvial deposits, in others they rise above the surface. Immense boulders of blue sienite were, at one period, scattered over the soil. The farmers, who at great expense of labour and gunpowder, have removed most of those that obstructed the plough, term them 'heathens', probably from the incessant contest they and their forefathers have waged with them from time immemorial."

Improvements in Scottish agriculture after 1760 restricted the area devoted to cattle grazing and forced the business of cattle rearing further north. The most profound effect of this was experienced in the North-East where a new mode of farming based on stock raising grew alongside and eventually surpassed in cost-effectiveness the traditional forms of arable farming. Demand from the South grew for the better quality cattle which Aberdeenshire was producing. By the end of the 18th century the beasts driven south from Aikey fair alone exceeded six thousand.

Gradually, new turnpike roads limited the freedom of passage of these great herds and the freedom of wayside grazing also became severely restricted. By 1836 the number of cattle passing through Tarves from Aikey Fair had dropped to about one-third of those counted on the corresponding day at the beginning of the century. The days of the great communal drives over Scotland's drove roads, with all the dust, clamour and excrement they left in their wake, were fast drawing to a close.

By early in the 19th century much of the cattle export trade had switched to steamer transit out of Aberdeen. In the 20 years to 1849, more than 150,000 head worth £3 million were exported from Aberdeen, and in 1849, alone, 7800 cattle and almost 700 tons of meat were loaded at the harbour. The first railway consignments went south in the following year, and the first weekly market was opened at the railway cattle station in Aberdeen in 1852.

The prosperity generated by the 'Improvers' in the North-East was not without its perils for the innocent and the unwary. That doyen of 19th century farming commentators, William Alexander, noted the eagerness of tenants to get on with improvements and their readiness to offer high rents in so doing. In that, however, there lurked danger, he said - and disaster for some. While many landed proprietors discharged their duty towards the land and their tenants in a spirited, equitable and even generous manner, tenants often went blindly on under the exhilaration of rising prices, to bite off more than they could chew. They often bound themselves for too much in rent and other commitments, bearing in mind their limited tenure and the one-sided nature of the statute law affecting landlord and tenant.

Alexander wrote:

> "The natural result was that he often did not obtain the just return to which his enterprise and active exertions entitled him. Our tenant farmers are, as a class, much poorer than they ought to have been. In the case of the landlords, the temptation to take the highest rents offered was undoubtedly great - not to say, irresistible. So, also, was the temptation to spend too freely personally."

Though Tarvesians did not suffer the worst excesses of the landlords, there was, nevertheless, a heavy stacking of the odds against the crofter and small farmer. It was this section of the community which, in the event, bore the heaviest cost of improvements effected in the Formartine countryside.

Alexander:

> "In all this the lairds had but a limited share. In many cases, where forty or fifty years ago they professed to assist the tenants by enabling them to participate in Government loans, they took care amply to recoup themselves by charging six per cent, or more, against the tenants for money for which they paid only three or three-and-a-half per cent. The loan, in short, was over three-fourths paid by the tenant during his nineteen-year lease; and then, at the end of the lease the laird felt no shame in adding to his exhorbitant greed by exacting as much of an increased rent as could be got by virtually exposing the tenant's improvements to public competition."

Nor did the danger to the smallholder's livelihood end there. Alexander highlighted another iniquitous practice lying in wait for the unwary:

> "No sooner was the lease out than they were apt to fall a prey to some grasping large farmer, if their little holdings were of a nature to tempt his cupidity. Or perhaps the laird or his factor concluded that it would be less trouble in management, and save cost in keeping up buildings, to extinguish the croft and let its occupants go elsewhere."

In the scramble, the crofter could, and often did, become a victim of the larger farmer. The well-heeled farmer knew that the croft contained soil which, having been well looked after, could be made to produce abundant crops, and seldom hesitated about playing his role in the eviction process.

Alexander commented:

> "The crofter, it might be, had spent the best part of his life in the reclamation of the little spot on the hillside where he had been allowed to make his home, and where he had done his honest part laboriously as cultivator, making a bare living without being able to put past anything for a rainy day, and in the expectation that his nest would not be disturbed. Yet, the proprietor, in his need or his greed, could not afford to give heed to sentimental associations, nor even to the claims of justice and fair dealing. If an advanced rent could be got, and no legal obstacle intervened, the crofter had to go to the wall. It was in vain to appeal to abstract principles of justice and equity, or to urge that property had its obligations as well as its rights; for until very recently the 'rights', so-called, of landed property were regarded with an almost superstitious reverence by the very class who had most reason to complain of their abuse."

This was a 'clearance' of a kind, one of the objectives being to ensure that old and worn-out crofters did not become a burden on the parish, while the laird had a better chance of getting his rent from the affluent farmer:

> "It is the opinion of those well qualified to speak that while a change from the old state of things had become absolutely necessary, the point where the proprietors, even the best of them, were in error was in practically confiscating the tenant's improvements by raising the rent whenever the lease expired."

It would be naive to believe that the Tarves landscape was unblemished by these practices, though it has to be said that under successive Earls of Aberdeen, the Haddo estate dealt generously with its tenants, large and small. This benevolence was repaid during the depression years of the 20th century when rent arrears spiralled in neighbouring rack-rented estates, while those on Haddo territory remained negligible.

Another commentator of the time wrote:

> "The keen competition for smallholdings arises, we believe, more from a desire in the heart to have a settled home than a sound calculation as to value. The experience of some wet and dreary term day in flitting the wife and bairns with their furniture and bedding is not a pleasant one, and undoubtedly makes many a man keen for a settled home at any price."

The hopelessness of the humble man's quest is evocatively recalled by Tarves-born David Kerr Cameron in his absorbing folk history of the Scottish farm touns, *The Ballad and the Plough* :

> "For the cottar man there was a way of escape from the tyranny of the grieve's (overseer's) watch: into a croft, one of those holdings that fretted the landscape between the fields of the big farm touns and nestled on the high hillsides, in the odd uninhabitable corners and on the inhospitable edge of the moor. They looked at times as though they had been thrust there, willy-nilly, by the land-greed of the bigger places, and that was about what happened.

> "They saw in the croft a chance to put their own foot tentatively on the farming ladder. And when they did so, these men took to crofting like a fever in the blood. It gripped them like women or whisky, and in spite of the damages of addiction they could see all around them. They believed they had the answer, that they could make sense of that impossible dream: sovereignty over a small patch of land with a self-sufficiency in body and soul."

For some, it was a forlorn hope in a heartbreak landscape, a pipe-dream in a lost land.

> "The result eventually was disillusionment. Years of dour crofting endurance honed them to the temper of hard steel and in time, as some solace for their frustration, they turned either to the kirk or whisky bottle, and whiles to both. In the dark week of crofting despair, it was a long time from Sabbath to Sabbath. The stark truth of it is that there was no independence, only a greater tyranny than the grieve ever imposed, from within and without."

No chronicler of William Alexander's time expressed as deep an appreciation as his of the small man's contribution to the agrarian economy of Aberdeenshire. Writing at the close of the 19th century, he said:

> "To them it is due that many hundreds of acres of barren moor have been brought under the plough within the last fifty or sixty years; and from his class, trained up in habits of industry, thrift and self-reliance, there have continued to go forth into various walks of life men and women fitted to act well their part under any circumstances: the main cause of regret being without doubt that in such limited proportion of numbers have these men and women been retained in connection with the soil as settled labourers, cottars, crofters and farmers, from the smallest tenant upwards."

In the following chapter, *Animal Farms*, Arthur Watson of Tarves - a member of the Tarves Heritage Project - reflects on another aspect of the Tarves farming scene - its rise to fame as a prime breeding ground for the Shorthorn and Aberdeen-Angus.

A Vanished Era

The mid-afternoon 'piece' was a welcome feature of the 'hairst' - as here (above) at Collynie during the 1920s.

A turn-of-the-century harvest in progress at Newseat of Tolquhon.

Pictures -THP

All Dressed Up

The 'power-houses' of the farming scene (above) - four magnificent Clydesdales in their finery. Flower-bedecked and harness gleaming (below) - a decorated horse and cart ready for a family seaside outing or competition at the local fair.

Pictures - THP

Work Horses

Clydesdales giving their all at a ploughing match (above), a popular and practical countryside pursuit. Below, docile but powerful, the Clydesdale was the great work-horse of the North-East.

Pictures - THP

Horsepower

The family wares (above) - three pairs of Clydesdale horses, a light horse for the gig and, far left, the bull. Below, a 'loon' and his horse. Waistcoat and nicky-tams were essential wear for the apprentice.

Pictures -THP

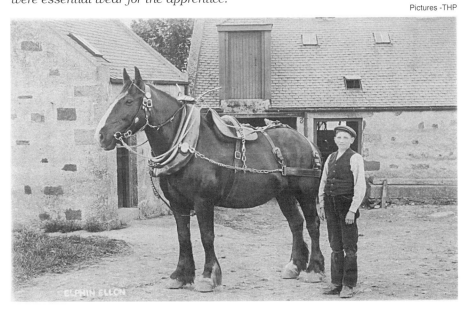

Jog-trot Days

The pace was slower in those jog-trot days. The pony and trap (above) was used by the well-off to get about the countryside. Below, there were no motor cars to bring hazards to this Tarves street 100 years ago. Part of the house was devoted to shoe repairing. An upstairs was added early this century. Next door was a blacksmith's premises. Pictures -THP

*Old-style crofter - the author's grandfather, William Porter, in his
cornfield at the Doulies, Tarves.*

An old-style croft, at Lang Lums, Schivas, long-since gone from the Tarves landscape. The occupant, James Cheyne, in his nineties, was said to have walked five miles to Tarves, and back, to cast his vote in 1895.

Picture -THP

Croft and Cottage

A Tarves croft in the 1890s (above) - the Doulies, near Raitshill, home to the author's great-grandparents, John Porter and Christina Annand, pictured with their youngest daughter Isabella in the 1890s (Picture D.K.Cameron).
Below, W.S. Cummings' cottage bakery, the first in the district, had just been opened when this picture was taken in 1893. The family lived above the shop. In 1993, the firm celebrated its centenary with BS 5750 quality accreditation (Picture - THP).

Faces From Another Time

The Tarves countryside abounded in worthies, some of the wandering kind like 'Beesom Jimmy' (top left) who made and repaired rough all-purpose brooms. Others, like Sandy Hay (top right), and 'Bailie Baron' (bottom right) were locals with idiosyncracies which endeared them to Tarvesians. John Petrie (bottom left) was the 'meenister's man', paid to keep a watch on the ponies and traps of those who came to worship at the parish church.

Pictures - THP

Chapter 17

Animal Farms

by Arthur Watson, Tarves

A S this book was in the final stages of preparation, farmers and the beef industry throughout the United Kingdom were coping with a world-wide ban on British beef exports. The ban was imposed by the European Union following outbreaks of BSE - 'mad cow disease' - but vigorous efforts were being mounted to seek compensation, restore confidence in British beef and have the embargo removed.

Nowhere was the ban felt more keenly than in Aberdeenshire. For the rich cornland that emerged from centuries of back-breaking toil became home, too, to the Shorthorn and the Aberdeen-Angus, symbols of top quality beef in markets the world over. Careful selection and breeding led to the Shorthorn becoming the most influential dual-purpose breed (beef and milk) in the Western World, and the Aberdeen-Angus became the yardstick against which the quality of all other beef cattle was measured.

The two breeds began to scale the heights to fame in the mid 19th century when better communications, improvement in feeding stuffs and a quickening market for fine beef ensured that cattle raising became a highly profitable part of Scottish farming. Instead of breeding lean cattle and driving them to the ancient cattle trysts for fattening elsewhere, farmers concentrated on rearing much fatter cattle for export by train and ship. The two breeds earned world renown and powerfully influenced the development of vast herds, notably in the United States and Argentina. Fortunes were made - and lost. Before the turn of the century a number of Formartine farms exuded the prosperity which Charles 'Hamewith' Murray captured when he wrote about 'Belcanny':

> "Belcanny is foggin' wi' sillar laid by,
> Wi' byres fu' o' feeders and pedigree kye,
> Wi' horse in fine fettle for plough or for harrow,
> An' a' the tools needit fae binder to barrow."

In the van of 19th century Shorthorn pioneers were Captain Barclay of Ury, Stonehaven, Amos Cruickshank of Sittyton, Newmachar, and the first of the famous Tarves breeders, Alexander Hay of Shethin. Hay purchased a Shorthorn bull called *Jerry* in 1827 from a herd in the Lothians. Its progeny showed such remarkable development that Hay's brother, William, who took over the tenancy at Shethin, acquired a number of females of the breed, establishing in 1834 the first Shorthorn herd north of the River Dee.

An excellent cattle judge and a skilled grazier and dealer, Hay introduced structured feeding instead of having the animals driven south as store cattle. He was the first to send animals south by train and by the 1850s the Shethin herd was considered to be the best in Scotland. He was the first in Aberdeenshire to win a prize at the Smithfield Club Show, the animal being a Hereford ox, and he was also the first to send cattle by rail to London. As the major technological advance of its time, the railway exerted a profound influence on the lives of communities, being able to transport people and bulk goods quickly and economically. The Aberdeenshire cattle trade prospered mightily, 45,000 animals passing through the Kittybrewster terminal in Aberdeen, in 1855. That later rose to 177,000 in one year. There was also a huge trade in fish, lime, stone, slates, timber and woollen and paper products.

After William Hay's death in 1854, the herd was taken over by his son-in-law, George Shepherd. By that time, good bulls were fetching high prices, though one for which George paid 200 guineas was responsible for some faulty progeny - "Jist fan ye think ye're a' richt, ye find ye nivver were farrer wrang! " George is reputed to have declared. Disillusioned, he sold the herd in 1863 - 50 cows, 20 two-year-olds, 24 yearling heifers, 17 heifer calves, seven bulls and 18 bull calves. Considering the embryonic nature of the breeding industry at that time, this was a very large herd, even for one of the largest farms in the parish. George Shepherd's son re-started the herd and gained some prominence in the North-East but on his death in 1902 the first herd of Tarves Shorthorns was dispersed for good.

So much for the first herd of Shorthorns. The second half of the 19th century was a time of unprecedented advance in agricultural practices, encouraging farmers to speculate in the sometimes risky craft of specialised stock breeding. Shorthorn herds were established in 1847 at Cairnbrogie by George Marr, and at Uppermill by his brother William S. Marr and son William. S. Marr, Junr. Following the early death of William Marr Junr. in 1904, the Uppermill herd was taken over by his cousin, John Marr, from Cairnbrogie, but dispersed in 1915 when he died.

At the fatstock shows at Birmingham and Smithfield in 1896 the champion Shorthorn was a heifer from James Black, Barthol Chapel. If there was ever a 'red letter' year in the history of the breed, however, it was in 1856 when, according to Isabella Bruce in her *History of Aberdeen Shorthorns*, the foundations were laid at Collynie of "what has been the greatest sire-producing herd of the passing generation and, in some respects, the most influential on any period of Shorthorn history." At the dispersal sale of Jonathan Whitehead's herd at Little Methlick in 1856, William Duthie, Snr., from Collynie, bought three cows at £ 41 each, a high price for females at that time. They were to become the trail-blazers for the greatest herd of all. Collynie's cattle were improvers in the front rank, noted for their size, hardy constitution, natural flesh, milking properties and uniformity of character and quality. In subsequent years, under William Duthie, Junr - the 'Shorthorn King,'- the herd expanded at Tillycairn and Tarves Farm. William was aided and succeeded by his nephew J. Duthie Webster.

At one of the early sales of pure-bred cattle, in 1896, a bull calf from the Collynie herd made 300 guineas, and from that sale 89 of the most highly priced animals went to English buyers, demonstrating that the breeders and cattlemen of Tarves were leading the way in developing and improving the breed.

Annual sales became the fashion, held in early October at Tillycairn and Uppermill. These attracted large numbers of buyers from South America, the USA, Canada, Europe and England. Local farmers and others engaged in agricultural pursuits also flocked to these sales to watch history being made and to gasp at the prices paid for Tarves cattle. A local newspaper report of the 1910 sales reported an imposing array of motor cars which were doubtless of as much interest to Tarvesians as were the animals. Large numbers also came by train to Oldmeldrum and Udny stations and the brakes in which they drove to the sales were ranged around the sale ring to create admirable grandstand viewing. At the 1910 sale, a bull calf made 1050 guineas, a breath-taking figure at the time but one that was to be bettered many times over within the next decade. And how very different all that was from 1891 when, at a Collynie sale, the average per animal was £ 12. 7s 1d, the top price being £ 21, and the total realised £ 160.

War inevitably creates a bonanza for agricultural products, and the First World War was no exception, with stock prices and averages increasing annually. A summit was reached at the Tillycairn sale in 1919 where 600 people spent an astonished 90 minutes in wintry conditions as witnesses to the dispersal of cattle worth more than £ 42,000. And shortly afterwards, at Uppermill, animals worth another £ 10,000 came under the hammer.

From the Collynie herd, the auctioneer disposed of 24 bulls and 15 heifer calves for £40,194, with a world-record price of 5300 guineas achieved for a 10-months-old bull, *Collynie Lavender King*. The purchaser was from Kent. From J. Duthie Webster's herd at Tarves Farm, four bulls and seven heifer calves fetched £ 2,325. The Uppermill sale was also hugely successful, with 10 bulls and nine heifer calves selling for £ 10,631. This included a record 2000 guineas for an eight-months-old heifer bound for Argentina. The total of £ 53,000 realised in one day was quite unprecedented.

A writer of the time commented:

"History was made, which will be recorded and talked of all the world over, wherever Shorthorn cattle are in vogue, and it is the proud boast of Shorthorn men that theirs is the breed upon which the sun never sets."

These fine animals flourished under the top priority treatment accorded them, and there was mustard-keen rivalry among the cattlemen who tended them, for topping the sales was a proud achievement indeed. It was a risky business, too, as James Burr emphasised when disposing of a herd at Mains of Schivas in 1933.

"If you want to lose money, start breeding Shorthorns. If you want
to make money, buy a lorry!"

John Sleigh, Newseat of Tolquhon, established a herd in 1935, which was
dispersed in 1980. He became well known as an exporter of cattle and sheep.

Uppermill, associated with Shorthorns from 1847 to 1915 during the
occupation of the Marr family, extended the lengthy alliance with the arrival in
1916 of James Durno and the long-established herd from Jackstown,
Rothienorman. The herd, which became known as the 'Uppermill Shorthorns',
has attained many distinctions in its 100 years and is the only Shorthorn herd
now remaining in Tarves and North-East Scotland. It is presently owned by
Miss Mary Durno,OBE. All registered breeders are obliged to keep details of all
births with names of sires and dams, and Uppermill's library contains registers
not only of the resident herd but of others from as far back as the early 1800s,
making it an irreplaceable record of the breed.

After the death of William Duthie in 1923, the Collynie herd became the
responsibility of his nephew, J. Duthie Webster. An obituary writer of the time
said this of the 'Shorthorn King':

"William Duthie was outstanding among the men of grit who
succeeded in reaching the highest pinnacles of fame in the
captivating but somewhat elusive industry of cattle breeding."

Following dispersal of the Collynie herd in 1937, the tenancy of Tillycairn went
to James Durno and the Uppermill Shorthorns moved from Uppermill to
Tillycairn, where they have been continuously bred for the past 59 years. Joint
sales with other breeds became centred on Perth and Aberdeen. At Perth in
1956 an Uppermill bull made a record price for the herd of 7100 guineas.

In 1955 there arrived at Cairnbrogie and Smiddyhill the well-known Bapton
herd from Kent belonging to Cecil Moores. It came from Kent by rail, the closed
branch line station at Oldmeldrum being specially re-opened to receive them.
A new arrival, unable to wait for the end of the long rail journey northwards,
was named *Northward Bound*. The herd was dispersed nine years later to a
Canadian buyer.

Diseases like pleuro-pneumonia and rinderpest, capable of wiping out entire
herds, were on-going problems for the early pioneers of the Shorthorn, Hereford
and Aberdeen-Angus breeds. Though ultimately defeated, they were replaced by
another - Foot and Mouth Disease - which appeared in the Tarves district in
1953 and 1960. The Uppermill herd was prevented from attending the annual
Perth sales of pedigree cattle, though a successful sale was staged at Tillycairn
in 1953 under extremely tight security and and strict precautions. The chief
herdsman for the Uppermill Shorthorns at Tillycairn for the past 30 years has
been Robert Minty, who has spent a lifetime with the breed, and taking
meticulous care of the herd book at Uppermill is Mrs Evelyn Gray who, like
many of the farm workers, has been many years with the Durno family.

The spotlight has been taken off the home-bred Shorthorns and the Aberdeen-Angus in recent years by Continental breeds like the Charolais, Limousin and Semmental which produce lean beef more economically, though admittedly of lower quality. Home breeders have been striving to raise bigger-bodied animals to see off the competition. Some success has been reported, with the Shorthorn showing possibilities of re-emerging as a proud leader among world cattle.

William Duthie's last message to the Shorthorn world was addressed to young breeders:

> "Buy the best, breed the best,
> Stick to it,
> Live up to your good cattle:
> Character is more than cash."

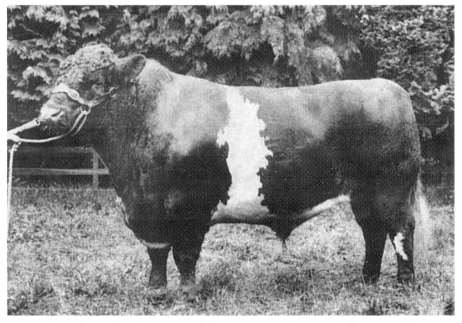

Chapelton Xile, Champion of Champions at the Royal Show in 1987

Picture - Miss Mary Durno

Doddies, Humlies and Aberdeens

Scotland had been rearing and exporting cattle, mostly black and small in build, along the drove roads since before the start of the Agricultural Revolution and the age of the 'Improvers'. As sweeping changes overtook traditional practices, progressive farmers turned their minds to ways of improving local breeds. The Industrial Revolution had wrought social change, a dramatic rise in population and an assured demand for more and better quality beef. Most cattle in the North-east were black, some horned, some without. A hornless variety, known as 'Doddies' was concentrated largely in the county of Angus, while other hornless types, known as 'Buchan Humlies', were congregated mostly in Aberdeenshire. It was to the hornless or 'polled' breeds that developers turned their attention in the late 18th century. Best known among the breeders of those early years were Hugh Watson of Keillor Angus, William McCombie of Tillyfour, Alford, Aberdeenshire, and Sir George McPherson-Grant of Ballindalloch, Banffshire. Their dedication, along with others, to creating an improved breed produced an all-black polled animal which was to become known the world over.

It is a story which has no parallel in cattle breeding history - so local were the origins, so rapid the progress made, and so successful the end-product. A conundrum which dogged breeders for many years focussed on the naming of the breed. Angus and Aberdeenshire were the principal areas of its development but to call it 'Aberdeen' would have offended breeders in Angus, and to name it 'Angus' would have had a similar reception in the more northerly county.

The need to form a Society and establish a Society Herd Book became urgent in the face of growing 'opposition' from the Shorthorn and Hereford breeds which were already set up in this way. In 1879 a large gathering of North-East breeders met at the Royal George Hotel, Perth, following the Highland and Agricultural Society Show, under the chairmanship of the Marquis of Huntly, and after much debate formed the *Polled Cattle Society*. The only local name on the committee was John Grant of Methlick.

The name did not meet with all-round approval, however. Apart from its vagueness, there were also other breeds of polled cattle. The deliberations rumbled on until, in 1907, it was officially changed to the *Aberdeen Angus Society*.

While the Shorthorn was looked upon as a great improver, it was also spoken of in Scotland as 'the great intruder'. Now, there was a truly local product and between them, the two breeds were to dominate the cattle world until well into the second half of the 20th century.

The Society's early committees contained many members of the landed aristocracy - the Marquis of Huntly, Sir George McPherson-Grant, the Marquis of Aberdeen, the Earl of Airlie, and the Hon Charles Carnegie, all of them forward-looking lairds interested in agricultural development within their estates. The new breed did not attain the same prominence in Tarves as did the Shorthorn, though drafts from the Mains of Haddo, Greenmyre and Gateside went forward a century or more ago to the sales of pure-bred cattle in Aberdeen.In more recent times, Mr E. Lee, Boolroad, Tarves, had a herd for a number of years.

The Aberdeen-Angus achieved huge successes at all the top agricultural shows and at Smithfield, as well as at cattle events throughout the world. Until the arrival of artificial insemination some 40 years ago, many farmers kept a bull. Like the Shorthorn breed, the Aberdeen-Angus has suffered competition from the Continent, though today there are 50 million animals world-wide.

Winners

Miss Mary Durno, OBE, and her late father, Dr James Durno, with the 'City of Perth' Perpetual Trophy for the supreme champion bull, which they won six times between 1967 and 1984.

Picture: Miss Mary Durno

Dairy farming, too, has played an important role on the agricultural scene at Tarves. In the distant past, the crofter kept a cow for a milk supply and the occasional making of cheese and butter. The better-off farmer kept two or perhaps three, supplying both the farmhouse and the farm workers.

With the great rise in population during the 19th century, the demand for milk soared and many farmers made dairying their principal business, especially where there was easy access to the railway. By the late 1920s motor transport had brought a new dimension to milk distribution and the industry flourished.

Of the many farms in the Tarves district which specialised in milk production, however, only five are engaged in dairying now - Mains of Cairnbrogie, Cairnbrogie, Uppermill, Oldmill of Schivas and Overton of Keithfield. Scientific applications which greatly increased the volume of milk produced by dairy cattle resulted in a serious milk surplus in the 1970s. Dairy farmers were offered Government compensation to come out of the dairying business. Though this partially resolved the dilemma, 'milk lakes' persisted and in 1984 quotas were introduced to limit the volume of milk for which farmers would be paid.

Other farmers continued to pursue the long-established tradition of rearing and feeding stock. Today, large herds of suckler cows can be seen on one farm, while another may have a substantial number of fattening cattle. A switch from turnips to silage as winter feed started 40 years ago and it is now unusual to come upon a field of turnips, the crop that so radically altered the pattern of agriculture some 150 years ago. Freisian and Holstein cattle have predominated on local dairy farms, though there is a handsome herd of Ayrshires at Oldmill of Schivas.

Sheep have been a common sight in the district for many years, numbers varying from 20 or 30 breeding ewes on smaller farms to ten times that number, with a shepherd, on the larger units. Sam Davidson, Northseat of Auchedly, was a noted breeder and judge of the Border Leicester breed during the early years of this century.

Recent years have seen some farmers specialise in crops like barley, wheat, oil seed rape, potatoes and oats - the latter once the principal cereal in the district. Many farms do not possess cattle at all today - an unthinkable situation 40 years ago. The introduction of subsidies during the Second World War to boost the country's food production has continued in a variety of forms ever since, contributing significantly to the healthy state of our agriculture today. Pig rearing is also undertaken in the parish, with farmers generally providing the buildings and labour and the pig company supplying the animals. Now almost entirely missing from local farmyards is the chatter of chickens or ducks and the once familiar spectacle of the strutting cockerel.

Mechanisation is as advanced on the farms of Tarves as anywhere in Europe. The farmer of earlier days would be thoroughly bemused by the high-tech monsters - wondrous machines, air-conditoned, heated and equipped with radio - which are the modern replacements for the scythe, the binder and the threshing mill.

Clydesdale - Powerhouse of Farming

Tarves was once home to the Clydesdale horse, powerhouse of the countryside for a century and more. The breed originated in the West of Scotland where Shire, Flemish and Dutch stallions were introduced in an endeavour to improve the size and strength of local breeds. It was named after the valley in which it emerged as a distinct breed in the 1830s. A breed society was founded and stud records established in 1878.

The animals' powerful build and their usually quiet disposition earned them the title of 'The Gentle Giants'. Besides their inestimable value to farming, Clydesdales were widely employed in forestry and haulage and were popular exports to Canada, the USA, Australia, New Zealand and other countries with burgeoning agricultural economies.

The breed was part of the folklore of the countryside, too. Sadly, however, many of these fine draught animals succumbed to a disease known as 'grass sickness', thought to have been introduced to this country during and after the First World War by horses imported from the Continent. The disease was invariably fatal. This, and the arrival of the Ferguson tractor and combine, brought inevitability to the disappearance of the Clydesdale from the North-East landscape.

The most prominent breeder at the turn of this century was James Kilpatrick, Craigie Mains, Kilmarnock, whose daughter arrived at Mains of Tolquhon, Tarves, as the wife of Alex Sleigh. Alex was a noted and highly respected Clydesdale breeder for over 40 years, disposing of his last horse in 1966. His father, John R. Sleigh, St John's Wells, Fyvie, and his grandfather had also been among the top breeders of their age.

Alex's daughter-in-law, Mrs Marjorie C. Sleigh of Tarves, told me that Alex had remembered well the golden days when stallions changed hands for upwards of £1000 and the head groom became rich on tips of a sovereign a time. He took over the 250-acre Mains of Tolquhon farm in 1923 at the tender age of 19, and in that very year won his first Clydesdale championship at Turriff Show. Just three years later, he won his first supreme championship at Aberdeen. At that time, and for many years afterwards, he maintained 20 horses in his stables, six of them working on the farm, the others employed in breeding and showing. In the 1930s, however, the district was severely blighted by grass scourge and in a short but disastrous period Alex lost 30 animals.

Between the 1920s and 1950s, Alex owned nine stallions which went out to service at the end of April each year, with a groom attending each animal. The longest-serving groom at Mains of Tolquhon was Doddie Gill, whose widow still resides in Tarves.

Marjorie Sleigh said:

> "He and other single farm workers stayed in the bothy and were fed in the farmhouse of Mains of Tolquhon. Grooms engaged for each stallion at the beginning of the season walked their individual farm districts - Dudwick, Ellon, Udny, Oldmeldrum, Inverurie, Deeside and Fyvie. Service was charged at £ 2. 00, with an additional £ 3. 00 when the mare was proved to be in foal. The groom's fee was 2s 6d."

One of the most celebrated Sleigh stallions, *Loyalist*, won the senior championship at Aberdeen Spring Show in 1942. Another, *Masterstroke*, was champion at the same venue in 1947. Returning in the teeth of a blizzard, with *Masterstroke* in a float, the groom, Maxie Forbes, found the Tolquhon farm road entirely blocked by snowdrifts. It was several anxious and energetic hours later before Maxie managed to bring the great and valuable beast home to its stable The snow was so deep that it reached the belly of the horse and he and the groom had to force a path uphill from the road-end to the farm, a mile away, in wretched weather conditions. Most farmers did not get home at all that day, abandoning their attempts and staying overnight with friends or in city hotels.

The stallion of the storm, *Masterstroke*, was one of Alex Sleigh's all-time favourites. It had won the Isle of Man Premium for him in 1941. A delegation visited Scotland to find a stallion for service on the island and it was another feather in Sleigh's cap when his stallion was selected for the task.

Marjorie Sleigh recalled:

> "At that time, Alex had three pairs of working horses and ten young colts and fillies - a beautiful sight in a lush green field of grass on a Spring day. The groom had to be up before 5 am to feed, muck, groom and exercise each stallion by walking him to the road-end and back every morning, seven days a week, before going to the farmhouse kitchen at 6 am for breakfast of brose, tea, oatcakes and bread."

In 1948, Alex's son Sandy, just 16, was obliged to come home from Edinburgh Academy to start his life with the Clydesdales. His mother, who died during his youth, was Peggy Kilpatrick, daughter of the famous Craigie Mains breeder whose memoirs, *My Seventy Years With Clydesdales*, attracted a wide readership. His dictum was:

> "There is no finality to the breeding of stock. The urge is ever to improve, and it is in the pursuit of that ideal that the real zest of breeding lies."

In the immediate post-Second World War years, Sandy was engaged on farm tours with members of the Tolquhon Stud, equipped with a float which took some of the drudgery out of the pedestrian circuits of old.

Marjorie Sleigh commented:

> "To show off their stallions and to try to book as many mares as possible, the groom would praise his own stallion and miscall another breeder's animal. He would have the mane and tail all tied up with ribbons to show the horse off to the best advantage. Such was the love and dedication that the worker showed his horse.

> "The working horses, male and female, were engaged in all manner of activities on the farm - ploughing, sowing oats and turnips, haymaking and trailing the coles home to the farmyard to build into stacks. They would also do orra work like cleaning ditches. At harvest time, three horses pulled one binder which cut the crop, while the rest of the men did the hard work of stooking the sheaves. The maid would bring out their 'pieces' in the afternoon - hot girdle scones and home-made jam to as many as a dozen men in the field. These teas were always most welcome as the men toiled and perspired all day long. At the end of the year,

the travelling threshing mill came to the farm for two or three days. Neighbouring farmers and workers came to help. They all had to be fed - up to 22 men for lunch in the farm kitchen of tattie soup, oatcakes and tapioca milk pudding, and perhaps the next day they would get mince, tatties and skirlie and semolina pudding."

The most coveted of all trophies in the Clydesdale world was the handsome Cawdor Cup. Alex Sleigh and his son Sandy won it at the Glasgow Stallion Show in 1956 when 110 horses competed. *Tolquhon Windsor*, a 10-month-old colt, was shown by Sandy with accustomed flourish - "beautifully polished bones, and a wealth of silky hair and action" said the Press. His father's right-hand man in stud management, Sandy was unsurpassed in the skills of preparing and handling a show horse. Sadly, he died in his prime.

The father and son team achieved the ultimate - outright ownership of the Cawdor Cup - by winning it in four successive years with different horses at the Glasgow Stallion Show and the Royal Highland Show. John Sleigh had achieved it 40 years earlier and borne it triumphantly back to Fyvie. Today, it has pride of place in the home of his great-grandson, Sandy Sleigh, another Tarves farmer.

A boy and his horse - the late Sandy Sleigh, when a very young boy, with his prize-winning Clydesdale at the Aberdeen Spring Show some 50 years ago.

Picture Mrs Marjorie Sleigh

The Road to Tarves

THE General Wade road building programme in Central Scotland in the mid-18th century did not reach the North-East. Travel was by foot or horse, with wheeled transport almost unknown. For many years, however, Tarves was on the only road linking Aberdeen with Formartine and Buchan. Now known as the Old Aberdeen Road, it left the 14th century Brig o' Balgownie - the first bridge over the River Don - and followed the high ground to the Hill of Tolquhon and down the steep brae to Tarves. Passing down Kirk Brae, it then headed for Raxton and Tanglandford to cross the River Ythan and reach the 13th century Old Abbey of Deer. The monks there are thought to have built the road to give them better communications with the town. Any wheeled vehicles travelling it depended on securing a trace up the steep Tolquhon Hill from a crofter who lived on the hillside and kept a horse for this purpose.

One of the first outcomes of the Turnpike Act of 1795 was a road from Aberdeen to Ellon, completed in 1799, with toll-gates at Balmedie and Ellon. It was 1830, however, before work was completed on the Murcar-Udny-Tarves road which we know today as the B999.Toll-gates were erected at Whitecairns and Pitmedden. By 1831 stage coaches were running between Aberdeen and Tarves, with a change of horses at what is now Udny Station Road. The toll-gates and houses were let by public auction - Whitecairns at £ 98 and Pitmedden at £ 40. Tolls were abolished in 1866.

In 1861, a railway line opened between Aberdeen, Udny and Ellon, making travel easier and popular. It also made a significant impact on the farming community. The line was extended to Peterhead and Fraserburgh, becoming known as the 'Buchan Line.' Branch lines opened later to Cruden Bay and Boddam and between Inverurie and Oldmeldrum. This gave the folk of Tarves access to the railway at three points - Udny, Ellon and Oldmeldrum. Horse buses were soon conveying passengers to the morning train at Udny and meeting the trains at night. The 7th Earl of Aberdeen was a railway enthusiast and in the late 1870s detailed plans were prepared for a branch line from Udny Station to Methlick via Udny Green and Tarves but the proposal foundered.

In the early 1920s, however, a motor bus service was started from Methlick, taking those who worked in Aberdeen into the city on Monday morning and returning with them on Friday night. This service - Kerrs Buses - developed in the inter-war years into a daily one between Aberdeen, Tarves and Methlick and heralded the death knell of the train. Passenger trains on the Buchan Line were withdrawn in 1965, though the freight service survived until 1979 when it, too, closed. Today, Tarves is very well served by the bus, with 14 daily services to Aberdeen and 15 from the city, as well as a limited service to Ellon. Today, as a reminder of why ancient travellers kept to the upland ways, there is recurrent flooding in the low-lying fields on either side of the road between Ythsie and Dinneswood. Melting winter snow, often up to a metre in depth, creates lakes which serve as a magnet to swans, ducks and other aquatic birds.

AW

Chapter 18

Country Claik

WINTER'S blast in 1894-95 besieged the countryside for three months. Roads around Tarves, especially those with high hedges, were cleared time after time, only to be filled to the brim once more by renewed storms. The barometer registered 49 degrees of frost in some districts and the village's water pumps had to be thawed out every morning for several weeks.

Just like today, the weather was a recurring topic in the 'claik'* of the countryside during that unusually dark and dismal winter. Stark portraits of Tarves then and in succeeding winters were painted in the columns of the *Tarves Letter*, a parish leaflet published by Duthie Webster, a leading light in the Tarves Literary Society. That august organisation, formed in 1888, was a debating society before flourishing, over a period of 60 years, as a literary group whose reputation extended well beyond the confines of the parish.

The organisation was a natural development of the Tarves Mutual Improvement Society, founded in 1865, which had as its principal objective promotion of the moral and intellectual improvement of its members. In its original form, meetings were held on alternate Tuesday evenings for the discussion of questions, the reading of essays or other subjects approved by a majority of members. There was an entry fee of 6d and a quarterly subscription of 3d. Members took turns in introducing subjects, intimating these for approval a fortnight in advance. Half-an-hour was allowed to deliver an essay, 20 minutes for a reading. Theological subjects were banned. In notes on privacy and good manners, the Society's prospectus stated:

> "Freedom of speech is allowed in discussion, but in order to give confidence to members there shall be no comparison of merits in the meetings, or anything permitted to transpire outside.

> "Should any member introduce offensive personal illusions during the discussion, it shall be the duty of the chairman to demand an apology; and should any member refuse to make such concession, he shall be liable to immediate expulsion."

claik - gossip, talk

In an age of change and improvement everywhere, the Society grew by leaps and bounds, and by the 1890s had 240 members on its roll - more than one-fifth of the adult population. The weather dominated its March 1895 newsletter:

> "We have still a few with us who can remember the much talked-about storm of '38. Mr William Duncan, Boghouse, remembers in that year harrowing snow in the middle of April to assist its departure from the village lands. The present storm began about Christmas and is still with us."

One wonders how in those dark days and bitterly cold nights some of Duncan's cronies even contrived to survive - 'Old Garland', for instance, living in a dilapidated thatched house on the hill-top at Tolquhon. Though the roof was virtually gone, the octogenarian had neither the funds nor the vigour to repair it. In order to at least keep dry, he had resorted to thatching his box bed! (*Thirty years on, though, in the 1920s, there was at least some light in the darkness - at Mill of Ythsie, 'Old Nauchty' had taken to making electricity with his mill wheel and had installed an electric light in his box bed! The light was extinguished when the wheel stopped. 'Nauchty' achieved this by pulling a string at his back door, but the impetus of the wheel was sufficient to keep the light going until 'Nauchty' was back in bed!*). How 'Old Garland' would have envied him!

During the 1894-95 winter, the village roadman, Alexander Macdonald, was said to have endured "a sore time trying to educate the farmers as to their duty about clearing the roads." The storm has been notable, not so much for the quantity of snow but for high winds and severe frosts.

The parish newsletter commented:

> "The village housewives have had a bad time. They might have done without water but when for days on end they could not see through their frost-bedimmed windows, the winter was felt to be severe indeed. Sledges are the order of the day. All kinds and conditions of them, from a big soap box on runners upwards, jingle merrily along.

> "The mail gig, though late, has been forward every day. The local postmen have gone on their daily rounds with praiseworthy pluck; while supplies of beef and bread have been distributed at the cost of much extra labour and expense. Wild birds suffered badly during the hard weather and many must have died.

> "Farm work was well forward at the year's end, but these ten weeks have kept things at a standstill. Few, even of the best prepared farmers, had store of turnips sufficient to outstand (sic) the storm, and turnips have been procured from the snow-clad and frost-bound fields with great difficulty. The quantity obtained under these circumstances was of necessity small, and the quality inferior. Fattening cattle have made little progress and the price is most disheartening. What a pity the farmer cannot pay his rent in kind instead of money! The Christmas market was a disastrous one - trade bad enough in Aberdeen but still worse in London."

While the winter was at its height - on 22 December 1894 - gales wrought havoc in the Tarves countryside:

> "It has been said that the Devil is the power of the air, and he must have broken loose entirely. About 10 am the hurricane burst upon us in a moment and continued for hours. Destruction in the Haddo House and Gight woods was terrible; and the beautiful avenue of holly trees at Tolquhon Castle will no more afford shade and shelter to straying lovers.One hundred thousand trees are said to have been blown down on the Haddo House estates alone.

> "In some parts the sight is sad indeed, whole areas being strewn with broken and battered trees but lately the pride and pleasure of all passers."

Sixty years later, when new growth had erased the damage of the 1894 winter, another great gale was to devastate the Tarves landscape on 31 January 1953.

In spite of it all, the social round of the 90s did not judder to a halt. The ploughmen's ball in December was rather short of women but the Bronie Lodge of Oddfellows' concert and ball was as crowded as usual. "Why call themselves odd," the newsletter asked, "when so far as we know most of these gentlemen are neither odd nor single!"

The annual Volunteer Party in February was as successful as ever, though attendance was down. Large numbers braved the icy blast to hear Literary Society lectures on the 'Army, Navy and Volunteers' by Messrs A. Coutts, Balgove, A.D. Massie, Tarves, and Lt. Sam Davidson, Auchedly; on 'Japan' by James Hay, Junr, Little Ythsie; on 'Music and Art' by Miss Davidson, Mains of Cairnbrogie, and Miss K. Strachan, Crichie. Sir Arthur Grant, from the great Monymusk family of farm improvers, lectured on 'China - with views.'

The newsletter was a fount of information about local folk. Miss Jeannie Shepherd, daughter of Ebenezer Shepherd, Keithfield, was reported as having come first of 700 in a national examination for telegraph clerks - the fourth local girl to have entered the Civil Service. The other three were from the Litlejohn family at Hardford, though one of them later quit to become a missionary. Several Tarvesians were reported to be doing excellent missionary work thousands of miles from home.

Indeed,there was news of parishioners from all over the globe:

> "Rapid means of communication have made the world small, and with such a Free Library as ours every inhabitant of Tarves can see and know the world from his own fireside. The word Scots means wanderers, and our national character does not belie the name. Sons and daughters of Tarves are to be found on every continent of the world. Our sympathies are world-wide."

Road conditions in the district were lambasted in the next issue :

> "The roads go from bad to worse and it is manifest that the law
> which allows unlimited traction traffic on the roads without charge
> must soon be altered. Light railways through such a district would
> do much to relieve the roads."

Extra taxation would have been highly unpopular, for the newsletter lamented:

> "Times are bad and taxes are already high. Tenants pay 1s 1d
> per £ for Parochial and County Council rates, and this is exclusive
> of special rates such as the Tarves water and drainage at 11d. The
> heaviest items of these taxes are the school rate at 8d; road rate
> 8d; and the poor rate eight pence halfpenny."

The £ 562 produced by the poor rate supported 43 paupers, eight of whom were
kept in the Combination Poorhouse at Maud - "a capitally managed institution
where the food, accommodation and attendance is all that could be desired."
This rosy description of conditions at the poorhouse is barely digestible today.
Hundreds who eked out a hand-to-mouth existence in that stern landscape had
lived in perpetual fear of "ending up in the poorhouse." But the Parochial Board
which managed the affairs of the poor consisted largely of well-to-do farmers,
with the schoolmaster as clerk. The business finished - and it was generally
hurried through - they adjourned as a body to the Inn for supper, followed by a
hot water and whisky punch.

It was known throughout the parish that many of the members went home
drunk from these comfortable soirees. After one such gathering, Morrison of
Hattonslap was driving home, much the worse of wear, when, at Uppermill, he
crashed into a phaeton driven by Argo of Braeside, a decent elder of Craigdam
Church. There was a terrible smash, for which Morrison was widely blamed.
Next morning, however, when the mishap was reported in the village, another
elder of Craigdam, local shoemaker Charlie Burr took a different view. "Braesie
(fellow elder Argo) had nae business to be on the road on a Board nicht!" he
said. That was a night, the souter added, when all decent citizens should keep
indoors.

The newsletter had been launched in the Spring of 1894. This was how it
described the village at that time:

> "The village itself changes little. It is still a place of a single street
> running East and West with the Square, formerly the village green,
> in the middle. Within the past 50 years some new houses have been
> built - the inn, the shop and house of A. Duthie & Co., Mrs
> Lumsden's shop, the doctor's house, the hospital, the bank house
> and Melvin Public Hall."

Though the railway had not reached Tarves - and never would - communications
with the outside world were well developed by this time. On weekdays, Morrison's
horse-bus connected at Udny with the morning train to Aberdeen and returned
to meet the 4. 50 service from the city in the afternoon. French, the haulier, ran
a weekday service to Aberdeen and the mail gig operated seven days a week.

The newsletter added:

> "He is a vera sma' crofter in these times that doesn'a keep a bit
> shaltie, and those of us belonging to the landless legion have still our
> legs, not to speak of bicycles.

> "We have two mails a day, the morning one being delivered by three
> runners all over the parish. A telegraph office was opened here in
> September and has done so well that the guarantee of £ 25 is not
> likely to be required.

> "This year, at the cost of £ 1000, a splendid drainage and water
> supply system with an irrigation farm has been provided for the
> village by the county council. This means an annual charge of 2s per
> £1 of rental for 50 years, of which, however, the Earl of Aberdeen has
> kindly consented to pay three-quarters. The promoters of the scheme
> had evidently ambitious expectations as to the expansion of Tarves
> in the future."

Tarves was swept by diptheria during the winter of 1896 and several deaths
were reported. School attendances fell by two-thirds and the school closed
during February. The epidemic gave impetus, however, to reform of the village's
drainage and sanitary arrangements as well as encouraging improvement of
other aspects of its appearance. The *Tarves Letter* reported:

> "The old, though picturesque thatched cottages are gone but they
> have made way for a wide and commanding entrance, which opens
> up to our view the Post and Telegraph Office and the handsome
> Public School buildings. The ground where the old houses stood
> has been planted with trees and neatly fenced, where, some day,
> we look forward to seeing a thriving, well-kept hawthorn hedge.

> "The Churchyard walls will soon also be covered with ivy. To make
> the village a little more romantic-looking, we might even aspire to a
> green to surround the new ornamental wooden pumps. But we do
> live in an age when only that which is useful and not beautiful is
> tolerated. All the houses facing the street have now a neat, tidy
> appearance, and not only have they a fair front, but the back
> premises are getting into better order.

> "Important and very beneficial alterations on the sites of the offices
> which are attached to many of the houses on the North side of the
> Square are now in progress, such as the removal of ash-pits and
> pig-styes to a greater distance from the houses, and the opening up
> of a new roadway behind the houses for the access of carts to
> enable these places to be kept clean. One would like to see a little
> more attention by those in authority to cleaning the roads or streets
> of the village. A frequent salutation of 'very dubby' is to be heard in
> place of the usual remark about the weather as one is plunging and
> plodding along the street in inches of mud."

Population drift from the countryside into the city had become pronounced by this time:

> "For single men, the wisdom of this seems doubtful, but for married men with young families, to whom fresh air and cheap food are essential, it seems madness. Yet, on one road leading into Aberdeen, last Whitsunday, over 70 flittings were counted, all making for the city. It was wretched weather, too, for the job.

> "If possible, let us have more crofts and small farms. They may not make money, but they make men."

Noting the long absence of Lord Aberdeen on tour as Governor-General of Canada, the newsletter commented:

> "It is a great honour to be a Governor-General but we'd rather smell the firs of Haddo House than all the pines of Canada."

Such was the esteem in which the heritor and his family were regarded by Tarvesians. The author has dipped again into the nostalgic feature article by Charles Davidson in Aberdeen's *Bon-Accord and Northern Pictorial* (1938)to savour the atmosphere of another occasion when the heritor brought joy to his tenantry. It was a halcyon day for all - the homecoming from honeymoon in June 1878 of the Earl and Countess of Aberdeen. Flags and triumphal arches abounded in the Formartine countryside. According to Davidson:

> "It was a long, patient wait, but at last we saw the dust from the cavalcade of farmers who, numbering several hundreds, escorted the carriage and six, with the smiling bride and bridegroom, to Haddo House. The postillions and scarlet outriders clattered along, slowing down to let us have a good look at the radiant bride, dressed in blue velvet, with her lovely fair hair and bewitching smile. To one at least it seemed as if the Fairy Princess of the books had come to life. And then, on the balcony of the House, amidst clamorous cheers, the charming Countess was presented to the multitude. On that same balcony, many years before, another Earl of Aberdeen, as Prime Minister, had appeared with Queen Victoria, leaning on his arm, when she visited to assure him of her trust in him after the censures of his opponents about the conduct of the Crimean War."

Davidson recounted the lavish entertainment showered on the tenantry at garden parties celebrating the return of the newlyweds :

> "I remember Lord Aberdeen going round and tapping the empty sherry casks and ordering a fresh supply. And one old wifie - fie on her! - I saw opening her capacious umbrella and raking in slices of cake. Fortunately, she was spotted by a footman who seized the umbrella and, holding it over her head, opened it wide to let all the slices fall to the ground. The greedy creature beat a hasty retreat."

When the beautiful chapel at Haddo House was opened, a London organist arrived to officiate. The chapel was filled to overflowing. The organist began with a fluty fugue and a toccata, musical forms unknown to the country folk. Davidson's tale has it that one worthy woman, asked what she thought of it all, said:

> "I couldna unnerstan't ava. It wis jist tooral-oot, tooral-oot tooral-oot toot toot! "

Throughout that landscape, amusements were simple and usually home-made.

Davidson:

> "I remember vividly the card parties that went on for days together at Hogmanay and Yule. The games were *Lant and Loo, Black Peter* and *Catch-the-Ten*, and there were all-night sittings. Since toddy was served at frequent intervals, there was a certain liveliness in the air. About the same time of year, the young fishermen from Collieston, about eleven miles away, came in boorachies round the farmhouses to serenade us with auld-farrant and sometimes far from Godly ballads. I can still see these men - Spanish types, whiskered like the St Kildans of a later period.
>
> "Then there was the yearly family excursion to Collieston - a tedious journey in a boxcart lined with sacks of straw. We took all our provisions with us. St Margaret's Fair in July was held on the Ordhill at Tarves and to it went people from far and near. At one time it rivalled Aikey Fair or St Sairs but gradually dwindled and died away. But what an experience for a boy! The stalls with gingerbread horses and dogs, the sweetie-vendors with their whirligeegies and their soople tams, the horse-coupers, the travelling tinkers, the cheapjacks with all their tricks, the fiddlers, the concertina-players, the neighing of horses, the shouting, the singing, the drinking - especially the drinking. Maudlin embracings, the smell of broth and beef and roasted hens, the grotesque dances of the half-fuddled performers - all this was a picture of , not the douce, canny Scot of tradition, but of the real Mackay. Christ's Kirk on the Green was a marrow to it, and Burns describes another such in the Holy Fair and Holy Willie. And there were some Holy Willies in the neighbourhood, but, as the Yank would say, 'they cut no ice', for we kent them ower weel."

Just as effective as temporary diversions from the daily grind were 'Meal-and-Ale' and 'Harvest Home' gatherings and the dances which followed on earthen barn floors, and the ceilidhs around kitchen fires in winter where each in turn took up the song, or the trampin' of the meal into the enormous meal girnal that had supplied the wants of many a poor fellow-creature in the time of famine.

"At such a time of stress," Davidson wrote," a poor woman came and offered my forebear her wedding-ring for a stone of meal. She went away rejoicing with her meal but her wedding ring still on her finger." Dance-masters toured the district, proceeding from farm-toun to farm-toun, with weekly rendezvous where dancing was taught :

"Thus everyone knew their steps, not like the lounge lizards of the present day who slither languidly around with such an air of refined boredom."

The countryside abounded in characters - the Auld Souter and the Young Souter, for instance. As a child, the Tarves writer sat entranced, on a low wooden stool, watching every step in the process of making or repairing a boot:

"And hearing the Auld Souter telling his awesome tales about ghosts and witches and warlocks, boodies and corpse candles. And all the time of his tale a drop like a stalagmite was gathering at the tip of his nose, I wondering when it would fall. When I told the Young Souter that I would soon be leaving for the Aberdeen Grammar School he said to me on parting that I would be deep in the mysteries of Oxycrotion, Etmology, Swinetax and Prosododdy!"

The age of the simpler, earthier life, was drawing to a close, however. Farm mechanisation, unstable market conditions and population drift transformed the countryside during the early years of the 20th century. Major James Keith of Pitmedden, reporting for the *New Statistical Account* in 1951,wrote:

"The 40s, 50s and 60s of last century were, on the whole, prosperous years for farmers, until cheap corn was imported from America. Prices for home-produced grain declined until in the 90s wheat was sold at £ 1 a quarter, oats being marketed at a still lower level. In the 1930s, oats could be bought at 12s to 15s a quarter whereas today the price is at least four times that amount."

The population of Tarves dropped from 2600 in 1881 to only 1850 in 1950, and the fall at Methlick over the same period was from 2160 to under 1500. In the 1870s, thousands of acres in the Formartine parishes had been reclaimed by farmers using casual labour at the rate of 1s a day plus midday meal. The process also began of farmers purchasing the acres they previously leased from the heritors. Most crofters were blind to the reality that land purchase on this scale posed a serious threat to the continued existence of their tiny plots.

Tarves-born author David Cameron comments:

"If it immured them in the past - divorcing them in the 1920s and 1930s from the machine-modernity of the farmtoun harvests around them and accentuating their loneness in the agricultural landscape - it was a pattern, none the less, that looked back more directly to the ritual harvests of a lost countryside. While the clackety-clack of the mechanical cutter-bar carried to them on the clear air of a fine harvest day the croft men wielded their scythes in their patchwork fields, looking anxiously over their shoulders in case the black clouds were massing behind them and the weather should break before they were done. Maybe they looked, too, at the worn women gathering and binding behind them."

The old crofts were destined to die. They were a collective anachronism in an entrepreneurial landscape. Recalling half-a-century as a major Formartine heritor, Lord Aberdeen, former Governor-General of Canada,who had been created 1st Marquis of Aberdeen and Temair in 1916, had this to say about the crofting crisis in the 1920s:

> "On the one hand it is admitted that the crofters have, in the past, formed in large measure the backbone of the population. On the other hand, there has been a steadily increasing difficulty in placing smallholdings on a satisfactory footing, except when the tenant has also a trade. In that case it is plain sailing; otherwise the question of erecting and maintaining the buildings presents serious difficulty."

The Population of Tarves 1755-1991

Notes: ◆ Accuracy of start year, 1755 (Dr Webster's Survey) is in doubt; ◆ There was no Census in 1941 ; ◆ Population of Scotland in 1801 was 1,608,420, but a century later had risen to 4,472,103; ◆ In 1750 more than half of Scotland's population lived North of the Central Belt, but by 1951 only one-fifth resided there; ◆ Census figures in the early 1930s revealed that 366,486 Scottish-born people were resident in England, 279,765 in Canada and 354,323 in the USA; ◆ In 1996 it was estimated that 1000 people resided in the village of Tarves and 2200 in the parish as a whole - still fewer than in the middle years of last century.

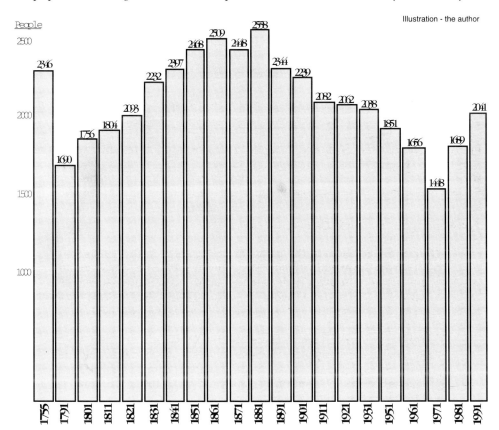

Illustration - the author

Chapter 19

A Terrible Price

THEY went off to war, the fearless young men of Tarves - carefree, jubilant almost - to fight for "Honour, Justice, Truth and Right." Patriotism welled within as they flocked to the recruiting offices. But they were to pay a terrible price. Their innocence would be buried in the mud and blood of Flanders. No fewer than 80 young men from Tarves and Barthol Chapel, most of them not yet 20, laid down their lives in the First World War. Another ten were to perish in the second global conflict. Those who returned from the horrors of the trenches did not find their native heath "a land fit for heroes to live in". It was easy, after the abominations of Mons, the Somme and Ypres, for young men to treat the pledges of politicians with contempt. For their promises were as bare as the apparently mindless future that stretched ahead. Their world had changed for ever. The eternal struggle on the land did not figure in their scheme of things - not for them the ancient touching of forelock to heritor and factor, nor for them the blind adherence to old ways and the prison-like environment of the croft. Behind them lay melancholy; ahead - upheaval and uncertainty.

These are the names of the sons of Tarves and Barthol Chapel who lost their lives in the two conflicts:

TARVES
1914-1918

Cpl Allan Aitken, Tarves; Pte Alex Allan, North Ythsie; Pte John Buchan, Schivas; Pte Francis Campbell, South Ythsie; Pte James Cooper, Mains of Tolquhon; Pte John Duffus, North Ythsie; Pte John Forrest, North Ythsie; Pte Rob Gray, Tarves; Sgt William R. Hay, East Shethin; Pte John Leslie, Raxton; Pte George McPherson, Ordhill; Pte Alf Matthew, Braiklay; Pte James Aitken, North Ythsie.

Pte William Beattie, Uppermill; L/Cpl William Bruce, Braiklay; Sgt Charles Chalmers, Craigies; Pte James Cowie, Schivas; Pte James Ewan, Auquhorthies; Pte Fred Gerrie, Schivas; 2nd Lt Alf C. Hay, South Ythsie; Pte George Jamieson, Haddo House; Chaplain William A. Macleod, Tarves; Pte Alex Marnoch, Nethermill; Cpl George Mearns, Gateside; Pte James Mearns, Gateside; Pte Gordon Dean Munro, Tarves; Pte Hugh Murray, Skilmafilly; 2nd Lt H.A.M. Pringle, Tarves.

Cpl Art Rennie, Auchnieve; Pte Rob Robertson, Auchedly; 2nd Lt John Sutherland, Tarves; Cpl John Taylor, Braiklay; Pte James White, Greenmire; Pte James Moir, Keithfield; Cpl William Morgan, Auquhorthies; Pte Henry Murray, Auquhorthies; Pte George Rae, Tolquhon; Pte George Rennie, Shethin; Pte Rob Robertson, Shethin; Pte John Tait, Keithfield; Pte Gil Tennant, Courtstone.

L/Cpl James Whyte, Tolquhon; Pte James Morrison, Ordhill; Pte Alex Murray, Boghouse; Pte James Mutch, Tolquhon; Pte Andrew Rennie, Hillhead; Pte James Robertson, Shethin; Pte Rob Sangster, Northseat, L/Cpl William Tait, Boolroad; PO William Urquhart, Braeside; Sgt James Wiseman, Tarves.

1939-45

Pte R.D. Fraser, Mains of Tolquhon; Pte W. Hill, Woodhill; Flt/Sgt H.G. Lunan, Tarves; AC1 W.J. Simpson, Keithfield; Sgt P.J. Taylor, Auchedly; Sgt A.J. Taylor, Tarves; Rflm A.W. Watson, Cairnfechil; Pte W. Williamson, North Ythsie; Pte P. Mitchell, Quilquox; Sgt J.H. Watson, Schivas.

BARTHOL CHAPEL
1914-18

Sgt James Andrew; Sgt James Hendry; Cpl George Henderson; L/Cpl John Bruce; L/Cpl William Davie; L/Cpl Robert S. Ross; Sapper Andrew Fraser; Pte Adam Black; Pte George G. Bruce; Pte Robert Coutts; Pte Charles G. Davidson; Pte Andrew Davie; Pte Robert Greig; Pte John Hutcheon.

Pte George Kiloh; Pte James Kiloh; Pte George Laing; Pte John Littlejohn; Pte Charles H. Low; Pte James G. Lumsden; Pte A. Campbell Morrison; Pte Alexander Reid; Pte Archibald Stewart; Pte William G. Stewart; Pte John Taylor; Pte Robert Taylor; Pte Alexander G. Watt.

Ceremony in the rain - the unveiling of Tarves War Memorial, 1922 Picture THP

Village Streets - 1

This was the somewhat empty prospect in Duthie Road at the turn of the century when none of the bungalows on the South side existed. The Melvin Hall is on the near right.   Picture - THP

Strangely bereft of the ubiquitous car - Tarves Square 100 years ago.   Picture-THP

Village Streets -2

This photograph of the Square at Tarves was taken shortly after the installation of
street lamps in 1895   Picture -THP

This photograph of the Eastern exit from Tarves says much about the tranquility
of an age without the motor car.   Picture-THP

Chapter 20

A Public Place

by Arthur Watson, Tarves

TARVES has been well served by its 120-year-old Melvin Public Hall. George Melvin, MA, Schoolmaster for 21 years, died in 1867, leaving the residue of his estate in trust for "some public purpose" in Tarves. William Duthie, one of the trustees, was the driving force in using the bequest to build a public hall which would replace an earlier and much-maligned meeting house nicknamed 'The Temple.'

While attending a social event at Haddo House in the early 1890s, William Duthie encountered Andrew Carnegie, by then an enthusiastic promoter and generous sponsor of libraries. Not one to allow a promising opportunity to pass, the man who would become known as the 'Shorthorn King' informed Carnegie that Tarves had been actively supporting the provisions of the Free Libraries Act since 1883. The philanthropist offered £100 to create a distinctive Library Room, built on the West side of the Melvin Hall and opened in 1892. It quickly acquired some 3000 books and became the envy of the district. At the time of Queen Victoria's Diamond Jubilee in 1897, sufficient public funds were raised to enable a second room, the Queen's Room, to be built on to the East front.

The first minute book for the Melvin Hall is missing, but the second one, covering the years between 1901 and 1959, is housed in the Local History Department of the North-East Library Service at Oldmeldrum. From it we learn that an extension was needed by as early as 1907. That year, substantial repairs to the building cost £267. 4s 5d. Use of the hall at that time for dances or other social functions cost £ 1. Rules issued in 1920 about letting a side room to an ex-servicemen's organisation were quite explicit in prohibiting "strong drink" or "gambling in any form."

After William Duthie's death in 1923, a legacy of £1000 provided the means to create the much-needed extension to the hall. A pitch pine floor was laid. A men's room was built on to one side at the North end and a ladies' room on the other, both equipped with toilets.

A kitchen and store were added on the East side. The cost of these improvements was £ 658.

There are frequent references in the minutes to the problems of heating the hall - a significant concern in a parish so subject to the vagaries of the Scottish climate. Two coal stoves on either side of the hall, whose cement bases are still visible, were not up to the task and were assisted by paraffin stoves from 1928. By 1940, the Grampian Electricity Company was supplying power at 8d per unit. Electric heaters were replaced in 1948 by a water heating system with radiators and a boiler. For some years now, heating has been from overhead installations.

The leasing arrangement with Haddo House was considered inappropriate and a feu charter was drawn up to replace it, the charter costing £ 1 and the legal charges £ 11. 15s 6d. An anonymous donation of £ 500 in 1938 was invested in War Stock, realising a steady income of £ 17. 10s a year.

Proposals for further hall extensions were made in 1945 and 1948 but it appears that neither Government nor local authorities attached much importance to this kind of activity at that period, extracting what they could from the income generated by the Melvin Hall. The accounts for 1945/46 reveal that £ 9. 10s was paid in income tax, £ 4. 15s in property tax, £ 1. 4s 6d as a contribution to 'war damage' and £ 20. 18s 10d in rates. Fortunately there is a more enlightened attitude today towards the value of a good, well-maintained and well-managed hall for the benefit of the community, with grants available for various purposes. In recent years the East side of the hall has been wholly modernised, with a new kitchen, ladies toilets and a small meeting room provided. Standards in the Queen's Room have also been raised.

This year - 1995/96 - has brought a long-awaited extension in the shape of building out a permanent stage at the North end - the end which was extended 70 years ago. At the same time, the hall interior has been refurbished and redecorated, and the floor has been cleaned and re-varnished. A very fine hall door has been fitted and the entrance has been been greatly improved. New regulations covering fire exits, and standards for toilets, lighting and access for the disabled have also been met. Equipment for sound and stage productions completes the task of fitting out the hall for the years ahead. The building is very heavily used by the community and is now ready to welcome another century.

Grants were made available by the Scottish Office, Grampian Region, Gordon District and the National Lottery. The trustees are obliged to meet a share of the costs from hall earnings and fund-raising projects.

The Carnegie Room became surplus to library needs 20 years ago when the NE Library Service started using mobile library vans. The room quickly filled up with junk, but it was adapted and in 1993 opened as the Tarves Heritage Project, a repository for village and parish records, of interest to residents, students and tourists alike, as well as those who seek their roots in Formartine.

Chapter 21

A Brave New World

THE world-wide scattering of folk today whose antecedents are in Tarves is a far cry indeed from the 18th century 'rockings' when the women of the parish assembled on moonlit nights with their rocks and reels to spin wool and flax and to gossip while the young folk danced or played games.

In the days of Empire, Tarvesians went out into a wider and altogether stranger world - as missionaries to China and deepest Africa, as planters to Assam and Ceylon, as tin miners to Bolivia or as pioneers in the great pulp and paper mills on the Canadian lakes. They made their mark in industry and commerce and in theology and the arts at home and abroad. When employment opportunities dried up at home, they became steel-founders and car-makers in the South, and many hitched successful careers to the discovery of oil in the North Sea.

The massacre of a whole generation of young men in the First World War deeply scarred the country parishes of the North-East. However well intentioned, the opening of Haddo House's policies in the glorious summer of 1919 for a succession of picnics and other events to celebrate the return of peace did little to still the sorrow of young widows, mothers and others who had lost loved ones in the mindless carnage in France.

The drift from the land accelerated during the 1930s and resumed after the Second World War as the call for labour was reduced by widespread mechanisation, the continuing enlargement of farms and the gradual demise of the crofts.

Through centuries of back-breaking grind, the soil, imperceptibly but surely, became kindly, and the farms prospered. It had been laboured for in time past by generations of gritty folk who were not destined to savour its solvency. The Psalmist's lines became appropriate in the 20th century countryside:

" He hath made peace in her borders
  and hath filled her with the finest of wheat."

Though fewer earned their living from the land, those who did clearly enjoyed vastly improved conditions and a freedom never known by their forebears. Better education also encouraged young people to enter the professions and to seek their fortunes outside the Formartine parishes. Many young women, preferring commercial training to domestic service, found employment in the towns.

Of the much improved living conditions, a contemporary account had this to say:

> "The hours of labour are now limited and wages are much higher. The farm worker can enjoy more leisure, a better house, greater opportunities for pleasure and wider interests. This is a mixed blessing, especially when young people would rather go to town than spend an evening in the village, for it leads to a growing lack of civic consciousness. The duty of caring for amenities is more and more falling upon the shoulders of the middle-aged, and the days of voluntary labour in any local project seem to have passed."

The Rev Alan J. Fraser, Methlick's minister, writing in 1950, took a somewhat jaundiced view of the influence of the church in the countryside at that time:

> "In these days the church is gradually losing its hold upon the hearts of the people. The necessity for Sunday labour during the years of war has encouraged this trend, for Sunday is becoming the day when the crofter can hire the use of a tractor and devote his attention to his land. With easy modern travel, Sunday is also a day of visiting when city dwellers may invade the country. Except for a few, it may be said that religion means but little to the countryman and his family. There is undoubtedly more happiness in the home but there is less real family life. The old ideal of a self-contained community has disappeared, for people have become more individual and tend to give themselves increasingly to interests outside the parish."

Writing for the *Statistical Account* about the same time, Major James Keith of Pitmedden reported that draining, careful cultivation and manuring had made the land rich and productive. The introduction of wild white clover 30 years earlier had revolutionised agriculture. Pastures became richer and the grazing season was extended by several weeks at each end. Almost 50 per cent more stock was carried, while third-year grass, once considered of little moment, was now highly valued. Many farms, he said, had changed from beef production to dairying, while the rearing of poultry for marketing and egg production had proved a valuable adjunct to the farmer's income. Great developments had taken place in the use of farm machinery, he said. The horse had been largely replaced by the tractor. The self-binder continued in use. On the larger farms, however, it was being replaced by the combine harvester.

He added:

> "A striking change has also taken place in the housing and wages
> of farm servants. The customary wage for a man employed at farm
> work at the beginning of the 19th century was £ 5 per annum;
> now, farm labourers earn more than that in a week, while dairy
> cattlemen's earnings, with perquisites, are £ 8 and sometimes even
> £ 10.

> "There has also been a great reduction in the number of hours
> worked on the farm during the last 20 years, the old-time 60-hour
> week having been replaced by one of 48 hours, with a half-day on
> Saturday and no Sunday duty except by special arrangement."

The *Statistical Account's* reporter at Tarves, the late John R. Allan, revealed that
although leases of 19 years and 14 years were still common, the lease was not
the bond it once had been. Many farms were held from year to year, under a
system of tacit re-location. A tenant, once accepted, could not be put out unless
the landlord proved either bad husbandry on the tenant's part or hardship on
his own.

"No cases have been brought to proof in the parish of Tarves,"he
commented,"which may say something for the husbandry of the tenants and
even more for the kindliness of the lairds."

The five, six or seven-year crop rotation persisted as the best regimen for the
land, with farmers on the better ground using wide variations of the old shifts.
Barley or even wheat could be taken three years in succession in the same field
and with good results.

"The Tarves ploughman has become a mechanic," Allan wrote. "There are still
five Clydesdale horses at Mains of Tolquhon and there are farmers who keep a
horse or a pair because they grew up with them, or for old times' sake, but in
general the parish has gone over to the tractor."

He added:

> "The price of progress is great expense, which Tarves farmers seem
> able to afford. The more expansive Tarves farmers are willing to try
> anything as long as their accountants and their bankers do not
> discourage them overmuch."

At the time of Allan's commentary - the 1950s - the village of Tarves, once a
muddy and stinking place with nothing to redeem its total lack of sanitation and
dearth of amenities, was a thriving community. It boasted a substantial general
merchant company, Adam Duthie & Company Ltd, founded 200 years before,
which, besides supplying all kinds of household goods, enjoyed a large trade in
seeds throughout the county and employed 15 people. The company's
dressmaker - deaf-mute Minnie Duncan - had retired and not been replaced -
"ane auld sang out of the days," he commented, " when the country merchant
sold lengths of coating, trousering, shirting and all the rest."

Allan added: "The country people bought the lengths and the merchant's tailor or dressmaker made them into more or less the shape of the customer."

The village had a butcher, a watchmaker and a large bakery employing 22 people. A boot factory had gone out of business. There was a blacksmith, a cycle mechanic, a motor mechanic, two joiners, a mason and a slater. There was an office of the Clydesdale & North of Scotland Bank - "a very large building fit to house all overdrafts." The church still used the old communion cups - two dated 1618 and the others 1754.

Allan may have had tongue in cheek when he reported:

> "There is no licensed grocer in the parish, which may be taken as a sign of remarkable sobriety among the inhabitants. There are, however, licensed houses in the adjoining parishes, some mighty convenient."

And, for good measure:

> "This is not to be taken that the people of Tarves are prone to inebrity. On the rare occasions when they are inebrious, they are never prone! "

There was a bustling social round in a community of people who "are of an independent mind and are not to be sat on."

The report continued:

> "Farm workers no longer flit every year in the hope (often disappointed) of finding a better master and a better house. Half-yearly engagements and feeing markets, always unsettling things, are all of the past. Wages are high. Employers are of necessity considerate. Men and their families remain in the same place and become established characters. The gain to the community is enormous."

While researching this book, I had the good fortune to encounter respected local historian and retired businessman Arthur Watson. A man who cares passionately about his community, Arthur is deeply involved in endeavours aimed at maintaining and improving parish amenities and preserving the story of its past. He was at the forefront of the drive, for instance, to establish a Tarves Heritage Project which now pulls together the historical threads of the village.

I am indebted to Arthur for an overview of parish affairs covering the past 50 years. He told me:

> "As our troops were demobilised at the end of the Second World War and former farm workers returned to the parish, the Land Army girls were disbanded. Prisoners of war who had worked on the farms were returned to their own countries, though some Polish soldiers chose to stay on. Indeed, the parents of our present

Head Teacher at Tarves were among them. Elderly farm workers who had carried on during the war finally retired, and something resembling pre-war days took shape in the rural districts.

"The high profile of agriculture during the hostilities was regarded by the Government as absolutely vital and, with the continuance of wartime subsidies during the peace, the outlook for life in the countryside looked bright."

Yet, fundamental changes lurked just around the corner. Fordson tractors had first appeared in the mid-30s, with wartime Lease-Lend arrangements bringing a great influx of American machines, as well as combine harvesters, into the Formartine landscape. A large number of Ferguson tractors also reached the North-East during the late 40s - " I can recall seeing a whole trainload standing at Ellon Station," Arthur said.

He added:

"The first model was petrol driven and, with petrol rationing in force until the summer of 1950, it was a means of acquiring petrol coupons for other purposes! Its greatest impact, however, was its introduction of hydraulic power to the agricultural world.

"Then came the home-produced combines. Maitland Mackie at North Ythsie was first in the Tarves area and I recall the arrival of his combine in 1950, along with three of the latest Ford diesel tractors and an Austin Sheerline car. I estimated the lot at about £ 10,000 - a fortune then. By the early 50s the tractor was supreme and the Clydesdale horse, after 150 years of sterling service in the countryside, virtually disappeared from the district, except for a handful of dedicated horse people like Alex Sleigh at Mains of Tolquhon who kept stallions until the 1960s."

As the early 2/3 (now 4/5)-furrow tractor ploughs and a wide range of labour-saving machinery appeared, horsemen were made redundant and another exodus from the land took place. In the search for alternative work, some moved to Aberdeen and other populous centres. Some emigrated and others resorted to acquiring new skills in the steelworks at Corby, 500 miles away - momentous transitions for men whose beings were inexorably bound up with the land. The queue of job seekers in the North-East was also lengthened by declines in shipbuilding, granite-quarrying, fishing and other traditional industries. As a reflection of this worrying time, the population of Tarves had by 1971 plummeted to a lowest-ever 1450. Empty cottar houses littered the landscape, were vandalised, or fell into a state of decay calling for demolition. Some became summer homes for well-off city folk. Except for those with healthy wallets, the countryside was in decline.

An entirely new dimension emerged, however, with the discovery of North Sea Oil in the early 70s. The North-East was thrust into an international spotlight.

All areas within easy commuting distance of Aberdeen were given a new lease of life - Stonehaven, Banchory, the new town of Westhill, Inverurie, Oldmeldrum, Tarves, Pitmedden, Ellon and Balmedie. Sleepy villages and small market towns doubled, even trebled, their rolls of residents during the next 15 years. Tottering cottar houses suddenly became hot property, highly desirable residences to those with cash to provide the mod cons.

It was boom time. The number of houses in Tarves - 66 in 1945 - had soared to 382 by 1996. A 130-house development was begun in 1974. The 1981 Census revealed a rise in population to 1680 persons but by 1991 this had spiralled to 2041 and the demand for housing continued.

Scattered throughout Aberdeenshire were pockets of housing originally created in the 40s and 50s for agricultural workers. In a few short years, however, there were no farm workers to occupy them. Most of the houses have now been sold to their tenants under the Government's right-to-buy scheme.

Despite the renewal which North Sea Oil brought to the North-East, the population of Tarves is still short of what it was 100 years ago. Arthur Watson told me:

> "The number of people deriving a living from the land has plummeted over the past 40 years. I well remember the situation at the three Ythsie farms, all of them dairy establishments, in the 1950s. With eight cottar houses, North Ythsie had over 60 people, including children, some working and living at home, some married, but visiting home whenever possible, and four or five living in the bothy, or chaumer as we call it. The total for the three farms was about 120. Today, none of the farms is in the dairy business and the population is about 30. The workforce for the three farms about 50 years ago was at least 30. Today, I doubt if the number of permanent employees exceeds six."

Arthur described how retail services in the countryside had also declined:

> "The fleet of vans - butcher, baker, grocer, fishman - that served the rural population started to diminish in the 1960s. Few have survived. Many rural shops and post offices have gone, though here in Tarves we still have a general store and post office and a baker and butcher. The motor car and supermarkets in places like Ellon and Inverurie have brought decline to the local retail scene. We don't even have a petrol filling station at Tarves now. I find it all rather sad. Fortunately, though, we do have a comprehensive range of other services to offer - two churches and a youth hall, two schools, a doctors' surgery, a garage, an electrician, joiner/undertaker, mason, blacksmith, taxi and bus services, a football field, two children's playing fields, a multi-purpose all-weather court, a village hall, bowling green, a hotel - the 'Aberdeen Arms'- and a pub - 'The Globe."

The first bank in Tarves, opened in 1850 on the site of today's Post Office, was a branch of the Aberdeen Town & County Bank. The agent in 1861 was William Duthie, aged only 21. The present bank and house were built in 1881. Duthie's nephew, J. Duthie Webster, succeeded him as agent, retiring in 1931. Subsequent managers included James Argo, W. Cameron, W.F. Whimster, George Brown, Ian Craig and William Grant. The Town & County Bank merged with the North of Scotland Bank, which in turn was absorbed by the Clydesdale Bank in 1950. As a result of major reorganisation in 1991/92, the now Australian-owned bank disposed of many local branches, including those at Methlick, Udny and Newburgh, replacing them with a mobile bank van. Tarves retained its banking facility as a sub-office of Ellon.

Arthur Watson is understandably critical of political activities which he fears are robbing the countryside of its character. He helped wage a hard campaign, for instance, against a Boundary Commission decision to transfer a substantial part of the parish to adjoining Methlick to create what the authorities claim will be "greater equality of population."

Arthur:

> "The boundaries go back to tribal times, with only very minor adjustments over the centuries. We were shattered by the proposal and fought it all the way, though in the end we had to concede defeat. Parishes no longer exist or are recognised as they once were. They are merely voting areas for local government purposes."

The Church relinquished some of its local powers with the introduction of the Poor Law Act of 1845 and the subsequent establishment of Parochial Boards. These undertook responsibility for Poor Relief, Public Health and Burial Grounds and, in 1854, the appointment of Parish Registrars to meet new regulations about the recording of births, marriages and deaths. Parish Councils arrived in 1894, the first Tarves one being chaired by William Duthie, the 'Shorthorn King' and comprising seven influential farmers, the Barthol Chapel minister and a representative from the village. "This was not very representative of the community and was, unfortunately, a situation that continued down the years." says Arthur. (Arthur was ultimately elected to represent Tarves on the local Ellon District Council, to find that of its 15 councillors all but two were farmers or local lairds).

Over the years the powers of the Parish Councils were extended, to include the levying of rates, acquisition of buildings for offices and land for recreation grounds, protection of rights of way and the provision of allotments. Local Government Re-organisation in 1974/75 established a two-tier system and a division of powers. The North-East, from Forres to Stonehaven, became Grampian Region. This was, in turn, sub-divided into five areas governed by District Councils, with Tarves in Gordon District.

From April 1996, however, Scotland returned to single-tier authorities, with Gordon District becoming a part of the larger area known as Aberdeenshire.

Arthur:

> "The old concept of a parish like Tarves standing on its own, with
> clearly defined boundaries, has been gradually eroded in recent years.
> The Northern part of the parish has been hived off to Methlick for all
> voting purposes and, along with Methlick and Oldmeldrum, is now
> known as the East Garioch Ward. The village of Tarves and the
> remainder of the parish, along with the parishes of Udny and Slains,
> make up the Ward of North Formartine. Before 1974, the area of
> North Formartine would have been represented by seven elected
> councillors. Now there is only one."

Tarves is in the Parliamentary Constituency of Gordon and its Member of
Parliament at July 1996 was Malcolm Bruce, a Liberal Democrat.

Arthur also believes that Britain's entry into Europe has been of highly
questionable benefit to Tarves:

> "Specialisation became the name of the game, encouraged by huge
> grants and subsidies under the Community's Common Agricultural
> Policy. The cereal barons, already prominent in parts of England,
> quickly influenced the scene here and our acres - or hectares - grew
> wheat and barley as never before, helping to create the huge
> surpluses which are now common throughout the Community. The
> cultivation of oil seed rape, helped by huge subsidy and the local
> climate, has also accelerated rapidly in recent years. Thus, many
> fields of yellow are likely to pepper the rural scene for many
> summers to come. The acreage of wheat, barley, oats and oil seed
> rape, as a proportion of the total at Tarves, was 40 per cent in 1957.
> By 1987 it had soared to 70 per cent - and some people wonder how
> surpluses come about!"

Arthur recalled how a farmer, as early as 1945, had forecast that farm work
would increasingly be undertaken by agricultural contractors, to the exclusion
of permanent staff:

> "Sadly he has been proved right. No longer are there to be found
> communities of families, especially on the larger farms, where
> everyone was identified with the farm and friendly rivalries often
> developed between different establishments."

Another tradition to disappear during the past half century has been the old
preference for Hogmanay and New Year instead of Christmas as a time of
holiday and celebration:

> "Christmas has come to replace what for Scotland was the 'holiest
> of holies' - Hogmanay. School records show that during last
> century the holiday began after Christmas. Children were given
> their presents - if there were any - at New Year.

"To shopkeepers and workers, Christmas was just a normal working day. But on New Year's Day everything stopped. Even the pubs closed, though the hotel remained open. Today, both periods are recognised as statutory holidays."

As this book went to the publishers in 1996 there were unmistakeable signs of renewed confidence in the rural scene, despite the temporary setback of BSE. The Aberdeenshire farming industry was enjoying a boost in investment - good for producers but beneficial, too, to the rural community in general.

A farming expert told me:

"Just as the recession years of the late 1980s became associated with borrowing to survive, so the mid-1990s are showing signs of becoming a period when farmers are once again borrowing to enhance the future strength of their business."

Prosperity had returned to village life, too. The family firm, Bain of Tarves, largest employer in the parish with 150 on its roll, was carving out an international reputation for quality venison, game and beef, supplying hotels and restaurants throughout Britain,and exporting game to Germany, France and the USA. The long-established bakery of W.S. Cumming Ltd celebrated its centenary in 1993 by becoming the first bakery in Scotland to be presented with the BS 5750 quality assurance certificate, an accolade sought by all those pursuing the modern quest for quality. The Dinneswood industrial site, started by Arthur Watson in 1950 with a Nissen hut and two petrol pumps, now houses a bus hiring company, an engineering business and a garage.

Haddo House, ancestral home of the Earls of Aberdeen, is now open to the public through the National Trust for Scotland. It has a country park and is home to an operatic and arts society of international renown. An art and sculpture gallery at Tolquhon, close to the beautifully preserved remains of the 16th century castle, has a widespread clientele.

A hydro-electric power line reached Tarves in 1939 but with the intervention of war the parish did not receive lighting until 1946. In 1976, Gordon District Council designated the village centre as a Conservation Area, ensuring its preservation and enhancement through careful control of development. The boundaries of the Conservation Area were drawn around the buildings of the Square and notable ones along the three main approach roads.

The Council's report identified a change in the village's role from that of merely providing facilities to sustain an agricultural economy to one of serving as both parish centre and dormitory settlement. It noted, however, that despite much new house-building, much of its architectural quality was unimpaired. The village's fundamental character was derived from the Square and the churchyard, it said. The variety of buildings and architecture and the essentially domestic scale, created a distinctly 'village-like' atmosphere, unlike larger settlements with their more regimented building styles and larger scales.

The Church and Kirkbrae Cottages formed "a compact unit which incorporates the most traditional features of 18th and 19th century developments in North-East Scotland." Kirkbrae was "the most architecturally cohesive terrace in the village." Also "worth preserving from damaging alterations" were the White House in the Square, the School and the Clydesdale Bank Building. Noted particularly were the turreted skylight over the school, the stained glass detailing in the fanlight over the school door and the decorative wrought-iron features on the gable of the bank.

Nothing symbolises the spirit of the new age in Tarves more positively than the parish's Heritage Project. For this is far more than a mere repository of historical records at the Melvin Hall. The Conservation Area was a valuable safeguard for the future but it was clear that much more could be achieved. From this was born a collective sense of the need to create a catalyst which would bring people together to work for the total benefit of the village.

A public meeting on 1 December 1992 gave birth to the Tarves Heritage Project, a properly constituted registered charity, complete with Business Plan, Management Committee and lots of enthusiasm - but no money! Separate projects and fund-raising committees were established.

The purpose of the Tarves Heritage Project is:

> "To encourage the preservation, exploration
> and development of our community inheritance."

Its aims are to:

◆ Provide a central facility for storing the records and artefacts of Tarves and neighbouring communities.

◆ Catalogue, make available and display material for study, research and general interest.

◆ Encourage, initiate and nurture creativity in the community.

◆ Preserve, maintain and enhance local sites of historical significance and record and revive local language, customs, traditions and skills.

◆ Ensure continuation of the Project.

The Projects Committee immediately set about its task of establishing teams to work on projects ranging from cleaning the stone circle area at Ythsie to encouraging craft work and re-establishing former cottage industries, collecting music associated with the countryside, re-establishing rights-of-way for walks around the village, and researching Church history. The fund-raising committee has organised barn dances, a St Margaret's Fair in the village Square, folk evenings, craft displays and 'meal-and-ale nights' as their contribution to a Gordon Doric Festival.

Kirkbrae Cottages (above) - "the most architecturally cohesive terrace in the village". Below, the White House in the Square - "must be protected from any damaging alterations".   Illustrations: Gordon D.C. Report

The Old School (below) - "much of the village architecture remains unimpaired."

A successful series of winter talks covered many aspects of North-East life. These events, coupled with tireless applications for a variety of grants, enabled the THP management committee to help fund refurbishment of the Melvin Hall as well as purchasing benches for siting along pathways. Initially, most of the funds raised went towards creating a centrepiece, or focal point, for the Heritage Project. The Carnegie Room at the the Melvin Hall has become a visitor centre where records and artefacts are held in safe-keeping for research work, and information is available on local heritage sites, walks, wildlife and leisure and tourist amenities.

50 Years of Change in Tarves

- **1946** Electric light arrives in the village. Ten prefab houses built.
- **1948/49** Tolquhon Avenue created, with three double Cruden-type houses, numbers 7-12.
- **1950** Dinneswood Garage opened (A. Watson).
- **1952-53** Red Cross built 1 double house, numbers 5/6; house, numbers 1/4 built.
- **1953** Building of houses 10-16 Marquis Cottages.
- **1954/55** Tolquhon Avenue Children's Playingfield laid out.
- **1955** G. Presly's butchers shop sold to John Bain.
- **1958** Huge voluntary effort creates Youth Hall.
- **1962-70** Mackie Avenue built.
- **1975/76** Mackie Crescent built.
- **1964** Cummings Bakery sold to J. Thain, Bakers, Aberdeen.
- **1965** Leask House built. Village Square tarred and trees planted.
- **1972** Duthie's shop sold.
- **1974/84** Stephens Estate built. Braiklay Avenue, Stuart Crescent, Pringle Avenue, Murray Avenue, Gordon Place and Old Aberdeen Road.
- **1976** Globe Inn opened. Blacksmith's shop taken over by Bill Higgins.
- **1977** Landscaped car parking in the Square completed.
- **1978** Post Office transferred to Duthie's shop.
- **1979** School became a Primary. Older scholars start bussing to Ellon.
- **1982** Hanover housing complex built.
- **1984** Doctors' surgery opened at Old School.Doctors Helen Stephen, Roy Burnett and Ronald Chisholm serving Tarves, Methlick and Pitmedden.
- **1991** Multi-purpose sports court built.
- **1992** Manse Brae corner improved and pavement to Square built.
- **1992/94** More new housing - Bede Way, Manse Walk and Forbes View, 50 houses.
- **1993** Tarves Heritage Project opened at Melvin Public Hall.
- **1995/96** Melvin Hall extended and refurbished.

The Organisations of Tarves, 1996

Telephone numbers are Tarves except where otherwise stated

TARVES PARISH CHURCH: Rev Leslie Barrett, The Manse   851250
SESSION CLERK: Miss Kathy Lawrie, Braiklay Cottage   851307
BIBLE CLASS: Mrs Ruth Barrett, The Manse   851250
YOUTH FELLOWSHIP: Mrs Eileen Galloway, 6 Braiklay Avenue   851407
   Richard Leavett, 24 Murray Avenue   851438
SUNDAY SCHOOL: Mrs Elizabeth Robinson, 1 Pringle Avenue   851841
   Mrs Fiona Thomson, 8 Manse Walk   851852
CHURCH CHOIR: Mrs Linda Mackie, Cairnhill   Ellon 761220
WOMAN'S GUILD: Mrs M. Bowen, 8 Gordon Place   851536
BOYS' BRIGADE, Captain: K. Moncur, Braiklay   851441
   Officers: Mike Perry, Tigh-na-Cruach   851389
   Ian Massie, 3 Mackie Crescent   851704
   Juniors: A. Clubb, Shieldaig, Ythanbank,   Ellon 761226
   D. Henderson, 38 Pringle Avenue   851746
   Anchor Boys: Mrs Linda Collie, 36 Pringle Avenue   851428
GUIDES: Mrs Janette McBoyle, 7 The Square   851851
BROWNIES (1st Tarves): Miss Fiona Ewen, 12 Braiklay Avenue   851394
   (2nd Tarves): Mrs Sue Reid, 4 Gordon Place   851424
RAINBOW GUIDES: Mrs Heather MacPherson, 30 Murray Avenue   851355
WEDNESDAY GROUP: Mrs Rosie Leavett, 24 Murray Avenue   851438
PARISH MAG. EDITOR: Mrs Frances Donaldson, Collingwood   851414
HALL COMMITTEE: Lindsay Cook, Little Meldrum   Ellon 761261
WRVS (Meals on Wheels): Mrs M. McCallum, Yarrow Cottage   851763
FRIENDSHIP CLUB: Arthur Watson, Glen Lomond   851288
BADMINTON (Junior): Mrs Jane Cattanach, 10 Pringle Avenue   851485
   (Senior): Stuart Cunningham, 26 Bede Way   851796
BOWLING (Indoor): Arthur Lashmar, 2 Gordon Place   851364
   (Outdoor): M. Presly, 78 Pringle Avenue   851415
RAMBLING: Mrs B. Wright, 21 Mackie Avenue   851722
KEEP FIT: Mrs J. Hollstein, Sonach Croft   851744
PARENT & TODDLER GROUP: Mrs Gillian Lappin, School Cottage   851869
PLAYGROUP: Mrs Jennifer Strachan, Roselea   851320
FOOTBALL: Ian Massie, 3 Mackie Crescent   851704
HADDO ARTS TRUST: Robert Lovie, Peatyard, Haddo House   851770
HADDO HOUSE CHOIR (Jun):   851666
   (Sen): Miss Ceri Thorburn, Haddo House   851665
BABY SITTING CIRCLE: Mrs S. Palmer, 25 Pringle Avenue   851383
DOCTORS & CHIROPODY : Surgery, The Square   851777
BRIDGE CLUB: Mrs K. Davidson. 4 Braiklay Avenue   851322
BRITISH LEGION (Men): J. Thomson, 1 Tree Road   851615
   (Women): Mrs Helen Massie, Ashvale   851205
DANCING (Ballet & Tap): Mrs E. Galloway, 6 Braiklay Avenue   851407
   (Highland): Mrs K. Ramsey, The Lilacs, Longside Road,   Mintlaw 622307
HANOVER COURT: Mrs Jean Jowett, 26 Hanover Court   851559
SCHOOL (Headmaster): Marek Gorski, Manse Road, Udny Green   Udny 842147
   (Parent/Teacher Assoc): Tim Eley, Na Caorainn, Craigdam   851304
   (School Board): Dr Kim Shearer, Craigiebrae   Ellon 761369
PIPING CLASS: Rev Leslie Barrett, The Manse   851250
COMMUNITY CLUB: John Thomson, 1 Tree Road   851615
POLICE: Police Station, Ellon   Ellon 720222
HERITAGE PROJECT: Mrs F. Crichton, Beechwood, Craigdam   851200
LIBRARY SERVICE: Every Wednesday afternoon 2.30 - 4.00pm

Chapter 22

Birds of the Wilderness

by Bill Rattray, Tarves

THE agricultural revolution brought with it fundamental changes in the social structure of the rural parishes as well as in farming methods. By the middle of the 19th century the growth of parish schools had ensured that literacy was widespread.

The conditions which developed and enriched the old ballads - illiteracy and, therefore, oral communication of songs through the generations - were fading. New social conditions re-defined the relationships between tenant farmers and labourers (or servants). As small farms were absorbed into larger ones, the displaced tenant became a servant of the man he once considered his equal. This created tension and conflict of interest, out of which grew what became known as the 'Bothy Ballad.'

Bothy ballads, or 'ploughman songs' as Gavin Greig* called them, described the social conditions of the farm servant during the period between 1840 and 1900, with themes related to the cycle of their lives. Feein' songs deal with the conditions of the feein' market where the servant hired himself out for a term, usually of six months. Others deal with ploughing and the relationship between horseman and horse; some tell of the harvest; most, however, regardless of subject, condemn the conditions of farm life for the servant.

Although known as 'bothy ballads', the songs were, in fact, 'chaumer ballads', for in the North-East of Scotland the 'kitchie' system was the most common form of domestic arrangement for the young servant. Farmers provided lodgings in a part of a steading building but meals were taken with the farmer's family or in an adjacent room, as opposed to a bothy which would have housed several workers. Only about five per cent of North-East farm servants lived in bothies.

Folk song tradition in the North-East was strong - the 'pop' music of its time and place, as it were. It obviously came easily to the farm servant, given the volume recorded by Gavin Greig. His collection, as well as ensuring we have a record, provides an insight to the life and experience of the farm labourer.

* ***Gavin Greig*** - *Folk-Song of the North-East. A series of articles published by Greig in the 'Buchan Observer' between December 1907 and June 1911*

The 'chaumer ploughman' songs can, in essence, be considered socio-historical documents, to be set alongside the more formal opinions and descriptions of the improvers. Theirs were opposing interests and social values - the new-style farmer eager to reduce costs, improve productivity and climb the class ladder; the servant keen to maintain his independence by regularly moving on and intent on resisting changes that the new economic conditions, couched in the language of efficiency, were creating. The regular movement - normally twice a year at the term times of Whitsun and Martinmas - reduced the power a farmer could exert over the servant and allowed the servant some degree of control over his life. Therefore, although the feein' market has frequently been described as a slave market, the servant had a vested interest in ensuring its continuance.* This conflict of interest - the farm servant wanting freedom at the expense of stability, and the farmer seeking productivity at the expense of the servant's conditions - led to a growing social divide.

Driving through the Tarves countryside today, we see well laid-out productive fields, mixed woodland, clean streams, double-glazed housing, good roads and expensive cars. The lifestyle many of us take for granted is very far removed from the experience of the average fee'd loon or first horseman of the mid-19th century. His was a life of unceasing, back-breaking toil. We can only imagine him under a blue-black sky, rain lashing and the wind tearing away his breath as he and horse drag large boulders to the field's edge - those memorial cairns to his labour still so familiar to us today. Perhaps those same stones were dragged into position by his ancient forebears.

At night, the horseman would have lain on his lumpy mattress and heard, below him, the crashes and bangs of loose doors, the rolling clanging of blown buckets as the wind howled through the stable, causing the disturbed horses to shuffle and clump; above him, the incessant racket of rain pelting on to the roof. The cold damp, mixed with the steamy manure wafting up from below, would sour the air he breathed. On still nights, it would have been rats in the rafters dropping their waste and other debris on to the weary lad below to keep him from his sleep. What did he have to look forward to but another day of grim toil in flooded clay parks? For breakfast - oatmeal, for dinner - oatmeal, and for supper - oatmeal.

It almost defies belief that out in the fields the simple rustic bard happily composed songs to the rhythm of his horse's hoof-beats as they worked in unison to plough a straight furrow, the sun warm on his back, the smell of rich newly-turned soil fresh in the air. The laverock would have been singing above, the yorlin calling from a nearby drystone dyke, the teuchat swooping and 'peesie-wheeping' all around him. No, the conditions which created the folksong of the ploughman reveal a different picture - one of greedy farmers, under-nourishment, poor living conditions, little respite from hard work, and low wages.

To some extent, we have come to romanticise the ploughman bard through the images of Burns' poetry. This has been built on by describing the songs as 'cornkisters', creating an idyll of ploughmen gathered for a 'bothy nicht' in the steading, glasses in hand, fire crackling and the songster rendering his new song to the dunt of his boots on the cornkist, all happy with their lot, knowing and accepting their place in the well-ordered social way of things. The content of the songs, mostly written in under-statement, is overlooked as we clothe them in nostalgia. Yet, given the conditions which created them, it is surprising how few are overtly political. To use them as a means of improving conditions was obviously not intended. It seems that the authors were simply following an ancient tradition of ballad-writing - recording experiences for their own sake, not for profit or personal gain, but perhaps to earn a little respect from fellow servants, enough to give them a sense of worth that put them above the animals whose welfare was valued more by the farmer.

What sparked Gavin Greig's interest in collecting the ballads was a recognition that they were dying. His interest was in the songs themselves as folk songs, not as social commentaries on the great changes which had taken place in agriculture in the North-East. Like most parishes, Tarves had ballads written about farms in the area. Sam Davidson, tenant farmer at Northseat of Auchedly, whose family had lived in the area since before the '45 Rebellion, passed a significant collection of songs to Greig, many of which were published in the *Buchan Observer* in the early years of this century. Sam was a friend of Greig, the two having met at Cuminestown when Sam was singing there. He was also a fiddle player and passed less common alternative tunes to Greig. The songs had been given to Sam by a farm servant and were copied by Greig from the original manuscript. They are significant, not only because they were the collection of a local man but because of their range, spanning as they do the era from the old ballads to the new chaumer folk song or bothy ballad.

Here, we deal with only three of the songs which are local to Tarves but form part of this unknown servant's collection - *The Tarves Rant*, *South Ythsie*, and *Nethermill.*

The Tarves Rant has as its focus the events surrounding an evening out in Tarves. It has been compared to *Tam o' Shanter* *, not for its literary merit but its description of an evening's revelry going badly wroing, followed by a warning to anyone else going to Tarves for a night out! *South Ythsie*, on the other hand, describes the work and people at the farm of South Ythsie in 1851/52. *Nethermill* describes the conditions of work at Nethermill farm and, in particular, the hard-driving 'Swaggers', the grieve. 'Swaggers' has a song all to himself, in fact, but we cannot claim it as a Tarves one since he was on a farm at Auchterless when it was written. Interestingly, the mill referred to in *Nethermill* is still with us today. There are at least four versions of *The Tarves Rant*, with at least three variants of the tune. The one given on the next page is the version of the anonymous farm servant whose manuscript copy was given to Greig by Sam Davidson. Greig said that the song was well-known in the locality. He wrote:

> "As a study of the farm servant 'out of the yoke,' it is one of the best things we have. The superior critic may despise such productions as mere 'strouds' but touches like what we have in verses 3 and 5 of *The Tarves Rant* are more intimate and

* *'The Ballad and the Folk' - David Buchan, RKP 1972*

illuminating than reams of pastoral poetry of the conventional type. No kind of minstrelsy, indeed, is more loyal to fact and truth than the ploughman song. Its purely literary value may be slight; but what it loses in inspiration it gains in sincerity and conviction."

The Tarves Rant

1. Gae ear to me ye gay young lads
that mean tae tak a spree,
I'll tell to you a story
Withoot a word o' lee.
My name I winna mention
It's hardly worth the while,
I dinna like to ruin mysel
nor spend my time in jile.

2. I canna work your horses
I canna haud yer ploo,
Nor cut nor build in harvest
But I can feed a coo.
It happened on an evening
To Tarves we did go,
To get a dram and hae some fun
The truth I'll let you know.

3. When we arrived at Tarves
tae Duthies we did pad,
And there we got some music
That made our hearts right glad.
The man that played the music
His name I needna hide,
He was a jolly ploughman lad
They ca'd him Ironside.

4. For treacle he tae Tarves came
For he was on his brose,
Some was there for boots and shoes
and some was there for clothes.
Few was there that I did know
and as few there knew me;
But there was one amongst the rest
That tried tae bully me.

5. It's then tae Philip's we did gang
to get a little fun;
I was so ensnared
Wi' the maiden o' the inn
She was a lovely maiden
The maiden that she be,
Twa rollin eyes, twa rosy cheeks,
and a lovely girl was she.

6. We sat and drank in merriment
we sat till we thought shame,
and to leave the tavern
and steer our course for hame.
It was there I lost my comrades
and on them I did cry,
and just at that moment
a lad in blue came by.

7. "I plainly tell to you gin
   ye dinna haud yer tongue,
   I'll get ye in tae custody
   and that before it's lang."
   He's ta'en me roughly by the arm
   and led me to the inn,
   It was there we fought in earnest
   for then it wisna in fun.

8. Surely I am a profligant
   a villain at the bone,
   Tae tear the coat from off his back
   and it being not his own.
   It was to get me till a room
   his strength he didna spare,
   But I did plainly show to him
   that it would need a pair.

9. It's soon assistance came to him
   they dragged me thro' a door,
   And I was made a prisoner
   and left to think it o'er.
   A few came into my head
   and up the window drew,
   Twa willing hands they pulled me out
   they didna like the blue.

10. I think the folk in Tarves
    a jail they'll need to get,
    For to lock up their prisoners
    and not let them escape.
    For I think it is a sin
    to break the Sabbath day,
    Searching for their prisoners,
    while they do run away.

11. A few mair words I've got to say
    but not to my disgrace,
    To Aberdeen they did me bring
    it's for to plead my case.
    When I received my sentence
    I received it like a shot,
    I had thirty shillings for a fine
    and fifteen for a coat.

12. Come all ye jolly ploughman lads
    that means to tak a spree,
    Fan ye gang tae Tarves
    dinna get upon the spree.
    Just go an get your errant
    and steer your course for hame,
    And when a row does begin
    ye winna get the blame.

In his notes to *South Ythsie* in the *Buchan Observer* article, Greig states that he had traced the author of the song as a William Forsyth who was engaged at the farm in the mid-1800s. Of particular interest in this song is the list of named individuals including, in the 15th verse, a 'jolly youth' called Davidson - perhaps a relative of Sam! The last verse paints a picture of the songster ploughman composing as he worked the land - maybe this image is not so far from the truth after all!

South Ythsie

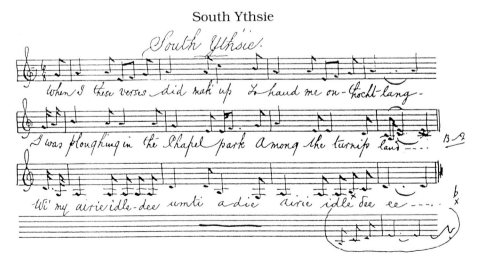

1. As I went down to Ellon Fair
   Ance on a day to fee
   Likewise an opportunity.
   My comrades for to see.
   Wi my airy eddle dum dady um
   My eddle dum dair a lee

2. And steerin' thro' the market,
   An auld neebor chanced to see;
   And when I stept up to him
   He asked was I to fee?

3. He told me he was leavin'
   Likewise his neebor tee;
   He said the grieve did want a hand
   And he thocht that I would dee.

4. He stept up unto the grieve,
   Says, "Here's a man to fee,
   I think he'll suit ye very weel
   If wi' him ye can agree."

5. He told to me some of the work,
   That I would have to do;
   He said I would have little else
   But cart and hold the ploo.

6. He asked at me my wages,
   What they were gaun to be;
   So in a short time after
   Wi' him I did agree.

7. I did engage wi' Johnnie Gray,
   The year o' fifty-one;
   Jist for to work his hinmost pair
   And be his little man.

8. Now to South Ythsie I am bound,
   The term bein' past;
   And trudgin' thro' the Chapel howe
   I cam' to it at last.

9. Straucht to the stable I did go,
   My horses for to view;
   They were a handsome pairie
   A chestnut and a blue.

10. So on the followin' mornin'
    We a' gaed to the ploo;
    But lang ere it was lowsin' time
    Sae sair's she gart me rue.

11. I held at her wi' a' my micht,
    And cam' but poorly on;
    The ither twa did lauch at me
    And at me they got fun.

12. But I complained unto the grieve,
    That she widna lay the fur;
    He said, " There is a new ane
    Jist ready to gang for."

13. Noo I've got hame my new ane,
    She pleased me unco weel;
    And I do think I am a'richt,
    I've got a better teel.

14. We hae a gallant foreman,
    His name is Jamie Watt;
    And for to drag the horses on,
    Indeed he isna slack.

15. Oor second man is Davidson;
    Indeed to tello the truth,
    It's I do like him very weel,
    He is a jolly youth.

16. And I mysel' the third man,
    My name it is Forsay,
    And I do my endeavour
    Their orders to obey.

17. The neist comes Willie Duncan,
    He's ready wi' a jest,
    Sometimes he doth work orra wark,
    Sometimes the orra beast.

18. We hae a topsman bailie,
    And Wallace is his name;
    He does his cattle off in style
    When he tak's doon his kaim.

19. Likewise we have another one,
    Oor orra beasts to sort,
    And sometimes in the mornin'
    To the barn doth resort.

20. Likewise we have a little boy,
    Oor eerants for to go;
    And when he's on an unco road
    Indeed he is some slow.

21. Likewise we have a housekeeper
    Our victuals to prepare,
    And everything that's in the house
    To keep into repair.

22. And likewise we have got a grieve,
    He is a quiet man;
    But for to tell the plain truth,
    His wark he canna plan.

23. Noo I hae wrocht this winter through,
    It's into fifty-twa,
    Still thinkin' on the month o' May
    That I micht win awa'.

24. At last the market it has come,
    And I am fee't again;
    I'm going back to Brackley,
    They call him Mr Bean.

25. Noo the twenty-sixth has come,
    It is the term day;
    I'll tak' my budgets on my back,-
    Fareweel to Johnnie Gray.

The song *Nethermill* appears in the last of the *Buchan Observer* articles. It was also written by Forsyth. Unfortunately, there is no recorded tune, but it is one of between 20 and 30 songs which form the central core of the 'bothy ballad.' Tarves can boast an association with at least six of them, either as songs specific to the area or in which the parish is given a mention. When Ellon, Fyvie and Methlick are added, we find there is a rich heritage of folksong in the Tarves district. It seems to have been common to adapt songs, alter the tune and the name and create a new ballad. Such is the case with *Little Ythsie*, which is *South Ythsie* to a different tune. This was not what we might regard today as plagiarism, but a normal part of the evolution of songs so common in the oral tradition.

Nethermill

1. It was about the term time
   When servants change their place,
   As I went down to Ellon Fair
   My fortune for to chase.
   Tirim fal de dal de dal,
   Tirim fal de dido;
   Tirim fal de dal de dal,
   Tirim fal de dee.

2. There was a farmer in this place
   He sought me to engage,
   It was na for his fancy man,
   Nor yet to be his page.

3. And when he sought me to engage,
   And told me all his plans
   He said, " I have my foreman,
   Ye'll be my second man."

4. It was to work his horses,
   Likewise to hold his ploo,
   But when that I went hame to him,
   Sae sairly as I did rue.

5. For early the next morning,
   'Twas sair against my will,
   When our grieve cam' to our
     sleeping-place,
   Demanding us to the mull.

6. Away down to the mull we go,
   And kindles up a light,
   And then we put the water on,
   And wrought wi' all our might.

7. And when the thrashing it was o'er,
   And faith it was na sport,
   And we to the stable go
   To gie our horse a sort.

8. And when that Swaggers he cam' round,
   To gie us out the line,
   He had the watch into his han'
   Just looking for the time.

9. "At seven ye'll gang to your brose,
   At eight ye'll gang and yoke,
   And work away as fast's ye can,
   For men's nae easy got.

10. " Ye'll clean your horses unco well,
    Likewise your harness too,
    And faith, my lads, ye winna stan'
    When ye gang to the ploo."

11. And when that we gang to the neeps
    It's still they cry for mair,
    For drivin' at them ilka day
    There is na time to spare.

12. Faith I'm sure it would gar you laugh,
    To hear him rowte and roar,
    And tear and twist his fuskers
    And rin frae door to door.

13. "My horsemen lads, ye winna stan',
    Be ye will ca awa;
    And let us get the plooin' tee,
    Ere we begin to saw.

14. "And when the sawin' does begin
    It's I will saw the seed,
    And full't up in my leisure hour,
    Just in the time I need.

15. "Ye bailie lads, ye'll gie's a hitch,
    Your master for to please,
    For if ye dinna labour hard
    Your temper he will tease."

16. Now all ye servant laddies,
    I fear ye'll get a gull *,
    If ye engage wi' Swaggers
    To gang to Nethermill.

17. And now my song it's at an end,
    I think I'll let ye be;
    But gang ye engage wi' Swaggers,
    The truth o' this ye'll see.

As well as the bothy ballads, Tarves has a strong association with fiddle music. Tunes like *Forbes Morrison of Tarves*, written by James Scott Skinner, and *The Tarves Trippers*, written by James Hardie of Methlick, are Strathspeys which enrich our musical heritage.

Fiddle music survives in the area as a much stronger legacy than the bothy ballads. The parish boasts its own Tarves Fiddlers, a group of local musicians who meet as occasion demands to play tunes in the new tradition of fiddle groups. Sadly, there is no such forum for the bothy ballad and, indeed, to create it could be false and simply add to the music hall caricature. The songs deserve more than that; they merit serious renditions by those who know the cadences and nuances of the 'doric' and have a sympathetic understanding of the people who wrote them. They deserve to live for what they are - the songs of proud, hard-working people who forged a landscape and fed a nation.

Greg referred to the ploughman songs as "birds of the wilderness":

"The bird of the wilderness has been caught and put in a gilded cage. In plain terms, can it survive?"

This question, which he put in an article for the *Buchan Field Club*, was concerned more with what was happening to the songs through collection, printing and editing:

"Their primitive strains are being reduced to conventional notation and clothed with up-to-date instrumental accompaniments."

The irony of this is that the songs could have been doomed - not because of Greig's reasoning but because the social conditions which created them in the first place gave way to a post First World War mechanised age.

* **get a gull** - be taken advantage of

This, coupled with the music hall and growing access to the media, not least the movie, saw the locals desert their culture in favour of an imported one.

This remains with us today as the children and grandchildren of the post Second World War generations derive their musical recreation largely from American imports. Yet, as this new musical style dominates the cultural preferences of our teenagers, we see the old music being adapted by modern 'folk' groups and re-defining itself. I recently saw a folk group with electrically amplified instruments hammer out *The Barnyards o' Delgaty* - the kids loved it!

Maybe the lesson is clear - we should not box our music and consign it to a particular time; it should, like the old ballads, adapt and change, grow and live, and remain alive albeit altered and, dare I say, improved?

The original writers would probably approve, even bemoaning the fact that they did not have the technology available to turn their simple rhymes into the exciting rhythms the modern band can provide.

The last word, as always, goes to the simple words of the *Tarves Rant* :

> " It's there we got some music
>   that made our hearts right glad."

Chapter 23

Church and Community

by The Rev Leslie McEwen Barrett, BD, FRICS

WHEN Henry Ford famously said "History is bunk", he sounded a useful warning to anyone attempting to record the complex events of the lives of communities. The task of presenting even a brief survey of our church and community in recent times seems to me to be fraught with difficulty because no such review would ever do full justice to the influences, changes and passions which are ever present where people live together in community with one another.

The long and eventful history of the Christian Church in this corner of Scotland from the earliest days of the Celtic Saints has been chronicled elsewhere. "The past is a foreign country," wrote L.P. Hartley, and it may as well be so as we read in the pages of this 'history' the curious stories and anecdotes of church life and religious influence from the past. Without a sympathetic understanding, however, of the social, cultural and political conditions of past times, it is too easy for us to judge superficially the actions and attitudes of the church and our ancestors. The many stories in these pages of censorious attitudes of the kirk towards that traditional hub of any community today - 'the tavern' for example - must be understood against a background of relative poverty and the availability of cheap strong drink which ruined the lives of families and individuals in earlier, less enlightened times. Today, most ministers are equally at home in pulpit or pub - "Tempora mutantur, et nos mutamur in illis" ("Times change, and we change with them")

The history of Christianity as a force in community life has always involved a great deal of change. In former days, the church has enriched the community as protector of the disadvantaged, the vulnerable and the weak, and as provider of the earliest forms of universal education and care of the sick and the poor. These functions, to a large extent, have now been taken over by the state or local authorities, but the community's debt to the kirk in pioneering such care is incalculable.

Today, these functions are carried on by our congregation, as part of the national Church of Scotland, in new ways beyond the parish where poverty and disadvantage exist at home in Scotland and in the developing world. They continue through our association with Christian Aid, Ekwendeni Hospital and the sponsorship by our Sunday School of Rastatutu, a young girl in far-away Africa, and the Church of Scotland's own Priority Areas Appeal, to name just a few of the recent initiatives for community care undertaken from our village alongside the continuing pastoral care within the community.

The visitor to Tarves today, returning after an absence of just one generation, could not fail to be impressed by the changes which have occurred in the village and countryside. An aerial view of the village in W. Douglas Simpson's *A Short History of Tarves*, published mid-century, shows the 'old village', a neat cluster of buildings centred on the Square and overlooked by the kirk to the eastmost corner of the photograph. Trim fields stretch away into the distance towards neighbouring parishes and, remarkably, not a single car or vehicle of any kind can be seen, either parked or moving on the roads and streets. Major changes have occurred within sight of the church which stands like a sentinel on its raised knoll surrounded by the kirkyard.

An aerial view of Tarves, showing how the village has recently spread its wings

Picture - THP

The revolution in farming techniques and increased mechanisation have caused a major shift away from the traditional farming economy upon which the life of the village depended until recent times. Many of the crofts and farm cottages in the parish which used to house farm workers have been sold and converted or extended by incoming families, and the land itself is now farmed by far fewer

men and increasing numbers of machines, often contracted for specific tasks
from outwith the parish. Far from causing a de-population of the area, these
changes in the traditional country ways have been accompanied by
considerable growth, driven by greater prosperity and diversity of life-styles
following a major influx of population based largely upon the North Sea Oil
Industry centred on Aberdeen. Increasing car-ownership has made Tarves an
attractive centre for commuting to employment outside the parish.

The village itself has grown in all directions. The post-war building boom was
responsible for an extension to the North and West where new housing was
constructed in Tolquhon Avenue, Mackie Avenue and Mackie Crescent. The fields
to the South-West were covered by a major development of 130 modern houses
built during a period of unprecedented community growth, begun in the 1970s
to accommodate housing demands created in the North-East during the early
years of rapid expansion in the oil industry. A small group of 'prefabs' on the
Northern fringe of the village was demolished to make way for an excellent
sheltered housing complex at Hanover Court, opened in September 1982, and
the latest phase of expansion involved the building of 50 new houses on fields in
front of the Manse in the early 1990s. Thus, in the space of 50 years, the
physical size of Tarves has more than doubled, with the majority of the
population employed beyond the parish, in Aberdeen and neighbouring towns.

I recall an Elder once breaking into ryhme:

> "Tarves wis a village,
> When I wis jist a loon...
> Noo, it's mair a toon."

The diversity within the population is reflected in the life of our community. The
rich tradition of community involvement stretching back over many years is
encouraged and kept alive by the many individuals who foster and encourage
village institutions. Much unsung work is done behind the scenes by men and
women who have the care of the village and its facilities very much at heart.
It would be wrong to single out particular individuals, but many of us have
reason to be grateful to these men and women who have made it their business
to ensure the smooth running of village committees, worked to provide or
improve village and community facilities and generally seen to it that Tarves is
an attractive, outgoing and welcoming place in which to live and bring up a
family. In this the church has always played its part through its programme of
youth work, fellowship and support for families from the youngest to the oldest.
The list of current village organisations given on Page 198 conveys some
impression of the wealth of activities and interest groups provided by and for
this small community.

On a personal note, in accepting the call to Tarves and Barthol Chapel, any
impression that this was a rural and, therefore, rustic parish, was quickly
dispelled when, within weeks of taking up residence in the Manse, we had
attended various plays, musical evenings, concerts and community events of
the highest calibre, including a Shakespeare production at Haddo which

included a Royal Prince in the cast and members of the Royal family, on holiday at Balmoral, as members of the audience! Social occasions, ceilidhs and Burns Suppers in the Melvin Hall regularly feature local talent and a winter programme of events draws in experts and guest speakers to discourse on matters of local history, the Doric language and literature and the natural history of the area. Village amenities include an excellent public hall, football pitches, an all-weather sports court and the church's own Youth Hall, created in the 1950s from the former steading buildings beside the Manse. In the wider life of the community, the involvement of the church is by no means confined to Sunday mornings. Church-based organisations encompass all ages and offer opportunitiues for fellowship and shared interests. Our Sunday School begins for children from the age of three and is impressive for the support it receives, with 81 youngsters and nine staff on the roll at the last statistical return. The Boys Brigade currently has over 50 boys within Anchor Boys and Junior and Senior companies. Tarves Guides and Brownies, though not a church organisation, attracts a similar number of girls. Bible Class and Youth Fellowship are available for teenagers and we are proud of our Woman's Guild, Choir (Junior and Senior), and the newly-formed and burgeoning Wednesday Group which meets for discussion and friendship each week in the homes of members.

No adequate measure exists for the impact of the church upon the community it is privileged to serve. There are two pieces of advice which I like to recall when we are brought face-to-face with the troublesome issues fof finance and numerical support. The first is that in the church we are not called to be successful; we are called only to be faithful to the tasks handed down to us from New Testament times. Secondly, it was a leading churchman who once said that "the church is the only organisation which exists for the benefit of those outside its membership." God has undoubtedly blessed and challenged us as the church of His Son, Jesus Christ, in Tarves and, I believe, will continue with us if we will only keep these things in the forefront of our minds.

Down the generations, as far back as I can see, the life of our church and community have been closely entwined, each giving to the other the mutual support which is the basis of any good relationship. The church has a conspicuous physical presence in the parish, our kirk overlooking the village square, but also a conspicuous spiritual presence through its life and worship and by many ways in which, though its members, it is represented in the life of the community.

Our *Welcome* leaflet states that "Tarves Kirk is the only place of worship in the parish and, as the parish church, we are committed to serve the religious needs of everyone living in the parish, regardless of denominational affiliation." Changes in the size of the community and shifts of population have had less effect on the life of the church than the revolution in attitudes and life-styles over the past 50 years. The post-war period signalled the beginning of a phase of reorganisation in church structures which is continuing today. In 1958 the former United Presbyterian Church at nearby Craigdam was closed for public worship and demolished, leaving a small cairn to mark the spot where this historic kirk had stood for some 200 years. Many of those who belonged to Craigdam Kirk have fond memories of it but dwindling numbers and economic necessity forced the closure of this and so many other small country kirks. The thinning of population in the countryside at that time, together with increasing mobility through car ownership, made it increasingly difficult for small, congregations to survive as independent units supporting a minister and maintaining their own buildings. Happily, the former members of Craigdam found a welcome and a new place to belong in Tarves Kirk. For some years after the closure an annual service was held at the cairn, often including baptisms.

In the same year,1958, the present 'linkage' was formed between the congregations of Barthol Chapel and Tarves. This continues to be a successful arrangement, with each congregation administering its own affairs. There is a 'quoad sacra'* constitution at Barthol Chapel, with a Kirk Session and Congregational Board, while Tarves continues under the old 'quoad omnia'* constitution, with Kirk Session only. The two congregations share their minister based at Tarves Manse, thus spreading the cost. On Sunday morning, worship at Barthol Chapel begins at 10. 00 am, after which the minister must dash the four and a half miles to Tarves for the service there at 11.15 a.m. This can be quite an adventure in winter months when snow often blocks the country roads. On several occasions it has been necessary to dig out and push the car free of snowdrifts in order to complete the journey!

Thus, while in living memory three separate congregations existed within the present-day parish of Tarves and Barthol Chapel, now there is but one charge served by one minister in place of the three. This has brought benefits to set alongside the losses, especially in that more lay people have taken on leadership roles within the church, notably in the kirk sessions. In 1952 Tarves Kirk Session numbered just 15, while today the number of Elders stands at 36. All the Elders in 1952 were male and most were local farmers. Today, the Session is made up almost equally of men and women from a variety of occupations. It is delightful to hear the great variety of accents - Welsh, English, Irish and dialects from many parts of Scotland - mingling with the local tongue at Session meetings today.

Though Tarves Kirk is the only formal place of worship in the parish today, that is not to say that the Church of Scotland is the only Christian denomination represented in the district. Several Tarves families belong to the Scottish Episcopal Church, the Roman Catholic Church and the Baptist Church, where congregational life is centred on nearby Ellon. There are one or two families whose attachments are to the Mormon Church, Evangelical churches or the Quaker Meeting House in Aberdeen.

The Chapel of Haddo House - "since 1881, when it was dedicated to the service of Almighty God, free from all ecclesiastical restrictions, has continued its ecumenical witness" - represents in concrete form the ecumenical spirit of the North-East, attracting preachers and theologians from a wide range of church traditions to conduct services. These, mainly evening, services often include leading churchmen from North and South of the border and from further afield,

* Under a **quoad omnia** constitution, the kirk session deals with all matters, spiritual and civil; under **quoad sacra** arrangements, however, the kirk session is concerned with spiritual matters only, with practical matters like property and finance being the responsibility of a congregational board.

who are invited to preach and afterwards to meet the congregation over supper given through the hospitality of Lady Aberdeen. Local clergy, who are also invited to conduct worship at Haddo have good reason to be thankful for this facility since it provides us with an opportunity to be part of a worshipping congregation in a beautiful setting on our doorstep, and to enjoy the fine music which is so much a part of the Haddo tradition.

The Rev John Pringle wears all the solemnity of a 19th century Church of Scotland minister. A Borderer, and son of a land steward, Mr Pringle ministered at Tarves for 45 years, first coming to the parish in 1871 to succeed the Tarves-born Rev Francis Knox.

A man of the modern age - the minister at Tarves today, the bagpipe-playing Rev Leslie Barrett, a qualified Chartered Surveyor who trained for the ministry at St Andrews and was inducted to Tarves in June 1991.

CONTRASTS

The Parochial Board of Tarves, 1862 (above), probably the earliest photograph of Tarves people - front l to r, G. Melvin, Schoolhouse; J. Duncan, Newseat of Tolquhon; P. McLaggan, Factor; J. Morrison, Hattonslap; Rev F. Knox, Minister; Dr Irvine; back row, l to r, G. Bean, Braiklay; W.S. Marr, Uppermill; G. Shepherd, Shethin; G. Garden, North Ythsie; A. Burnett, Keithfield; T. Milne, Gateside.   Picture THP

The photograph on the page opposite, taken by Tarves photographer, Innes Stephen, after morning worship on 10 March 1996, shows members of the Kirk Session and officials of Tarves Parish Church as well as leaders of uniformed organisations. They are:

Front row *(seated at floor level)* : *Rev Leslie Barrett, Minister; William Howie, Beadle; Margaret Robb, Reader.*

Second row *(seated) l to r: John Mackie; Kathy Lawrie, Session Clerk; Dawson Henderson; Sarah Haws; Fiona Ewen; Linda Tait; Ian Massie.*

Third row *(central): Edward Hay; Edith Innes; James Lynch.*

Fourth row *(l to r): Edward Morrison; Mary Bowen; Elizabeth Rothnie; Rosie Leavett; Robin Rothnie.*

Standing *(l to r): Mike Ogg; Sandy Sleigh; Anne Moncur; George Emslie; Sandy Gibb; Alison Walker; Neville Trainer; Arthur Watson; Helen Hainton; Alistair Murdoch; Beth Reid; Andy Clubb; Rosa Dickie; Doreen Gray; Doreen Brown; Dr Gordon Laing; Eileen Galloway; Janet Sladdin; Gladys Murdoch; David Presly; Linda Mackie, Organist; Ken Moncur; James Mathewson, Senior Elder; Andy Duff; Heather MacPherson; Mike Perry; Ruth Barrett, Bible Class Leader; Janette Ross; Ian Craig, Treasurer.*

One of my predecessors described Tarves as "the best parish in the Church of Scotland." Recent times have been years of rapid growth and change, presenting many challenges to a community long settled in its ways and steeped in tradition. Happily, few would doubt that the changes have been accommodated in a creditable spirit of tolerance, yet imaginatively grasping the opportunities for renewal which growth in size and population have brought to village and parish.

The expansion of the community has undoubtedly been a blessing, bringing an influx of people to support village businesses and institutions and keep alive many features of village life which cannot, these days, easily be sustained by very small numbers. The church has benefited, along with the whole community, from the newcomers who have helped to enrich the life and worship of the congregation and have offered their gifts and talents in the service of our kirk and in the administration of its affairs.

The North-East is a hospitable place and it is a tribute to those who have lived here for generations that the transition of recent times has been managed with grace and intelligent sensitivity for the needs of all the community.

Wise newcomers, too, have quickly learned to value and respect the native traditions and ways of doing things. The church and community today is a happy blend of old and new, tradition and modernity, which sit well together in pew and village street, each making its own distinctive contribution to the common life of the parish.

◆

INDEX

A

Abbey of Arbroath, 8, 97
Abbey of Deer, 170
Abercrummy, Sir Alexander, 8
Aberdeen Angus, 159, 163-4
Aberdeen, Earls of, 51, 54, 117, 119-22, 139, 148
Agricola, 3
Aikey Brae, battle, 10
Aikey, fair, 39
Alexander, William, 142, 147-9
Allan, John R., 188-9
Allan, William, 70
Amenities, village, 210-11
Anderson, Rev George, 52-3, 96
Andet, 6
Angelwell, 64
Arthur, Alexander, 18
Auchedly, 22, 55, 76-7, 201
Auchedly, Mill of, 55-6
Auchinive, Mayns of, 55
Auchneive, 19, 21, 58
Auchterlonie, Rev D.K., 95
Auquhorthies, 10, 51, 61-2, 78, 81, 95

B

Bain of Tarves, 194
Balconny, Sir Archibald, 8
Balgove, 19, 22, 64
Ballads, 88, 199
Balliols, 7
Bank, 192
Bapton, herd, 162
Barclay, Cpt. of Ury, 29, 159
Barclay, Patrick, 27-8
Baron courts, 18-20
Barra Hill, battle, 10
Barrett, Rev Leslie, 208
Barthol Chapel, 66, 95-6, 130, 139
Bartholomew, Saint, 96
Beaker folk, 1-2
Bede House 50, 98-99
Beginnings, 1-8
Bennachie, 3, 42
Black, James, 160
Black Kalendar, 70
Bloodsuckers, 31
Boghouse, 18-20, 63, 172
Bohemia, 15-16
Boolroad, 21
Bothies, 87-88, 199
Boundary Commission, 192
Braes o'Gight, 3
Braeside, 19, 63, 174
Braiklay, 15, 21, 26
Brechullath, 8
Brechin, family, 19
Brig o' Dee, battle, 12, 123
Broadward of Shives, 67
Bronie, 21
Bronie Lodge, 173
Bronze Age, 3
Brose, 87
Brown, Rev William, 93
Bruce, Sir Edward, 10
Bruce, Robert, 7-9
BSE, 159
Buchan, harrying of, 10
Buchan Line, 170
Buchan Observer, 201, 205
Buses, 170
Burr, James, 161
Byron, Lord, 118

C

Cairdseat, 19, 22, 64
Cairnbrogie, 3, 8, 22, 51, 68, 77, 125, 160, 162, 165
Cairnbrogie, Mains of, 165
Cairnbrogie, New, 68
Cairnbrogie, Old, 68
Cairnbrogie, Newplace of, 69
Cairnfechil, 3, 22
Cairns, 1, 3
Caldhame, 18-19
Cameron, David K., 88, 149, 178
Canmore, 7
Carnegie, Andrew, 184
Catto, Lord, 126
Ceilidhs, 177
Celts, 3
Charming, 76-77
Christianity, arrival of, 6
Christian Aid, 209
Chyldkeeper, 52
Cloister Seat, 22
Clothing, 39
Clydesdale, horse, 166-9, 190
Clydesdale, bank, 189, 192
Collieston, 177
Collynie, 22, 95, 160-2
Colm, Saint, 6
Combine, harvester, 187, 190
Common Agricultural Policy, 193
Community Care, 209
Computers, 128, 140
Comyns, 7, 9-10
Conservation Area, 194-5
Cook Collection, 124
Cornkisters, 200
Corshill, 61
Cotton, Bruce, 105
Cot-touns, 37
Coucher Cairn, 3, 19, 65
County Park, 194
Courtstone, 22
Covenanters, 11-13, 117, 123-4
Craig, William, 16
Craigdam, church, 211-2
Craigdam, school, 130
Craigdarra, 55, 93, 95
Craigdoune, 60
Craigie, Mains of, 60
Craigie of Shethin, 55-6, 109
Craigies, 2, 124
Crofts, 147-9, 178-9
Cromwell, 13
Crop Rotation, 143
Cumming, William S., 105
Cumming, W.S. Ltd., 194

D

Dalforkie, 65
Dame's School, 135
Dance masters, 177-8
Darien Scheme, 54, 84, 115
Davidson, Archibald, 32
Davidson, Charles, 135, 176
Davidson, Ian, 97
Davidson, Sam, 125, 173, 201
Davidson, window, 105
Death rate, 46-7
Deer, Abbey of, 170
Dempster, 19
Devenick, Saint, 6
Diet, 39, 87, 145
Dinneswood, 194
Diptheria, 175

D (cont.)

Disruption, 132
Doddies, cattle, 163
Donald, Lord of the Isles, 10
Doulies, 21
Drainage, 143, 175
Drinking, 16, 90-3, 208
Drostan, Saint, 6
Drove roads, 39, 146
Droving, 39-40
Drumbreck, 22
Duncan, William, 172
Durno, family, 162
Duthie & Co., 188
Duthie, William, 95, 135, 160-3, 184, 192
Dykes, 143

E

Earlesfoord, 68
Education (Scotland) Act, 132
Ellon, 17, 170
Ellon Academy, 139
Ellon Presbytery, 14-16
Enclosures, 143
European Community, 193

F

Fairs, 177
Falkirk Tryst, 39
Famine, 42-47
Feeing markets, 87-8, 145, 189, 199-200
Ferm-touns, 37
Feudalism, 17-23
Fiddle, music, 206
Flitting, 88, 176, 189
Flood, 42
Foor & Mouth, 162
Forbes, Auquhorthies, 51
Forbes, Tolquhon, 14, 18, 51, 54, 98-99, 109, 111, 114-5
Forbes, Hugh, 86, 126
Forbes, Maxie, 167
Forbes, Sir Samuel, 22
Fordyce, Bailie William, 78, 81
Formartine, 6-7
Fraser, Rev Alan J., 187
Free Church, 132
Fuchill, 8, 19, 52, 64-5
Fullfoord, 65
Fyvie Castle, 7

G

Galfridus de Wellys, 8, 97
Games, 177
Garden, Mary, 135-7
Gardyne, Rev Thomas, 14, 16, 24, 26, 30-1, 126
Gateside, 21
Germok, Rev Thomas, 24
Gight, castle, 118
Gill, Doddie, 167
Glencoe, massacre, 49
Gordon, Agnes, 26-8
Gordon, Sir John, 11-13
Gordons, famous, 119-122
Gordon, Tillyhilt, 14-16, 26-7
Gordon, memorial church, 95
Gorski, Marek, 139
Gowlie, burn, 22
Grant, Sir Archibald, 85
Grass sickness, 167

Grassums, 86, 143
Gray, George, 51
Gray, family, 125-6
Greed, 83, 88, 147-8, 200
Greig, Gavin, 199
Greig, William, 52, 54, 129

H

Haddo, 12-13, 22, 26, 117, 138, 148, 173,
   176-7, 184, 194, 212
Haltoun Slapp, 65, 174
Hanging, in public, 71, 74-76
Hangman, 70
Harlaw, battle, 10-11
Harrying, of Buchan, 10
Harvest Home, 177
Hay, family, 26, 124, 159-60
Herons, 118, 138
Historic Scotland, 98
Horse bus, 174
Hospital, 135-6
Housing, 37-39
Howe, Rev Alexander, 32
Howff, 126
Humlies (cattle), 163
Huntly, Marquis of, 13-14

I

Ice Age, 1
Illegitimacy, 33-34
Inverurie, 9-10, 17, 37, 170
Inverurie, battle of, 141
Improvers, 83-85, 141-2
Iron Age, 3
Ironhill, 22
Irvine, Alexander Forbes, 3

J

Jacobites, 84
Jaffray, Bailie Alexander, 12
James VI, at Tolquhon, 13, 111-2
Jamieson, William, 82
Johnson, Alexander, 26
Johnston, George, 51
Johnston, Robert, 115

K

Keith, Major James, 124, 178, 187
Keith, James, 47, 51, 54
Keithfield, 22
Kellebrae, 62
Kelly, Helen, 34
Kelly, Place of, 11-12, 54, 117
Kerrs Buses, 170
Kidnappers, 78
Kilpatrick, James, 167
Kirk Session, 212, 214-15
Kirkfoord, 65
Kirk-touns, 37
Kitchie system, 199
Knolls, Rev Alexander, 85-86
Knox, Rev Francis, 36, 101, 130, 142,
   144-46

L

Lady Well, 77
Laverockland, 19

Leverocklyes, 65
Leslie, Barbara, 25
Lethenty, 10
Library, 173, 184
Lion, William the, 8
Local Government, reorganisation, 192
Logie, Cpt John, 13
Logierieve, 22
Lowrie, John, 15, 129
Lumsden, Henry, 8
Lumsden, John, 8

M

MacAlpin, Kenneth, 7
Macbeth, 7
MacDonald, Alexander, 172
Machar, Saint, 6
Mackie, Maitland, 190
Mad Cow Disease, 159
Mails, 175
Mains of Craigie, 55
Malcolm 11, King, 7
Man, James, 19
Manse, Tarves, 53
Manure, 143-44
Mar, Earl of, 10
Marr, family, 125, 160, 162
Marr, George, 18
Martin, Saint, 6
Martin's Land, 6
Maurice of Tarves, 8, 97
McNaughton, George, 132
Meal & Ale, 177
Meal, prices 43
Mearns, Dr Duncan, 96
Melvin, George, 133-35, 184
Melvin Public Hall, 135, 184-5
Mercer, Rev John, 27-28
Merchants, Tarves, 52
Meldrum, Bailie George, 19
Middle Boghouse, 63
Middleton, James, 52
Mill, John, 15
Mill, William, 129
Milne, David, 21
Milton, 8
Mill-touns, 37
Mill of Shives, 67
Ministers (Tarvest list), 105-8
Missionaries, 173, 186
Mitchell, Rev Thomas, 37, 40, 100
Mitchell, William, 25
Moir, Rev James, 24
Money values, 8
Mons Graupius, battle, 8
Montglay, 67
Mosside, 19, 65
Multure, 18
Mungo, Saint, 6
Munro, Rev John, 8
Murdebur, Saint, 6, 97
Myreton, Sir Thomas, 8

N

National Trust, Scotland, 117, 123, 194
Nethermill, 201, 205
Nether Tillycairn, 55
Newburgh, 17, 37
Nether Kirktoune, 66
Nether Woodhill, 68
Newplace of Cairnbrogie, 69

Newseat, 18-19, 63
Newseat of Shives, 67
Newton, 8
Ninian, Saint, 6, 98
Norsemen, 6-7
North Sea Oil, 190-91, 210
Northseat, 55-56, 125, 166

O

Oddfellows, 173
Ogilvie, George, 77
Ogilvy, Alexander, 8, 24
Old Balgove, 19
Oldmeldrum, 9, 17, 22, 37, 170
Oldmill of Shivas, 165
Old Garland, 172
Old Nauchty, 172
Old Pretender, 84
Oldtoun of Fuchill, 19
Ordhill, 177
Overboghouse, 19-20, 63
Overhill, 55-56,
Overkirktoune, 66
Over Tillycairn, 55
Over Woodhill, 68

P

Parish Councils, 192
Parochial Board, 174, 214
Parochial system, 6
Picktillum, 22
Picts, 3, 6-7
Pirie, George, 133
Pitmedden, 10, 12, 22, 122-4, 170
Ploughman songs, 199-200
Poll Tax, 47-48, 51, 57, 59
Poor Relief, 45, 174, 192, 208-9
Population, 84, 145, 176, 178-9, 186-7,
   190-1, 210
Potato, 143
Pottery, 2
Premier Earl, 121, 126
Preston, Sir Henry, 10, 109
Preston's Tower, 109, 112, 116
Prices, food, 87
Private lives, 24-34

Q

Quakers, 85
Quilraxe, 67

R

Railway, 160, 165, 170
Raitshill, 6, 19, 22, 34, 63, 87
Raths, 6
Rattray, Bill, 199
Raxton, 21, 55-6, 76, 124, 170
Reformation, 24-5, 129
Reoch, Donald, 24
Rents, 85
Rhymer, Thomas the, 118
Rinderpest, 162
Rinnin' Minister, 93
Roads, 170, 174
Robertson, Rev Patrick, 93-4
Rockings, 186
Rose, Rev John, 37, 85-87
Rotation, 143, 188
Rotherham Plough, 84

S

Sabbath, 89-92
Sackcloth, 25, 29, 92
Saints, 6
St Margaret's Fair, 177
Schivas, 2, 51-2, 66-7, 86, 125-7
Schivas, Mains of, 161
Schools, 54, 128-140
School reports, 132
Seaton, family, 12-13, 123-4
Secessionists, 93-5
Sex, 25-28
Sheithin, Craigie of, 56
Shethin, 13, 21, 52, 55, 76, 109, 124-5,
    144, 159-60
Shepherd, family, 124, 160
Shithin, Maynes of, 56
Shithin, Mill of, 56
Shorthorns, 124-5, 159-62
Shorthorn King, 95, 160
Silage, 166
Silvermoss, 64
Simpson, W. Douglas, 2, 6, 25, 209
Skilmathillie, 66
Sleigh, family, 162-9, 190
Slobatts, 65
Smiddyhill, 8, 21, 68, 162
South Craigie, 55, 60
Stage coaches, 170
Starvation, 43, 86, 126-7
Stockings, 86-87
Stone Age, 1
Strachan, Dr John, 96
Suaill of Tillelt, 61
Sympill, William, 8, 96

T

Tacitus, 3
Taixali, 6
Tanglanford, 170
Tarves, Heritage Project, 185, 189, 195-7
Tarves, Tarves Letter, 171
Tarves, Literary Society, 171, 173
Tarves, Mutual Improvement Society, 171
Tarves, Organisations, 198
Tarves, Volunteers, 173
Tavern, 90-3, 208
Telegraph office, 175
Term time, 88
Ternan, Saint, 6
Thanages, 6-7
Thirlage, 143
Thomvan, 55, 58
Thornroan, 22
Threshing, 144, 169
Tileilt, Overmill of, 55
Tileilt, Maynes of, 55, 58
Tilielt, Overheids of, 55, 58
Tillelt, Nethermill of, 58
Tillelt, Newton of, 58
Tilliecorthie, 16
Tillycairn, 3, 21, 58, 160-2
Tillyeve, 21
Tillygonie, 21, 47, 54, 67, 77
Tillygreig, 21
Tillyhilt, 14, 16, 21, 26-7, 52, 55
Tolquhon, aisle, 98, 111
Tolquhon, castle, 13, 18, 20-3, 62,
    109-116, 173
Tolquhon, hill of, 170, 172
Tolquhon, gallery, 194
Tolquhon, Mains of, 2, 167, 190

Tolquhon, Mill of, 19-20, 52, 63
Tractor, 188, 190
Trot, of Turriff, 13
Truancy, 139
Tulicarthyn, 8
Tulielt, 8
Tull, Jethro, 84
Tullidaff, Rev Thomas, 25
Turnips, 143-44
Turnpike Act, 170
Typhus, 46

U-Z

Udny, Academy, 132
Udny, helen, 26
Udny, Station, 170
Underwasles, 67
Uppermill, 160-5
Urns, 2
Vicarage, 8
Vikings, 6-7
Wages, 85, 87, 145, 188
Walk Milne of Rakstoune, 61
War, 180
War dead, 180-1
Water supplies, 40, 175
Watson, Arthur, 159, 170, 184, 189
Webster, J. Duthie, 160-2, 171, 192
Wedderbyres, 52, 68
Wester Craigie, 55, 60
Wester Kilnary, 64
Whistling kirk, 104
Whitecairns, 170
Wife, sale of, 30
Williamson, Peter, 80-82
Witchcraft, 74-77
Worcester, battle of, 54, 114
Wood, Isobel, 26
Wood, Margaret & Lilias, 26
Wysack, Malie, 77
Ythsie, 18, 19, 21, 170, 191
Ythsie, Little, 18, 19, 62, 142
Ythsie, Meikle, 19, 63
Ythsie, Mill of, 18, 19, 63, 172
Ythsie, North, 1, 2, 190
Ythsie, Prop of, 41, 117
Ythsie, South, 1, 2, 4, 52, 201